WAY PAY   DEATHS

LOFTY   BLOOD   SERANG - P.O.
   ·20   ·20   MOULMEIN
 3·30   2·55
 1·00   1·60   AT SEA.
    —   3·00   TANZUN (60)   A.B - E. THOMPSON - FEVER
 4·50   4·50   "   C. - - SCOTT   - DYSENTE
 5·13   5·13   "   "
 5·50   4·35
 8·30   7·60   BEKE TAUG (40) O.D - D. KITCHER   "
 3·50(appx) 2·40   "
    ?   ·30   "   "CHSHIP - F. KING   "ULCER INTH
    ?   — —   "   " AB - J HANNAFORD - MALNUT
25·23   31·93   "
             2·00   RETPU (30) CH·STO - G. GILES   - DYSENTER
                           "   SIG. A. DAVIES   "
Cme   Cowie.   "   O.D - W. LEWIS   "
rly Bowers Ulcer. leg THAMBYUZAYAT (BASE) Sto. - Stokes
A. Brown Dysentery   (Bo) A.B. - S. O'Brien   "
J. Burley   "   (31)
J. Daley
P. Gibbs   (55) A.B. - J Hodge   Fever
J. Mickey   "   L/s F. Nash   Beri-Ber
J. Douglas Beri-beri (35)   "   AB   L. Partridge Dysente
H. Wilkinson Dysentery   "   AB Doc Neil
H Cilby   ?   "   AB "Kango" Willis
A Cayne   "   Sto - Woodhead
R Costoin   "   P.O. G. Bolshaw
R. Talbot   (55) "   G. Harris
R. Trimble   " AB R. Ryan   Perforated St
H. Pole   42   " O.D P. Donnelly Dysente
- MacDonald ?   " E.R.A J. Matthews
T Herman   (105) A.B. H Nicholls Dysenter
A Lund   (60) (100) Tel. P. Nelson
E Dundon   (60) " AB W. Bevon
P Donaghue Malnutrition   (105) Sto - Anderson Dysen

ARTHUR'S WAR

ARTHUR'S WAR

ARTHUR BANCROFT

with

JOHN HARMAN

VIKING
an imprint of
PENGUIN BOOKS

VIKING

Published by the Penguin Group
Penguin Group (Australia)
250 Camberwell Road, Camberwell, Victoria 3124, Australia
(a division of Pearson Australia Group Pty Ltd)
Penguin Group (USA) Inc.
375 Hudson Street, New York, New York 10014, USA
Penguin Group (Canada)
90 Eglinton Avenue East, Suite 700, Toronto, Canada ON M4P 2Y3
(a division of Pearson Penguin Canada Inc.)
Penguin Books Ltd
80 Strand, London WC2R 0RL England
Penguin Ireland
25 St Stephen's Green, Dublin 2, Ireland
(a division of Penguin Books Ltd)
Penguin Books India Pvt Ltd
11 Community Centre, Panchsheel Park, New Delhi – 110 017, India
Penguin Group (NZ)
67 Apollo Drive, Rosedale, North Shore 0632, New Zealand
(a division of Pearson New Zealand Ltd)
Penguin Books (South Africa) (Pty) Ltd
24 Sturdee Avenue, Rosebank, Johannesburg 2196, South Africa

Penguin Books Ltd, Registered Offices: 80 Strand, London, WC2R 0RL, England

First published by Penguin Group (Australia), 2010

1 3 5 7 9 10 8 6 4 2

Text copyright © Arthur Bancroft and John Harman 2010

The moral right of the author has been asserted

Cover design by Tony Palmer © Penguin Group (Australia)
Text design by Marina Messiha © Penguin Group (Australia)
Cover photograph of beach: Paul Edmondson/Getty Images
Author photograph by Alison Harman
Maps drawn by Damien Demaj, DEMAP
Typeset in 12.5/18 Fairfield Light by Post Pre-press Group, Brisbane, Queensland
Printed and bound in Australia by McPherson's Printing Group, Maryborough, Victoria

National Library of Australia
Cataloguing-in-Publication data:

Bancroft, Arthur.
Arthur's war / Arthur Bancroft with John Harman.
ISBN: 9780670073467 (hbk.)
Includes index.
Bancroft, Arthur. World War, 1939–1945 – Prisoners and prisons, Japanese – Biography.
World War, 1939–1945 – Personal narratives, Australian.
Other Authors/Contributors: Harman, John Frank, 1942–

940.547252092

penguin.com.au

This book is dedicated to Mirla, my loving wife, for her support and understanding over the past sixty-five years, and to all the men of HMAS *Perth*, both those who came back as well as those who never made it home.

CONTENTS

Sumatra

Telok Betong
(Bandar Lampung)

Sunda

Krakatoa Island

D U T C H

Indian Ocean

Princes Island

Java Head

BATTLE OF THE SUNDA STRAIT

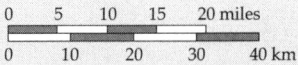

0	5	10	15	20 miles
0	10	20	30	40 km

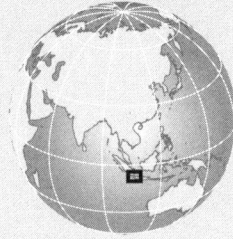

Java Sea

Houston
sunk

Perth
sunk

Strait

Babi Island

St Nicholas
Point

Merak

Bantam
Bay

Sangiang
Island

Bantam

Serang

Batavia
(Jakarta)

Tanjong
Priok

EAST INDIES
(INDONESIA)

Bekasi

Lubuan

Java

Bogor

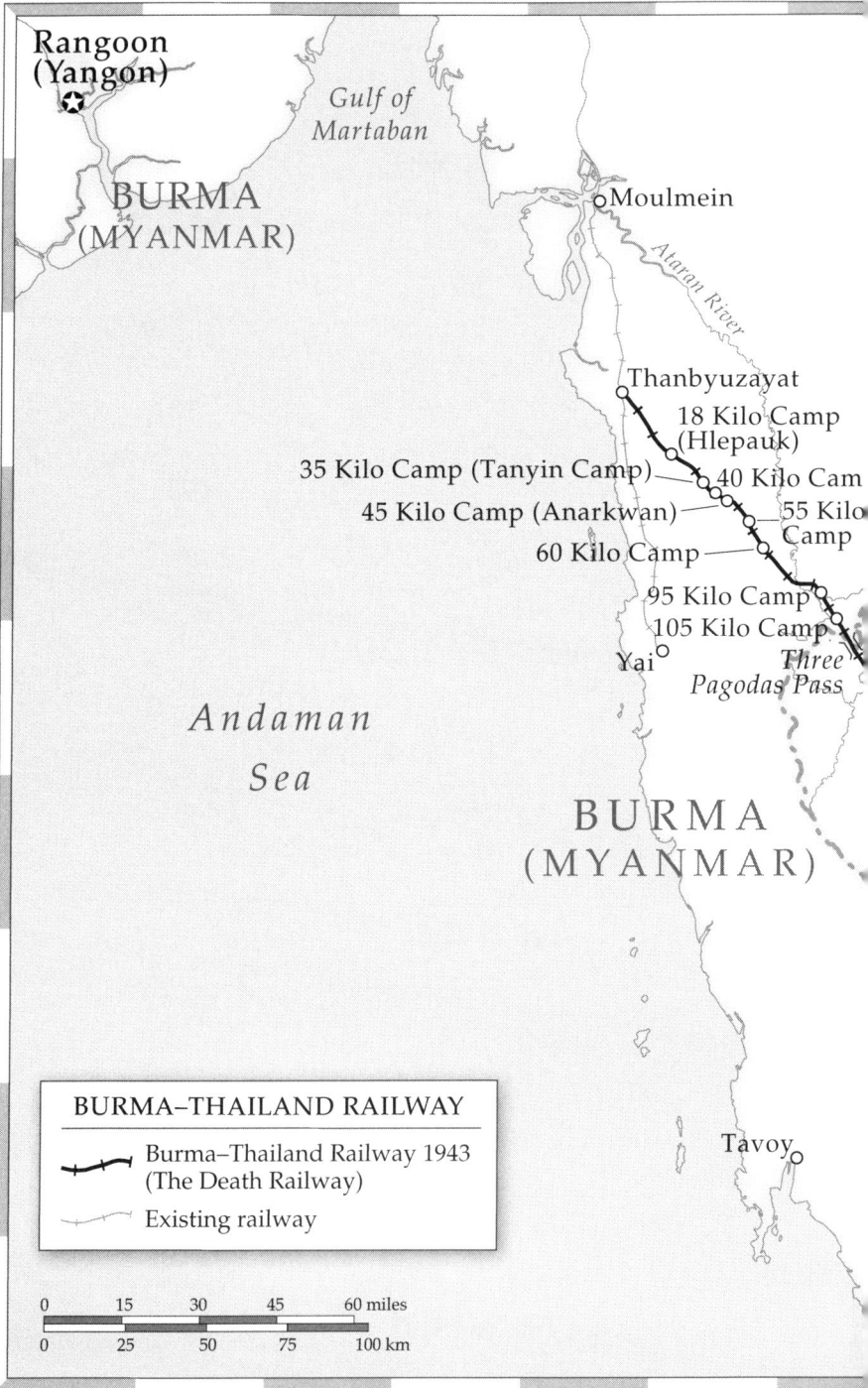

Rangoon
(Yangon)
✪

*Gulf of
Martaban*

BURMA
(MYANMAR)

Moulmein

Ataran River

Thanbyuzayat

18 Kilo Camp
(Hlepauk)

35 Kilo Camp (Tanyin Camp)

40 Kilo Cam

45 Kilo Camp (Anarkwan)

55 Kilo
Camp

60 Kilo Camp

95 Kilo Camp

105 Kilo Camp

Yai

*Three
Pagodas Pass*

*Andaman
Sea*

BURMA
(MYANMAR)

Tavoy

BURMA–THAILAND RAILWAY

Burma–Thailand Railway 1943
(The Death Railway)

Existing railway

0	15	30	45	60 miles
0	25	50	75	100 km

SIAM
(THAILAND)

Mae Khlong
River

Menam Kwai
Noi River

Tha Chin River

Chao Phraya River

Hintok Road Prison Camp
Hell Fire Pass

Tamarkan Camp
Kanburi (Kanchanaburi)

Nakom
Paton

Ban Pong

Bangkok

Bight of
Bangkok

To Mergui
85 km
(53 miles)

1

Battler Blood

The night is as bright as day with star shells bursting and the muzzle flashes of the eight-inch guns on the heavy cruisers blowing the hell out of the Houston *next to us, while the searchlights of the Japanese destroyers are lighting up our ship like a cinema screen. The noise is terrific, the booming of our guns and the screaming of their shells numbing my mind to everything except what I have been trained to do.*

The Japs are closing in for the kill, a Jap destroyer so close I can see one of their gunners behind their four-inch guns. A bloke just like me doing what I am doing, only with a lot more effect. We have run out of ammunition and are firing star shells at the Japs – about as useful as tennis balls against a tank. But we have to show we still have teeth, that the Perth *isn't going down without a fight.*

Suddenly, the ship lurches as if she's taken a punch. Another torpedo, again on the starboard side. I glance at Lofty. That has to be the killer blow. Slowly she begins listing and soon over the din we hear the captain's voice through the loudspeakers, 'Abandon ship, every man for himself. Good luck.' I don't know it but those are probably the last words the captain will ever say.

My mates and I have been working the forward four-inch gun on the port side and I never thought I'd find myself abandoning it but already I am scrambling across the deck towards the starboard railing. Lots of blokes are moving in the opposite direction, to the port side but, though it's closer to the water, I think it's more dangerous. As I reach the railing there's a bright flash and a loud explosion behind me. The forward gun deck – the place where moments before I was loading shells – has taken a direct hit.

Clambering over the railing, I slide down the hull into the sea. The water is warm – and covered in something thick and sticky. Oil. For a moment I panic. All it needs is a small flame and the sea will ignite. I will be burned to death in the middle of Sunda Strait. Luckily, nothing around us is on fire. I take a deep breath and blow into the mouth tube of my life jacket.

It is darker down at the surface of the sea and around me in the blackness I can hear men calling out, some shouting – one bloke, closer to the ship, is screaming in agony. Dark, anonymous shapes thresh the water and a couple of bodies float past me, face down. With a jolt I realise they are probably dead.

With my 'Mae West' inflated I am lifted a little out of the water – and the oil. Nearby I hear one of the petty officers call out. I can't see him but his voice is calm, like he's in the drill hall. 'Remember your training, lads. Don't let the oil get in your eyes. And for God's sake, don't swallow any. If this stuff gets in your stomach or your lungs, you'll die in agony.'

I check around in the darkness for Lofty, Marcus, Merv, Harvey *and the rest of my mates but I can't see any of them. I look back at the* Perth. *She is going down by the bows, the stern lifting far up into the night sky, silhouetted against the bright lights of our enemy. I think of my bunk, my locker and the little bit of space I'd called my own. Everything I own is on board that ship and inside that locker: a wristwatch my mum and dad bought me when I joined up; letters from them and my brothers and sisters and, dearest and most precious of all, letters from Mirla and a special photo of her taken in Kings Park a couple of days before I had left to join the* Perth.

Everything – all of it sinking beneath the waves. I am appalled, and stupidly hear myself crying out, 'There goes my home.'

It is now sixty-eight years since it happened, yet every day – and there have been almost twenty-five thousand of them – I have thought about it. Some incident or person, almost all of them dead, has flickered into my mind and for a few seconds or even minutes I have been back: loading a four-inch gun under fire on a stricken ship, or struggling to stay afloat in the middle of an oil-slicked sea, or striving to exist in a stinking POW camp in the middle of the Burma Railway.

Sometimes I wonder how exactly I managed to survive while other men around me died. Some of them were better men than me: quicker, stronger, more intelligent. Not that I was weak or stupid, but many of the blokes we lost were the flower of our generation. Maybe they were unlucky because, for sure, luck had a lot to do with whether you lived or died back then. And I reckon I *was* lucky; not that you could call what happened to any of us lucky, but living through it and coming home and getting on with life has to count for something, I reckon.

Yet, maybe my survival was down to not much more than simply being true-blue. Somehow, no matter what, I managed to stay cheerful and almost always expected to survive: expected to come home to my mum and dad and sisters and brothers and the girl I knew I was going to marry. That attitude, that Aussie optimism, that 'She'll be right, mate', was true for almost all of us, especially in the camps.

Most of the time we were optimistic, particularly in comparison to the British soldiers who were there with us. I got to know quite a lot of the Brits and many of them, individually, were good blokes. But, as a group, they were more pessimistic than our mob: they had to work hard at keeping their spirits up and their officers hardly ever bothered with them. As a result, I think more of them succumbed to malaria and dysentery and beriberi and all the other bloody stuff rife in the camps.

But our officers cared for us, and we always had each other – Aussie mateship kept a lot of blokes going who might otherwise have died. I reckon I was one of them. I had some good mates back then. Not all of them got back home. And there were times when even my optimism was tested and, very occasionally, I wondered if I was actually going to make it. But mostly I reckoned I would come through.

Of course there may have been other reasons why I survived.

But, look . . . I'm getting ahead of myself here. I ought to start at the beginning.

***

By the time the First World War broke out, my father, who was a builder, had lost an eye through a ricocheting nail and the index finger on his right hand. So when he volunteered for the Australian Naval & Military Expeditionary Force, they took one look at him and told him he was unfit for military service. Clearly, the army thought he wouldn't be a lot of use to them: if he squinted to sight his rifle he'd be blind, and even if he could see the enemy he didn't have a finger to pull the trigger. So they sent him home.

Yet although my dad was judged not fit enough for the army he was pretty fit in a lot of other ways, for between 1910 and 1921 he made my mother pregnant seven times. I was the youngest of the seven children, born with flaming red hair on 24 November, 1921. I had two older brothers and four sisters.

They say boys with older sisters tend to be spoiled. I don't know about that, but I do know I had a happy childhood, even though I was raised right through the Depression. My childhood was as typically Australian as you could get. Just like my family history, I suppose.

My grandfather, Edward Bancroft, who was also a builder, had emigrated from a village called Dunham Massey in Cheshire, a county of rolling green pastures in the north-west of England. He arrived in Cooktown, Queensland, on the steamship *Scotland* in September 1882. Three years later he married my grandmother, the beautiful, flaming-haired Alice McQuaid, an Irish immigrant whose family were also newly arrived in Australia. Edward and Alice had four children, all born in Brisbane. Harold, my dad, was the eldest.

In 1896, after the family home in Breakfast Creek was flooded out, Edward and Alice decided to move and, with four children under ten, took passage on a ship and sailed halfway around Australia to Albany. From there they trekked north: 800 kilometres overland to Coolgardie in the Goldfields where grandfather Edward reckoned there were good prospects for someone in the construction business. Coincidentally, just like my father, Edward had lost an eye plying his trade as a builder.

Life in the heat and dust of the barren Goldfields at the turn of the twentieth century was pretty rugged and it must have been especially hard on red-haired, pale-skinned Alice who, being Irish and from a lush, verdant country would have yearned for green grass and the gently falling rain. Five years after arriving in Coolgardie she committed suicide. Dad was about thirteen then. Two years later the 500-kilometre water pipeline from Mundaring Weir engineered by C Y O'Connor, himself an Irishman, was finally pushed through and suddenly the Goldfields were getting twenty-million litres of water a day. But by then O'Connor, too, had committed suicide.

After Alice's tragic death Edward shifted the family around the state for a few years, first to Fremantle, then to York, where my father met my mother, and then to Trayning, about 200 kilometres north-east of Perth, where he took up land and built a hessian humpy with a corrugated-iron roof. My dad, who by then had also become a builder, helped build it. The farm on which the humpy stood is still called Dunham Farm.

Harold, my dad, married Susie Hayden in 1910. My mother was another descendant of Irish immigrants; her father George, who had settled in York and enrolled as a Pensioner Guard, was mentioned in the York census of 1865 as having assisted in the capture of the notorious bushranger, Moondyne Joe.

My parents lived a typically rural life: each day after my older brothers and sisters came along, my mother drove them 9 kilometres to school in a horse and sulky. Later, Harold moved the family into Trayning, where Susie ran a boarding house. Later, in 1927, six years after I had been born in a hospital in Fremantle, he and my mother decided to shift the family to the city of Perth.

I remember very little about the farm and life in Trayning; almost all of my early memories date from after we moved into the city. We first moved to Crawley, a small suburb down river from the city where I went to Nedlands Primary School. Although it was a city suburb, I remember Crawley as mostly rural. Virtually in the shadow of Mount Eliza, which a few years before had been renamed Kings Park, there was, close to our house in Caporn Street, a reserve where my mates and I would play. The bush stretched all the way down to the banks of the River Swan at Matilda Bay. Sticking out into the river at the southern end of the bay was a spit of land, Pelican Point, at the end of which was a hut belonging to the 1st Pelican Point Sea Scouts. I asked my dad if I could join and so I became, at six years old, a Sea Cub. It was a good choice. I was in the Sea Cubs, and subsequently the Sea Scouts, for years and became a strong swimmer.

After a couple of years in Crawley we moved into a small, Federation-style house in Subiaco Road, Subiaco, so-called after the leader of a group of Benedictine monks who came from Subiaco in Italy and who had settled in the area in the 1850s. The suburb, west of the city and even closer to Kings Park, was leafy and mainly residential, with quiet, wide, tree-lined streets. Almost an extension of the park, Subiaco was slightly genteel and considered, at least by those who lived in it, to be a cut above most of the other city suburbs. For me it was a warm and friendly place; safe for us kids to play in the street even though our house was pretty close to the Perth–Fremantle railway line. More importantly, we were even closer to Subiaco Oval, which was just over the road from our house.

Like any Aussie kid, I was raised on sport and played cricket and football every waking moment I wasn't at school. By that time my dad had become heavily involved with the Subiaco Football Club. In fact, when he retired as a builder, he became Head Steward of the Western Australian National Football Club. Not only that, but my brother Harold, who was eleven years older than me, had started pulling on the maroon guernsey and was playing for Subiaco. Sometimes I went along with him as his bag boy, or ball boy or boot boy – any kind of boy, so long as I could get in to see the game! But most Saturdays I had to resort to climbing the great Moreton Bay fig tree directly over the road from our front gate. It was a hard climb, the trunk was huge and smooth and the lowest branches were about 3 metres up. But that didn't deter me or my mates, for once up in the tree we would edge along a branch until we were across the fence and then make the 3.5-metre drop into the ground. If the stewards saw us they didn't do anything about it. Maybe they reckoned that any kid who made that difficult climb and then risked his neck on the long drop deserved to see the game for free.

One thing was for certain: very few of us could pay our way into the ground. It was the late 1920s and times were hard. Like the rest of the world Australia was in the grip of the Depression. Sometimes my father had work; often he didn't, and he had a big family to feed. I earned a few coppers by selling the evening paper, the *Daily News*, around Nedlands and Subiaco.

But even though most people were doing it tough, I never remember going without good food, or being short of clothes to put on my back. Of course, almost all my clothes were 'hand-me-downs' from my two older brothers, mainly from Les who was three years older than me, although some of the things I wore had been around more than ten years and had originally come down from Harold via Les. Like all mothers back then my mother would patch garments and preserve them for years, and days after I had inherited something 'new' I'd still be walking around smelling of mothballs and lavender. None of my mates mentioned it; mainly, I guess, because they often smelled the same.

One item my parents didn't have to spend much money on was shoes. Like most Aussie kids, I never wore them. Well, not if I could help it. Every morning my mother would send me off to Thomas Street School in my clean, well-worn clothes and polished shoes and every morning as soon as I got around the corner, off the shoes would come.

I enjoyed school. The lessons weren't difficult and I especially liked maths but what I most liked about school was the sport. In fact, what I mainly remember about that period in my childhood are hot days and the smell of the eucalyptus trees in the park where we played football and cricket continually. Every day in the school holidays, and most days after school, my mates would come around and shout for me. Back then your mates didn't come into your house. Instead they stood outside the house and hollered for you. 'Blood! Are ya there, Blood?'

Blood was my nickname. I was the only one in the family with red hair, Alice McQuaid's DNA having skipped an entire generation, plus all my siblings, to infect only me. Of course, with flaming red hair I had been called 'Blue' or 'Bluey'; even 'Coppertop', for a while, though my hair was more red than copper. But in the end it was 'Bloodnut', shortened to 'Blood', that finally stuck and was universally used and accepted. Well, not universally. My mother didn't care for it, and when my mates came around to shout, 'Blood, are ya comin' out?' she would march to the front door, open it and query, in her best, Sunday Subiaco voice, 'Do you mean Arthur?'

'Arthur?' my mates would laugh. 'Nah, we want Blood.'

When I was twelve I left Thomas Street School and attended Claremont State High School. By then I'd become a strong swimmer and was a member of the Nedlands Swimming Club where I swam in a lot of competitions and even had a few wins. At Claremont I played cricket for the school and eventually became captain of the school football team where, naturally, I was called 'Captain Blood'.

One of my teachers at Claremont High was Miss Tangney, who taught us English. She was a good teacher, though pretty strict, who took a personal interest in all her pupils. She was particularly interested in politics and very active in the local ALP. It was from Miss Tangney that I got my love of reading and good books.

I grew into a lanky kid and was pretty strong for my age and within a couple of years I was not only playing football for the school but also for the West Subiaco Metropolitan Football Association. Then, when I was fifteen, I was lucky enough to be selected to play halfback for the Western Australian Schoolboy Football Team.

Oh, you beauty! It was such an enormous privilege to play footie for the state – I was as proud as I could possibly be.

Not long afterwards our coach told us that an interstate football carnival was to be held in Adelaide and that our team would be travelling to it. I remember my excitement. I had never been out of the state before, though I was a bit worried about how my parents would pay for the trip until the coach told us that the State would be paying. Even so, it was 1936, the Depression was still on and my parents had to stretch to find the money for all the extras a trip to Adelaide would involve.

One of the other blokes in the team was a full-forward called Allan Wilkinson. Allan was a first-class all-round sportsman and a really good footie player. Truth to tell, he was a bit of a goal sneak and though our team didn't win the final in Adelaide, Allan was the individual player selected out of all the footballers as the 'fairest and best' in the whole tournament. Being fair in a game of football was important back then.

I got on well with Allan, even though he was a pupil at Perth Boys' School, which was considered pretty snobby, at least in comparison to Claremont State High, and after we came back from Adelaide we became good friends. His house, also in Subiaco, was less than a kilometre from mine and I used to visit him often.

Allan's father had fought in France in the First World War and been badly gassed. After hospitalisation in England he had returned to Western Australia to hold an important position in the State Legislature as Clerk of the Legislative Assembly. Unfortunately, the poor bloke never really recovered from the damage to his lungs and was often ill. He died when Allan was eleven. Now,

Allan, his mother and his sister were Legacy Wards, which meant that a Legatee looked after the family.

The Legacy Club had been created after the First World War to take care of the widows and children of servicemen who had either been killed in action or subsequently died of their wounds. In fact Legacy sponsored him to twelve months' free education at the prestigious Scotch College because Allan was so good at sport.

Mirla, Allan's sister, was just as good at sport as he was. After a few chats with her I discovered that she was a member of the Perth Athletic Club where she was both a runner and a hurdler, that she was a keen swimmer and hockey player and that not only did she play tennis for her school team but had just won a scholarship to Leederville Tennis Club where she was to receive twelve months free coaching.

Mirla was my kind of girl. I reckoned anyone, even a girl, who was that good and versatile at sport had to be all right. But I discovered there was more to Mirla than just sport. Not only had she been a prefect in standard seven at Perth Girls' School, the following year she'd been made a class prefect. Yet, even though she was clever enough to have gone on to take her Leaving Certificate, Mirla had decided to leave school early so she could help support her mother who was taking care of her family on an inadequate war widow's pension. Just before she was about to leave Perth Girls', the headmistress called Mirla into her office to ask her to consider staying on. When Mirla asked why, the headmistress told her that she had been selected to be the school's Head Girl for the following year. A lot of people would have been swayed by such an honour but Mirla had made up her mind and explained to the headmistress the reasons for her decision.

I liked my mate Allan a lot and enjoyed going to see him at his house. But I reckoned I was beginning to like his sister even more, which is why I went to their house so often. Almost every Sunday morning would find me at their place, calling for Allan on the way to footie training at Rosalie Park oval, and often I would go back to his house for a meal. Usually I'd help with the washing up and after I'd washed a plate I'd flip it (a bit like a frisbee, forty years later) to Allan who was waiting at the other side of the kitchen, dishcloth in hand, as first receiver. Allan had enormous hands and never once dropped a plate, though his mother, fearful of her dinner service ending up as bits of broken crockery, watched our antics in alarm. Mirla laughed at our performance and sometimes I caught her watching me, which only made me want to show off even more.

Like her brother, Mirla was conscientious and hard working and after leaving school she got a twelve-month sponsorship from the Legacy Club to go to Underwood Business College to be a shorthand typist and bookkeeper. At the end of that year she passed her Junior Certificate with flying colours. By that time I was seeing quite a lot of her.

I took my Junior Certificate on my fifteenth birthday and left school shortly afterwards. For a while I thought of taking a job as a telegraphist in the post office but instead took a job as a clerk in the State Lands Department. The job was all right as a way of bringing a little money into the household, but I knew it wasn't what I wanted to do for the rest of my life. Then a family connection who had just returned from London where he had been working in a bank told me a job was going in the Fremantle branch of the Union Bank of Australia. It was a long shot but after a moment's thought I decided I'd apply. I was pretty young for a job in a bank but I saw no reason not to give it a go. I had matriculated at the age of fifteen, which was early, but pretty much everything in my life up to that point had been early. I had gone to school a year earlier than most and I seemed to have spent a lot of my life in the company of older boys, striving to keep up.

Anyway, I went down to Freo for an interview with the bank manager and once in his office I told him I thought I was the right bloke for the job, even though I was much younger than the rest of his clerks. That manager took a bit of persuading but in the end there must have been something about me that he liked as he gave me the position.

Returning home on the train I was quietly pleased. I'd always been good at maths and now I thought maybe banking might be a good career for me. But I was also pleased with myself on another count: I'd had the nerve to actually go into the manager's office and persuade him to give me the job. I was a child of the Depression and had learned long before that nobody was ever going to give me anything unless I got off my backside and persuaded them to give it to me. Even as a youngster I knew that if I wanted to get ahead I would have to work hard all my life. But, more than that, if I wanted good things to happen to me, then it would be down to me to *make* them happen. I didn't realise it then but that assertive attitude, that ability to stand up and ask for what I wanted, would one day save my life.

I started working in the Fremantle branch of the bank and did all right as a junior clerk. But while things were travelling well for me personally – holding down a good job that could turn into a worthwhile career, playing footy for a first-class team and going out with Mirla, the prettiest girl in Australia – things were not looking so good for the rest of the world.

For about five or six years a bloke called Adolf Hitler had been stirring things up in Europe. I hadn't taken a lot of notice in the early years because I was too young, and later because there were a lot of other things happening in my life. But increasingly there was talk in the papers and in the pubs of war in Europe. To a lot of people the thought of another war was unimaginable. They couldn't believe it might start all over again. So many of them, like Mirla and her family, had suffered the loss of a loved one on account of the First World War. But the newspapers were turning gloomy and no one in Australia believed that the British Prime Minister, Neville Chamberlain, had solved anything when he came back from Munich waving his scrap of paper, which, signed by Hitler, was supposed to guarantee no war. What with the annexation of Austria and the invasion of Czechoslovakia, matters were coming to a head.

But that was Europe – and Europe was on the other side of the world. Except that, now Germany was allied with Japan, there were rumours that if there was a war in Europe, Japan might attack Australia in order to strengthen her power in the region the Brits quaintly called the 'Far East'. Well, it may have been the Far East to the Brits but for us in Australia it was the Near North. With Japan invading China there was already a war going on there and most people were keeping a wary eye on what was happening.

Yet the mood in the streets and in the press wasn't melancholy. There was quite a lot to be cheerful about: the country was coming out of the Depression, there was more work and, generally speaking, people were pretty happy, even though there was a quiet mood of resignation that pretty soon we might be having another biff with Jerry.

In between playing footy, seeing my mates and going out with Mirla, I listened to all the talk and concluded that if there was a war I would feel it my duty to go and fight for King and Country. Australia was part of the Empire: if Britain went to war there was no question that Australia would be right there alongside her. And anyway, going away to war was a pretty exciting prospect, especially if I could join the Royal Australian Air Force (RAAF) and learn to fly. I reckoned if there was a war I'd join up immediately – get in before it was all over. At just on six feet, I'd grown into a pretty strong bloke who could take care of himself if he had to. Joining up would probably be a bit of fun. And through playing so much sport, I knew what it was to be part of a team: how to do as I was told, how to do my bit. I told my parents what I intended to do if war broke out but they weren't overjoyed with my plans. They were very reluctant and told me that, because I was under eighteen, they would have to give their written permission for me to go away to war.

War was declared on 3 September, 1939 when Prime Minister Robert Menzies made his famous 'melancholy duty' speech. I didn't hear it and in fact didn't even know the war was on until the following day, when someone in the bank told me. Mirla heard the news talking to the girl who lived next door to her. She immediately thought that as the last war had lasted four years, this one was bound to only last for two.

A few days after the war's outbreak I was sent to Beverley, a small country town in the wheat belt, to work in the branch there.

It was a minor promotion and in some ways I was pleased to go, though I knew I'd miss Mirla as we were going very steady then. By the time of my eighteenth birthday the war was already more than ten weeks old, and the day after I went down to the Post Office to get the form to join up, after which all I had to do was get my parents' permission to put my name down for the RAAF. It took some doing but I finally managed it. I had always fancied flying, though as I had grown so tall I was a bit worried I might be over the height limit to be a fighter pilot. But, at least I could be a member of an aircrew, I reckoned. I expected the RAAF would want to snap up blokes like me. So I went for my medical and, passing that with flying colours, waited for them to call me up . . . and waited . . . and waited . . . and waited.

I heard nothing for twelve months. Meanwhile, I was being moved around the bank's branches in the larger wheat belt towns east of Perth – first to Northam, then to York – to cover for blokes who were going off to the war. It was a frustrating time and I reckon the only things that kept me going were Mirla's letters and the opportunity of playing football and cricket for the various local teams.

Finally, I returned to Perth to work in a city branch. It was late 1940 and I'd still had no word from the RAAF. Meanwhile, Harold, my eldest brother, was talking about joining the RAAF and Lesley, the next one, was signing on for the army. Even my sister, Win, was thinking of joining up. Everywhere there were posters of a tough-looking digger with his sleeves rolled up and holding a rifle with the headline 'One In – All In. Join the AIF Today'. Well, it seemed to me that it was 'all in' except for Arthur Bancroft.

In the end, I couldn't wait any longer. Because I was under

twenty-one I needed a letter from my employer releasing me to join up. My divisional manager was pleased to give it to me and told me my job would be waiting when I came back.

I didn't take a lot of notice of what he said at the time, though his words were to come back to me later. They were one of the many small things that would keep me going. But then I was eager to get into the war before it was all over. So I marched off to the recruiting office in Fremantle to sign up for the Royal Australian Navy.

Mirla's Story

They called him 'Blood' on account of his flaming red hair. Some of my girlfriends didn't like boys with red hair, but I fancied Arthur right from the start. He was tall, which I liked because I was so short. He also had a kind of quiet, cheeky smile that I responded to. Not that I was thinking much about boys when we met. I was fourteen and only just growing aware of the opposite sex. Mainly I spent time with Arthur because of sport; I was sports mad and so was he. Along with my brother Allan we would talk sport for hours. But while Allan was self-assured and extroverted, Arthur was quieter: almost shy. I liked that about him too. Not that he was a wuss. I admired him when he stood up for himself and especially when he went to get the job in the bank. When, later, the bank sent him away to work, he asked if he could write to me . . . penpals, so to speak. I said yes and he wrote me lovely letters: full of fun and humour and interesting things. He was a good drawer too; he would do little pen and ink sketches on the letters; even on the envelopes. I suppose it was his letters that started me thinking about him romantically.

2

The War on Our Doorstep

'Take the pistol out of the holster,' the chief petty officer murmurs.

I do as I'm ordered, slipping the weapon out of its canvas holster. The weapon – it's a Webley – is heavy, maybe four or five pounds. I heft it in my hand, reassured by its substance. 'It's got a kick like a mule,' he adds. 'Let's hope you don't have to fire it.' He takes it from me and cracks open the chamber. Silently, under the solitary, dull light of the wardroom, I watch him slip six shining brass shells into the chambers. 'This is a loaded gun, Bancroft. Be careful what you do with it.' His voice is quiet; sonorous with authority.

He slides the pistol back into the holster, which he buttons before giving me the gun belt. Awkwardly, I slip the lanyard over my head and buckle on the belt, realising I should have done it the other way around. On the scuffed wooden table before me lie a whistle and a torch. The whistle is attached to another lanyard. I take it and slip it around my neck before picking up the torch.

'You know the drill?' I nod, but this being the navy I know the PO is going to tell me all over again. 'Anyone sneaking around in the dark,

19

anyone who shouldn't be there – you challenge them. All right? Shine the torch on them and tell the buggers to stand still. If they don't, if they run for it, blow the whistle and go after them. If they still won't stop, then —' He nods at the holster pulling down on my right hip, 'take that out and shoot the buggers. You got it?'

'Yes, Chief.'

'Off you go, then. And be careful.'

Outside, and with the wardroom door closed behind me, the Perth's *deck is as black as an admiral's wallet. The ship is completely blacked out and all my mates are asleep in their hammocks. Everywhere around the gun deck is in deep shadow.*

I finger my whistle and touch the holstered gun for reassurance before unbuttoning the holster. If there's someone out there ready to jump me, at least I want the chance of drawing my pistol, though how cowboys like Tom Mix ever managed the quick draw defeats me. I reckon it'll take me ten minutes to draw this bloody thing out of its holster. It'll be like hauling a bucket of coal off my hip. And what if I do get the bloody thing out – what happens, I wonder, if I actually have to fire it?

The loom of my torch lights up the sheen of the steel bulkheads. Surrounded by all this steel and with the distinct possibility I'll miss what I'm aiming at, there's a serious chance of a ricocheting bullet. I feel my blood run cold as I realise that if I do see someone and open fire, it'll likely be me who ends up with a bullet in my bum.

Of course joining the Royal Australian Navy (RAN) wasn't as simple as I'd imagined it would be. Even in a war there were forms to be filled in and paper-pushers to placate.

I went into the navy recruiting office in Fremantle High Street with all my documents and signed permissions from my parents and my employer and was immediately instructed to fill in yet more forms. As I was anxious to get on with it I did as I was told, though I remember thinking that if filling in bits of paper won wars, then we would all be home by Christmas.

Once all the bumph had been completed to the satisfaction of the naval bloke behind the desk he told me I had to go for a medical. 'Why?' I asked. 'I'm as fit as a Mallee bull.'

The bloke gazed at me and shook his head. 'Regulations. You can't join the navy if you're not fit.'

I was eighteen, going on nineteen, stood six foot tall and weighed well over twelve stone. I played every sport imaginable and had even pulled on the maroon-and-gold guernsey of the Subiaco Football Club at least half-a-dozen times. It seemed blindingly obvious to me that I was fit and I told the bloke so.

He stared at me mordantly. 'You can't be sure of that,' he said darkly. 'You could have some disease you don't know about. Your heart could be weak.' I stared back at him. Bloody hell, I thought, if the navy is full of jokers like this one, I'll be fighting the war from a funeral parlour.

So I duly went straight off for my medical, which was held in a surgery next to the recruiting office. By a strange coincidence the doctor conducting my medical was the same doc who had brought me into the world. Dr Field-Martell was a well-known medic in Fremantle, so I suppose it wasn't unusual that he would be doing his bit for the navy, though he gave no indication that he remembered me. Not surprising really, I thought. The last time the doc had seen me I was stark-naked and he was smacking my backside. He gave me a thorough examination and as I was pulling on my shirt I asked him how I had done. He smiled. 'You'll do. You're pretty fit. I'm putting you down as A1.' I was tempted to say, 'I could have told you that,' but I held my tongue.

Immediately after my medical I was directed to another office to attend an interview with a uniformed bloke who looked to me to be some kind of senior recruiting officer. Seated across a desk he shuffled lots of pieces of paper before telling me that I could enlist in the navy only if I was prepared to join the communications branch as a communications cadet. I tried to keep the surprise off my face. I couldn't understand it. First the RAAF wasn't interested in me and now the navy was saying I could only join under certain conditions. 'Why?' I asked.

'Because of your educational qualifications,' he said pleasantly. 'You have your Junior School Certificate. You did well in maths and English and you work in a bank. We need men of your education to be signallers and radiomen. It's an important task, Bancroft. If our ships can't communicate, they can't fight effectively.'

Well, that sounded pretty good to me. Actually, I wouldn't have cared which branch of the service I joined; all I wanted was to join up and fight a war. But to be recruited into the senior service in order to perform an important duty like signalling and radio communications sounded as if I had landed on my feet. After shuffling more bits of paper, the officer pushed one across the desk and told me to sign on the dotted line. After I signed we stood up and the officer shook my hand. 'Congratulations,' he said, 'you're in the navy.'

It was 18 November, 1940, a warm, sunny day, and completely unremarkable in the history of the war except that it was the day I enlisted in the Royal Australian Navy and became Ordinary Seaman Second Class A Bancroft, number F 3239.

I was elated and walked out of the office as though I was on air. Halfway out of the building I realised I was missing a vital piece of information. I hurried back inside to where the officer was gathering up the bumph.

'What happens now?' I asked.

'Oh, don't worry,' he said airily, 'we'll send for you when we're ready.'

As soon as I got home, I told my parents what I had done. The first thing my mother said was, 'Well, at least I know you can swim.' That surprised me. She had been dead-set against me going into the RAAF, yet she seemed okay about the navy. I asked her why that was. 'I didn't want you joining the air force,' she said, 'because I knew you couldn't fly.' I laughed. In a funny kind of way there was logic to my mother's thinking. But, underneath their natural concern, I think my mum and dad were pleased I was going to do my bit. So was I. I couldn't wait to get stuck in.

But that's what I did. I waited . . . and waited . . . and waited.

For two weeks I kicked my heels.

Every day I hurried to the post box to see if I had my orders. Nothing. Then, at last, arriving home from the bank, my mother told me an official-looking letter had come for me. I grabbed it off the hallstand and ripped it open. It was from the RAAF, telling me my application to join the air force had been accepted. I stared at it in confusion. I had almost forgotten I'd applied to the

RAAF and now, a year later, they were telling me I could join up! I didn't understand it. Had the brass hats in the Australian military decided to play games with me? Was I going to have to wait a year before the navy decided to call me up too? I dashed off a letter to the RAAF telling them I had joined the navy instead and reminding them that, as the navy was the senior service, I couldn't transfer out to join the RAAF. I enjoyed telling them that bit.

But after posting the letter I was back to the tedious business of waiting to hear from the navy. Why didn't they get on with it? There was a war going on and I wanted to get into it. I was nineteen and itching to get into the scrap, though part of me also felt it was my duty to go.

The news out of Europe was not good. France had fallen and much of the British army had only escaped annihilation through a miracle called Dunkirk. The air war that Winston Churchill was calling the Battle of Britain had been won, though everyone said it was by the skin of our teeth, and now London and other big cities in Britain were being blitzed. We stood alone. The Russians had allied with the Nazis and the Americans didn't want to know. Our side – the Empire and all it stood for – appeared to be retreating on all fronts and I reckoned that things would never get better until Arthur Bancroft, RAN, got into the fight.

Finally, the letter arrived ordering me to report to Leeuwin Naval Depot in Fremantle and it was with a great sense of relief and excitement that I packed a small bag and took the train to Freo. The barracks were a series of brick built buildings, mainly two-story, close to the foreshore. It was a good posting: I was on pretty familiar territory and less than 20 kilometres away from home.

The first few weeks of training went quickly. I wouldn't have said naval training was easy but it wasn't that hard either. I joined a hut of about thirty young blokes, all of us from very different backgrounds and parts of the state. The main thing we had to learn was to do as we were told without question, but after a couple of incidences when we were insubordinate or queried orders and ended up on fatigues, cleaning out the dunnies, we got the point.

We had plenty of physical exercise to get us fit, which I enjoyed, and almost from day one we were into learning semaphore and Morse code using the big Addis lamps. The navy regime was tough but not brutal; the facilities bare and unadorned, yet not completely spartan. The petty officers were regular navy; hard men but fair. Their job was to bend all us young blokes to the navy's will – to bend us but not break us. I think they did a good job. One thing the navy did supply in abundance was food. Good food – and plenty of it, which was just as well as every day we were up at six and when we weren't marching and parading and generally square-bashing, we were doing physical training or rifle drill or sitting in a classroom trying to remember what all the flags signified.

The hardest thing I had to do in my early navy days was learn how to climb into a hammock. At night our barrack room, which was called the mess deck, was strung with hammocks, below each of which was a small locker. The hammock and the locker was our home: that's where we kept all our personal possessions. Everything else in our universe belonged to the navy. On our first night in the mess, with thirty unslung hammocks hanging motionless in the still, warm air, the PO demonstrated how to climb into one. He made it look easy. Then we were ordered to do the same. Thinking this was a piece of cake, I swung myself up into my hammock – and promptly fell out the other side. I would have been embarrassed, except that most of my new mates were doing the same thing – the wooden barrack-room floor resounded to the thud of dropping bodies. The PO was not impressed. He hadn't ordered anyone to fall out of their hammocks! he bellowed. Once more he ordered us to climb into our hammocks. Most of us disobeyed the order and fell out again. I managed to cling onto mine like a koala in a cyclone for a couple of seconds before falling out.

It took four or five attempts to finally master it, and I reckon that PO was chuckling to himself all the time he was shouting at us. I discovered that the secret was to throw yourself into the hammock without any hesitation. You had to act it as if it was alive and knew you were trying to climb into it. If it knew you were coming, then, at the last moment, it would deliberately move away from you and deposit you on your bum on the floor. So, the secret was to creep up on it and throw yourself in before the hammock was aware of your presence. Maybe it was a crazy concept, but it worked for me.

After a few weeks in barracks we were given a pass to allow us home for Christmas. Like everyone I had been issued with a brand-spanking new white naval uniform, which basically fitted me where it touched. I took it home to my mum who did things to it so it fitted me a treat. I put it on and went to see Mirla. Even though I was just an ordinary seaman, second class, I felt like a million dollars. I think she was suitably impressed. I spent as much of that Christmas leave as possible with Mirla before returning to barracks.

Not long into the New Year I had my first day at sea when I was ordered to join a minesweeper taking a naval diver out to a ship moored in Gage Roads. It was a good experience: we weren't far out into the ocean but just a single day's opportunity to put to sea as a seaman was exhilarating. I couldn't wait to get through my training and join a ship.

Later, back at barracks, we were told some sad news. Two young, newly enlisted naval ratings had drowned in an exercise off Garden Island, a few kilometres south of the naval depot. They were to be buried with full military honours and I was selected as one of the honour guard. We trained all day every day until the funeral: the slow-march, how to reverently lift and lower the coffins, how to fire our rifles in perfect synchronisation. Unlike some of the country boys in the barracks I had never handled a rifle before, so I worked particularly hard on my rifle skills.

On the day everything went off like clockwork: we did the funeral march in total lockstep and fired our rifles in perfect unison over the open graves. Though it was a sad occasion, I felt the honour of moving and acting in total harmony with my comrades as we showed our last respects. It was only afterwards I realised that this was the first funeral I had ever attended.

Slowly, the navy was forging us into a disciplined body of men. Now we were practicing with the big Addis lamps and the semaphore flags down at the foreshore, where the petty officers, with thunder flashes and smoke, tried to simulate the conditions we would experience under fire.

One of the lads I got to know was Dennis Robinson. Dennis stood out like a sore thumb as he was practically the only bloke on the whole depot with a car. All the officers possessed were bikes. Dennis's family had a big store down south, in Albany, and were pretty well-off. A lot of the officers would look sideways at him when he drove in after a weekend's leave and sometimes the petty officers gave him a hard time just because he was in the money.

Marching back from practice one afternoon I heard my name being called by a PO who detailed me off to see an officer. I wondered what I had done. We new naval ratings didn't see much of officers; they were like gods from some other planet. Told to stand easy in front of the officer's desk I waited for a blasting for some unknown misdemeanour. 'I hear you're a bit of a sportsman, Bancroft,' he said. 'Play football for Subiaco.'

'Yessir.'

'Do you play cricket too?'

'Yessir.'

'Good. We have a match against the army next week. You're in the team. That's all. Dismiss.'

Come the day, the navy bussed us out to North Freo Oval. There were rumours that this was a bit of a needle match; that the army had won the last couple of contests and that the officers were expecting us to extract some revenge. I went in at number three and pretty soon got the measure of their bowlers. I batted away for well over an hour until, suddenly, after scoring a four, the small crowd broke into applause. 'What's that all about?' I asked the wicketkeeper.

The army bloke looked at me in surprise. 'It's because you've scored a hundred, dimwit. Don't you know how many runs you've scored?'

28

The fact was, I didn't. I had been slogging away with no notion of the score. Anyway, I knew enough to raise my cap in acknowledgment of the applause from the small crowd and went back to the crease. The upshot of my score, along with everyone else's, was that we beat the army and everyone looked pleased. Even our petty officers, who only smiled once a year and then only in secret, looked happy.

Back at the clubhouse, someone asked me, 'What are you drinking, Bancroft?'

With a shock I realised he meant alcohol. There was only one drink I'd heard regularly mentioned in my house. 'I'll have a shandy, sir. Thank you.'

He looked surprised. 'A shandy? Are you sure? Oh, very well.'

Sipping it, I realised it was the first alcohol I had ever tasted, though, the navy being the navy, it wasn't going to be the last, of course.

Our time at HMAS *Leeuwin* was coming to an end. It had been a good six months. I had learned a lot and felt as if I was on my way to becoming a fully-fledged seaman. Yet I had been able to get home regularly to see Mirla and my family and now, with the start of the football season, I had even managed to get a couple of games for Subiaco. Life seemed good.

Then things went haywire. I developed a series of boils on my neck. At first they were painful but not serious, however they wouldn't go away and pretty soon they were turning into a series of very painful carbuncles. The medical officer took one look at them and immediately assigned me to the sick bay. When I protested he gave me a steely look. 'Don't argue, Bancroft. I need to know why you are getting those things. They can be dangerous. And anyway, they're contagious, so I want you isolated.'

So that was it. I was practically marched off to the hospital and only had time to make a quick telephone call to Mirla to tell her I wouldn't be back that weekend. She was disappointed, but seemed slightly less than sympathetic about my condition. 'Well,' she said, 'now that you'll be lying in bed all day, why don't you write me a long letter for a change?'

Mirla had been complaining for a while that my letters to her were too brief. She didn't seem to understand that the navy kept us pretty busy and didn't put writing to girlfriends high on its list of priorities. But now I had no excuse. Okay, I thought, Mirla's right. There's no reason not to write her a long letter – so I will.

As soon as I was able, I crept to the heads and liberated half a toilet roll on which I wrote her a really long letter. You could write on toilet rolls in those days. It ran to about a dozen sheets.

After a while my carbuncles disappeared as suddenly and as unaccountably as they had come. The doctor had no explanation for them and after two weeks in the sick bay he signed me out as fit. I packed up my kit and went back to my barracks. They were empty. All the lads with whom I had trained had been posted to Flinders Naval Depot in Victoria to continue their training. With a shock I realised I was on my own.

I asked a PO what was to happen to me. He told me that, as I had missed the draft this time, I would have to wait until the next one had finished their training before being posted to Flinders. 'But that could be months,' I moaned.

'It's going to be a nice easy number for you, Bancroft,' the PO said. 'You can do your training all over again and be close to your family for another few months.'

I stared at him. I could see why a bloke would think like that, but a nice easy number was not what I had joined up for. I asked to see the commanding officer. The next day I was marched into his office and stood to attention in front of his desk. 'What's your problem, Bancroft?' he snapped.

I should have been scared witless, fronting up before the CO like that, and maybe I was a little, but mainly I felt determined. 'Sir, I joined the navy to fight a war. I've been here six months and now everyone else who joined up to fight a war with me has been posted and I'm still here. They say I'll be here for another few months.'

'That's right. You'll have to wait until the next draft has finished their communications training before you can be posted.'

'Is there no way I can be posted sooner, sir?'

'Not in communications, no. Only if you were an ordinary seaman.'

I thought for about ten seconds. 'Sir, request permission to become an ordinary seaman.'

The CO looked surprised. 'Are you telling me you want to be demoted to ordinary seaman so you can be posted sooner?'

'Yessir.'

'Why?'

'Like I say, sir, I joined up to fight a war.'

The ghost of a smile crossed the CO's face. 'Very well. If that's what you want, you'll be posted to Flinders in the next couple of weeks.'

***

We got a good notion of what Flinders was going to be like the moment we got off the train after the four-day journey across the Nullarbor. Arriving at the station in the middle of the night, we discovered there was no transport to take us to the depot so the petty officer sent to meet us ordered us to double march – practically run – with all our kit, more than a mile to the barracks.

Once we were in our mess the PO ordered a detail to organise a cup of hot tea for all the lads. 'Austin, Bancroft, Bruce!' he shouted.

We leapt up. 'Yes, Chief.' In fact he wasn't a chief petty officer but we had noticed that the petty officers liked it when we called them Chief.

'Go and get hot tea for everyone.'

Early the following morning the same PO marched into the mess. 'Austin, Bancroft and Bruce,' he bellowed, 'double away and get morning tea and rations for the men.'

I stood up. I could see the way this was going, and if I and the other blokes allowed it to continue our lives at Flinders would be hell. 'Excuse me, Chief,' I piped up. He gazed at me with the standard petty-officer look: wary and suspicious, like I was a troublesome horse he might have to shoot. 'Do you know the alphabet?'

The look hardened, as if he was getting ready to fire. 'You trying to be funny?'

'No, Chief. But the way it's going, Austin, Bancroft and Bruce are going to win this war all by themselves.'

His eyes narrowed. Was he going to pull the trigger and have me up before the CO for insubordination? Then the look softened – very slightly. 'Fair enough,' he said and, glancing at his roster, called out the last three names on the list.

32

In comparison to HMAS *Leeuwin*, Flinders Naval Depot, otherwise known as HMAS *Cerberus*, was huge, though it didn't take me long to feel at home as out of my class of twenty ordinary seamen, sixteen were from WA. The training for ordinary seamen, like that for signallers, was intense. If I had thought we were busy at *Leeuwin*, here at Flinders we were close to frantic. But we were discovering the sinews of war: gunnery theory and practice; how to load and fire the big guns; seven weeks of torpedo training; learning how to handle mines and depth charges and the searchlights; rifle drill and practice. In my first rifle practice I scored only fifty-five out of a hundred, but over the course of the following months I managed to edge that up to seventy-five, which was at least the pass grade. And when we weren't learning the art of ordnance we were marching and drilling or being subjected to intense physical training. Time at Flinders rocketed past and I was astonished to find I had been there three months before I managed to cross the Nullarbor on a four-day train journey to get home for two weeks of leave.

A few weeks into my time at Flinders I had gotten a phone call. It was from the South Melbourne Football Club. Apparently someone at Subi Football Club had called South Melbourne and told them I was a useful player, so a bloke travelled the hundred or so kilometres down from Melbourne to talk to me about playing for South Melbourne while I was at Flinders. I was rapt. South Melbourne was a semi-pro club; what today we would call Premier League. It was a considerable cut above playing for Subiaco or the navy. Of course, I said yes.

Unfortunately, word got out that I had been approached by the club and a few days later I was ordered to report to the commanding officer. Once more I wondered what the hell I had done wrong as I was marched into his office and snatched off my cap.

'What's this I hear, Bancroft?' he snapped. 'You've agreed to play football for South Melbourne?'

'Yessir.' Pretty pleased with myself, I was expecting some kind of compliment. I should have known better. This was the navy. The navy didn't do compliments.

'Well now, Bancroft. Did you join the navy to play football or to fight a war?'

I thought it was a pretty stupid question – not that I was about to tell the CO that. But he must have known from my records that I had demoted myself so I could get into the war quicker. 'To fight a war, sir.'

'Very well. Which means you don't have time to go off playing football, do you? Tell them you can't play. You're too busy getting ready to fight a war. That's all.'

I was pretty peeved. The navy had denied me a chance to play for a really ace team. But I was even more irritated a week later when I was ordered, by no less than the CO himself, to play football for the navy against the army. In fact the CO saw to it that I played a lot of sport at Flinders. Apart from football, I played soccer and rugby union as well as a bit of cricket. Getting ready to fight a war apparently was not an impediment to me playing sport – so long as it was for the navy.

When on my next leave I told my father what had happened, he was hopping mad. 'You had a chance to play for a team in the Victoria League and this officer denied it to you? Who does he think he is?' It took me a while to calm my dad down and explain

34

to him that, in the navy, the commanding officer was God. In fact, I told him, at Flinders Naval Depot, the CO was so much of a god that even God called him God.

Though I never got to play for South Melbourne, I had a lot of good games playing for the navy. Armed services football was pretty big, and we played a lot of crack teams in the VFL. In one game I was going pretty well until the opposition moved a man onto me who ensured that I never got another kick of the ball. After the game they told me the bloke had won a Brownlow Medal.

Merv O'Donoughue, one of the blokes I played with on the navy team, was also from Perth. Merv was a good player, strong and aggressive, and we built up a good rapport on the field and became good mates off it.

By the October of 1941 I and all my mates had completed our basic training at Flinders. I had been in the navy for eleven months and had just been made up to ordinary seaman first class. I was itching to be posted to a ship.

When we finally received our posting I was over the moon. I was to serve on the light cruiser, HMAS *Perth* – a boy from Perth serving on a ship called *Perth*. You beauty! What's more, a lot of my mates from WA had also been posted to the *Perth*. Aside from my closest mates – Lofty Nagle, Marcus Clark and Merv O'Donoughue – some of the other lads were Harvey Gilbey, Norm Fuller, Les Bruce (known as 'Egghead'), Harry Larcombe, Charlie Thompson and Jim Hewitt – the list went on and on. In all, there were fourteen of us WA boys ordered to join the *Perth* from Flinders and we were a rip-roaring, boisterous mob. There wasn't a bad bloke among us.

We were also rapt to be joining the *Perth* because she was a fighting ship. For nearly a year she had been patrolling in the eastern Mediterranean; taking part in the invasion and subsequent evacuation of Greece and Crete while fighting off repeated attacks by German and Italian aircraft. Then, only six months before, she had been involved in the Battle of Cape Matapan in which ships of the British and Australian navies had sunk three Italian heavy cruisers and two destroyers for the loss of only a couple of torpedo bombers. Wherever there was action, it seemed *Perth* was in the thick of it. She was definitely the ship for me.

I joined her in October 1941 after she had been lying up in Sydney's Cockatoo Dockyard undergoing a major refit. Now she had been moved to Garden Island and the first moment I saw her, my heart leapt – exactly the way it did when I caught sight of Mirla after months away.

It was a bright sunny day and, even though she had suffered damage from enemy action, the *Perth* looked dazzling. Nothing could hide her true nature despite the fact that they were still repairing her – there was scaffolding on her superstructure, and there was the loud clatter of riveting and the sparks of the welders were arcing out onto the deck. This was a pedigree ship of war: sleek and powerful and bristling with guns. Just looking at her made my blood race and my heart swell with pride.

With much of the repairs almost completed, the *Perth* was now in the process of being repainted. Naturally, all the new recruits were immediately given a brush and paint tin and told to get stuck in. When we weren't painting we were scrubbing the decks and generally getting the ship to look her very best before we put to sea. We got into it willingly; we were so proud of her.

Because of the work still being undertaken on the ship, there wasn't enough room for us new lads to sleep aboard, so we were accommodated at HMAS *Kuttabul*, the accommodation ship moored alongside Garden Island. From there we had magnificent views of the harbour. For most of the *Perth* boys it was the first time we had been in Sydney and we were hoping to get some leave to explore the city. Though *Kuttabul* was only accessible by water, there were plenty of ferries across the harbour to the city. I fancied taking the ferry to Manley where Dorothy, one of my sisters, had settled after she had married. I got across to visit her a few times and usually took some of my washing. She was always pleased to see me, though I can't say she was as delighted to see my dirty clothes. A couple of times a few of us took the ferry across the harbour to see the beaches on the north shore, while a few of the lads talked about taking a look at the notorious Kings Cross.

Then, just as we thought we might get a little leave, we were moved 40 kilometres out of the city, to Liverpool Army camp. The reason, they told us, was lack of accommodation at *Kuttabul*.

Being deposited as a bunch of naval ratings into the very heart of the AIF at Liverpool Camp was a challenge for us, especially as on one side of our billets we had the AIF, while on the other was a battalion of blokes from the territorial army – 'chocos' we called them, meaning chocolate soldiers, with the implication that they were soft and couldn't fight.

We navy lads were ordered to exercise with the army and to join with it in drills and marching. We reckoned we were as smart as the army and could drill as well as they could, though of course they had a different opinion. They were especially scathing about our open order drill and reckoned none of us knew how to fire a rifle. So, pretty soon, we had fixed up a rifle-shooting contest in which, it was rumoured, all the smart money was on the army boys wiping the floor with us. As it turned out, we beat the army handsomely. We heard that quite a lot of senior army brass lost money on the contest so we were a pretty cocky bunch of naval ratings when, about a week later, we marched smartly out of the camp gates on our way back to the *Perth*.

With her new paintwork *Perth* was looking really great; like a sleek, well-muscled hunting dog, straining at the leash. As soon as we were back we heard that she had a new skipper, Captain Hector M. L. Waller, DSO RAN. 'Hec' Waller was well known in the navy. He had been commander of the 10th Destroyer Flotilla in the Mediterranean and, aboard HMAS *Stuart*, had seen a lot of action, including taking part in the Battle of Cape Matapan. It was the perfect combination: we had a fighting ship and now had a fighting captain.

Back on board we were into more drills, including closing up as quickly as possible to action stations. We also practiced abandoning ship, an exercise I didn't much care for. I didn't like to think that we would ever have to abandon the *Perth*. At that time we were also assigned our duties on the ship. Naturally, the navy being the navy, someone decided not to give me the job I'd been trained for.

At Flinders I had been trained mainly as a gun layer on the four-inch guns. It was a pretty heavy duty, entailing every few seconds lifting a shell weighing about seventy pounds and carrying it across the deck from the starboard hoist before heaving it into one of the breeches of the guns.

But instead of being assigned to one of the ship's four-inch guns, I was ordered below decks, to a position above the forward magazine where I would be loading six-inch shells onto the hoist to be taken to the guns above. As the six-inch shells weighed over a hundred pounds and I was a big, strong lad, I could see why the navy had given me the job. But it wasn't what I was trained for. What's more, I didn't want to be below decks in a battle. I wanted to be topside, where I could see what was happening and where I knew I would be taking part in the fight.

A couple of days after I had been assigned the job below decks, Lofty told me there was a position as a gun layer on P1: the forward, portside four-inch gun. I thought about it for all of ten seconds before deciding to do what I had done in civvy street – to front up and ask for the job. I went in search of the petty officer in charge of the gun deck and said, 'I believe you're looking for a gun layer.' I went on to tell him that, as I had been trained on the four-inch guns at Flinders, I would like the job. He appraised me for a few seconds, giving me the usual petty-officer look, and then replied, 'Yes, all right, lad. You'll do.'

I was delighted. I was serving on a great ship under a great skipper and now doing a job I was trained to do. Of course, I wasn't to know it then, but many of the blokes serving in the forward magazine didn't make it out when the *Perth* later went down.

Like everyone on board I was anxious to put to sea and get on with our sea trails and exercises. But a mysterious succession of accidents and incidents had held us up. The ship was being repaired by welders and fitters from the dockyards who we called 'dockyard mateys'. Most of them, we were told, were pretty militant union men with a lot of Communists in their numbers. Certainly they were in no hurry to repair the *Perth*; even I could see they spent a lot more of their time sitting around drinking tea and playing cards than they did fixing up the ship to put back to sea. There were a few ugly incidents between some of the ratings and the mateys when the ratings accused them of sabotage and being fifth columnists. I couldn't understand it. Even if the repairers were Communists, why wouldn't they want the *Perth* to get to sea and fight? Hitler had invaded Russia back in May, so now Joe Stalin was on our side. But the evidence was irrefutable. Someone was sabotaging the repair of the *Perth*; the after magazine had been flooded – something which couldn't possibly happen by accident – and a lot of the new wiring had been damaged and needed to be replaced. It wasn't a happy situation; some of our own people were fighting us. The captain was livid and ordered that the ship be patrolled at night by armed sailors with orders to shoot anyone lurking about who didn't stand still when challenged.

I was selected to patrol on the first night. The petty officer took me into the wardroom and issued me with a torch, a whistle and a loaded revolver. The PO gave me my instructions and sent me out into the dark. I was on patrol for the entire four-hour watch, creeping around the gun deck and a couple of decks below where, what with the blackout, it was as dark as Hitler's heart. I didn't see anyone, which was just as well as my main worry was that if I had to fire, not only would I likely miss, but I would stand a good chance of being hit by the ricochet.

At last, towards the end of November, the *Perth* was ready to go to sea and we put out into the Southern Pacific for sea trials and exercises. The skipper had us at it hard: for hours we practiced closing up and action stations as *Perth* went through her paces. She was a lovely vessel: all of us felt the exhilarating thrill when the skipper ordered her worked up to full speed and she surged through the water. At full bore her Parsons turbines could take her to over 30 knots – more than 60 kilometres an hour – and we loved it. It was as if *Perth* was made for the sea and we, her crew, were made for her. I'd never thought about it before but I was beginning to understand what all the old salts knew but never admitted: A sailor could fall in love with his ship.

After our exercises we crossed the Tasman and put in to Auckland which none of us ratings had ever seen before. After a few days patrolling off Auckland harbour we sailed back to Sydney and moored up.

In Sydney, a lot of the lads were given a long weekend pass. I drew the short straw and had to stay on board. Suddenly, early on Monday morning, the ship's klaxon opened up, shattering the peace. I was already on the gun deck as the Number Two's voice came over the Tannoy: 'Action Stations, Action Stations.'

To my ordinary seaman's mind, sounding action stations with half the ship's complement still ashore was pretty stupid. But as I wasn't about to question naval authority, I grabbed my flash mask and tin hat and closed up to my position at the guns. I was the only rating there, the rest of my watch were still sleeping it off somewhere in Sydney. I stood to my position as a live shell popped up from the starboard hoist. I humped it across the deck to the port gun, slotted into the breech of the gun and stood ready. A petty officer rushed past.

'What do I do, Chief?' I asked.

'Do your best, lad.'

I stared at his disappearing back in surprise. What the hell did that mean? Was I supposed to practice operating the gun on my own? It was possible, but the rate of fire with one man on a four-inch gun was ludicrous.

I stood closed up for about twenty minutes until another PO came past. 'What the hell's happening, Chief?' I pleaded.

He stopped and gave me a queer look. 'Haven't you heard?'

'Heard? No, I haven't heard anything. I've been stood to here. Why, what's happened?'

'The Japanese have bombed the American base at Pearl Harbour. The Japs are in the war. We're expecting their planes over at any moment.'

Mirla's Story

After he went into the navy Arthur continued writing to me regularly, and whenever he got leave from the depot in Fremantle he would come to see me. I suppose you could say we were 'stepping out', but though we kissed a little, we were a long way from being intimate. We seemed more like good friends than a romantically attached couple. But his chatty letters, along with their quirky but talented little drawings, remained interesting and full of fun – even though I thought they were often too short. And, above all, Arthur made me laugh.

Especially when I got his 'long' letter.

As always, I checked the letterbox on my way to work. I had secured a good job at MacRobertson-Miller Aviation, a small airline that operated ten-seater aircraft on flights from Perth to Darwin. The aircraft stopped off at about a dozen airfields in the bush en route to Darwin, and I was responsible for booking passengers onto the flights. What with the war, we were very busy. Dashing out, I saw there was a letter and was thrilled. I opened it on the bus, slitting the envelope open with a nail file, and pulled out the letter. Imagine my horror when a long streamer of toilet paper unfurled in my hand! The bloke in the seat next to me nearly had a fit: he was staring wide-eyed and in horror at the crazy girl beside him, obviously wondering what I was going to do next. I felt my face go as red as a beetroot as I stuffed the toilet-roll letter back into its envelope. I read it when I got to work and then showed it to the girls in my office. I told them what had happened on the bus and we all had a great laugh.

Then Arthur was posted to Flinders Naval Depot in Victoria. He could have stayed in Fremantle for a few more months but he wangled it to get there quicker and to get into the war. Of course I admired him for that, even though I would have liked him to stay close so we could carry on regularly seeing each other. But there was a war on, and what any of us wanted in our personal lives had to take second place. It was then – when he was sent away to the other side of the continent – that I suddenly realised how much I felt for him. My feelings had gone beyond enjoying his letters and liking his company and laughing at his jokes and antics. With him on the other side of the country, so much further from me and so much closer to the war, I realised I was falling in love.

3

The Best and Worst of Times

I am an automaton; a small cog in the marvellous fighting machine called the Perth. *I dart across the deck to haul another heavy four-inch shell up from the hoist. I turn and, for an instant, glance up. The Zeros are coming in low: tongues of fire leaping from the leading edges of their wings. They are machine-gunning us, though if there are bullets whizzing past my head or ricocheting off the deck I am unaware of them. My mind is locked on to my job: feed the guns. The guns are hungry: eight barrels each hurtling more than ten shells a minutes into the air. Better than anything we ever did in training – though even in training we were good. But this is the real thing. Men in planes are trying to kill us. Our job – my job – is to kill them first. Only I don't think about that. I don't think about anything except ramming the next shell home into the breech. Somewhere in my peripheral vision I am conscious of Lofty and Marcus; the part of their faces not covered by their flash masks are set and intense as I guess mine is. The navy has trained us superbly. There is no fear here; no notion that death could be millimetres away. Our only focus is doing what we have been trained to do.*

Suddenly we hear the order to cease fire. I look up. The Zeros have sheered away and have already cleared the harbour. Low over the water they are winging out to sea. Everyone is grinning. We have seen the bastards off. I glance around to check what damage has been done. None to the ship that I can see, but the doors to the godowns, the small warehouses on the quayside, have been blown askew by the percussion of our guns and inside their murky interiors I can make out stacked cases of gin and whiskey and rum along with thousands of cartons of cigarettes.

Some of the lads give a small cheer and immediately swing across the narrow gap between the ship's railing and the quayside and form a human chain to liberate as much of the booze and cigarettes as they can. I watch them and burst into laughter. Thirty seconds ago these same blokes were part of a totally focused and efficient killing machine, fighting off a determined enemy. Now, they are busily swiping a stack of illicit grog and as many smokes as possible before the ship's officers twig to what's going on.

If that's not typical bloody navy – then I don't know what is.

Of course the Japs didn't come, though we remained ready for them, closed up at action stations. All morning I watched the blokes streaming back on board from weekend leave, their cheerful faces clenching the moment they heard the news. For hours we stood tight to the guns: fused to the ship, as much a part of her as the rivets in her hull, like protective sons around a threatened mother.

In an instant our world had changed. We had expected to go to war in the north – to steam 10 000 miles into another hemisphere before we fired our guns. But now the war had come to us; the enemy somewhere over the horizon to the east; maybe within a day's sailing of Sydney Harbour.

Two days later we heard that Japanese torpedo bombers had sunk the British battleship HMS *Prince of Wales* and the battle cruiser *Repulse* off the coast of Malaya. We stared at each in silence. The *Prince of Wales* displaced 44 000 tons, had fourteen-inch guns and fifteen-inch thick armour plating. *Repulse* was pretty much the same. If, we asked each other silently, the Japs could sink capital ships like those, what chance did *Perth*, at 7000 tons and armed with six-inch popguns, have? We soon put the question aside. It did no good to be thinking like that. We had a job to do and we had to get on with it. We reckoned when the *Perth* came up against the Japs, we would do all right.

The threat of imminent battle coalesced us. We who had been good mates before were suddenly as close as brothers. Curiously, I found my vision narrowing, my focus sharpening onto the things that really mattered: discovering that the warm thoughts I had been harbouring of King and Country, duty and Empire, were evaporating. Patriotic notions of what we were fighting for were turning misty and diffuse; so dispersed in fact that they had somehow become wrapped in the flag fluttering at our stern. Now I reckoned that when I went into battle I would be fighting for two things: my ship and my mates.

The navy was great for mateship. Long before Pearl Harbor I had made good mates with some of the blokes in the first intake of communications cadets at *Leeuwin* and even more with the mob at Flinders, where so many of our mess were West Australian boys isolated in deepest Victoria. It was with three of my mates, Harvey Gilbey, Norm Fuller and Les Bruce, that I shared, at the navy's insistence and the navy's expense, a flat in Kings Cross.

Returning from our brief sojourn at Liverpool Army Camp, some of us were told there was no room for us to mess at *Kuttabul*. The navy was pretty laid back about it. 'There's no room, lads,' a sub-lieutenant told us.

'So, what do we do, sir?'

'Find some digs, of course. A flat or a bed and breakfast. The navy will pay.'

They were magic words. We jumped aboard the next ferry and took ourselves to Kings Cross where, in Tower Street, we found a suitable two-bedroom flat on the second story of a small unit. We were there about three weeks, during which time we formed the fervent hope that the war would never end. We had a ripper time.

Our job for most of that period was to operate one of the navy's 32-foot cutters that plied between the shore and the navy's ships moored out in the harbour. We delivered mail, orders and officers to the ships and brought back other officers and mail to the shore. The four of us were the crew under an amiable, easy-going PO. It was fine November weather and we spent our days being serenaded by the sound of the small engine as we chugged around Sydney Harbour with nothing to do except look smart in our white uniforms and smartly execute all the navy drills for handling a naval cutter. I don't know if we impressed the captains, commanders and even the odd vice-admiral whom we ferried across the placid blue water, but we certainly impressed ourselves.

Those were our days. Our nights were even more fun. Living

in the flat we had no mess duties so we had every night off. Kings Cross was vibrant and, despite the blackout, bustling with life until late into the evening. The place was filled with sailors and young women, many of whom we presumed were prostitutes, though, unlike the old salts, we young lads were much too afraid to go anywhere near them. We just stared.

Most evenings we took the ferry over to Luna Park, where entry was free to members of the armed services. The first time the four of us walked through the gates the band broke into 'All the Nice Girls Love a Sailor'. We were certainly hoping so! There were dances every night except Sunday at the Luna and, of course, there was all the fun of the fair with a big ferris wheel and dodgems cars and lots of sideshows. And we noticed too that where there was a fun fair, there were pretty girls – and where there were pretty girls there were sailors.

In some ways it was, as Charles Dickens put it, 'the best of times and the worst of times'. There was a war on and young blokes were going away to it, some never to return. Yet Sydney was vital and alive and filled with uniforms – mainly naval uniforms. It seemed as if everyone was pulling together and doing their best to have a good time; trying to make the most of a bad situation.

Well . . . not everyone. In Hyde Park one of the volunteer organisations had set up a canteen where they served free meals to navy, army and air-force personnel. As it was close to our flat in Kings Cross, the lads and I used it a lot. One evening I noticed a curious-looking sailor being served a meal. He was a leading seaman: I knew that from the fouled anchor on the upper-right sleeve of his uniform. Only his rank badge should have been on his upper *left* sleeve. The bloke was a bloody impostor, chiselling a free meal. I marched across to him, the others right behind me. He saw us coming and I could tell from the sudden dart of fear in his eyes that he knew he'd been sussed. 'Get the hell out here,' I snarled. He took one look at us and scuttled away. Yet the incident left a sour taste in my mouth. We were supposed to all be in this bloody war together – yet there were spivs and bludgers pulling on a uniform that they had no right to wear and taking advantage of the situation. It made me as mad as a meat axe to think there were people out there trying to get something for nothing out of the war effort when we could have the Japs on our doorstep at any moment. To my mind what that bloke was doing was the total opposite of good mateship.

Of the lads in the flat, I suppose I was closest to Harvey. He was older than the rest of us, already married and, when I first got to know him at Flinders, he was waiting to become a father for the first time. Harvey was a quiet, softly spoken kind of bloke, small in stature and neat, both in his person and in everything he did. Everybody liked him – he was Mister Nice Guy. However, at Flinders, as most of his naval pay was going back home to take care of his pregnant wife, Harvey didn't have the same amount of cash as the rest of us to spend on beer. By that time, of course, along with all the other things the navy had taught me, it had taught me to drink. So, as I had money in my pocket and Harvey and I were mates, I stood him a good few beers.

About halfway through our time at Flinders some of us were given two weeks' leave. Harvey and I took the train across the Nullarbor and after a couple of days arrived in Kalgoorlie, the last stop on the long, tedious journey before Perth. At Kalgoorlie Harvey was surprised to hear his name being called on the station loudspeaker. He went to the station master's office to find a telegram waiting for him. Telegrams in wartime were not generally good news but this one was – the best news. Harvey was a dad. He had a new son. Mother and baby were doing fine. Well, we couldn't allow this great event to go uncelebrated, and as we had a few hours' stopover we headed for the station bar.

I was a bit worried at the time as I had another carbuncle on my neck and was praying I wouldn't be forced to repeat my experience at *Leeuwin* and end up in the sick bay. This one was a real corker and was giving me gyp. However, there's no doubt in my mind that the best possible cure for carbuncles is to wet a newborn baby's head. I noticed with every beer going down in the noisy, smoke-filled station bar, that the pain on my neck lessened. In fact, by the time Harvey and I managed to stagger back onto the train, I couldn't feel the carbuncle at all – though, to be honest, by that stage there were quite a few body parts I couldn't feel. Thank God we had about ten hours to sober up before we got into Perth. There we shook hands and separated: me anxious to see Mirla and to catch up with my family, Harvey eager to see his new son.

On the gundeck of P1, my closest mates were 'Lofty' Nagle and Marcus Clark. We were a fearsome trio. At six feet tall, I was the little'un: Lofty was six-foot two and Marcus six three. Merv, who was also a big bloke at six two, was the other member of our special mob, though he wasn't with us on P1 – he was assigned to one of the six-inch guns. Although none of us were looking for trouble when we went drinking in Sydney, I noticed a lot of other blokes gave us a wide berth. It made us chuckle; Lofty especially was as gentle as a lamb. He was the quietest of the quartet: serious and thoughtful, although he could be quite a laugh and loon about when the mood took him. Merv was pretty quiet too, although he would talk about football till the cows came home.

Marcus was quite the opposite of Lofty. He had worked as a salesman for WD & HO Wills, the cigarette company, and was full of the typical salesman's banter and jokes. Marcus had spent a couple of years selling cigarettes to publicans in the wheat belt and had an inexhaustible supply of funny stories. What with his size and sunny disposition, he was a character everyone remembered.

I suppose I was the bridge between the others. I wasn't as serious and studied as Lofty; not quite as obsessed with football as Merv; and couldn't match Marcus in the joke-telling personal-charisma department. But as a small mob of mates we were inseparable – as tight as brothers – especially after Pearl Harbour.

I got on well with everyone in the gun crew, though in the navy, as in any organisation where there are a lot of blokes, you had to stake out your territory and be ready to assert yourself. There were about a dozen of us to each gun and at least half of the blokes on the gundeck had seen action in the Mediterranean. We new ratings respected them for that; they had experienced battle and we hadn't. I suppose all of us new blokes were wondering how we would act when the time came. The old salts, for their part, pulled our legs a little, telling us we were green and untested, but by and large they didn't make a big thing out of our not seeing action. Except for one rating. He kept on about it and was forever telling us, 'You blokes haven't seen action yet. Wait till yer do, then you'll know what it's all about. Some of you will be filling your pants.'

If I'd known then what I know now, I would have said that the bloke had a problem with being under fire and was trying to displace it through putting us new ratings down. But back then all I knew was that his constant niggling was beginning to grate on my nerves. One morning, after he'd started yet again telling us, 'You have no idea what war is like. Wait until you see action. Then you'll know what it's all about,' I bailed up to him.

'Considering we haven't seen any war yet, how about you and me having our own little war right now?'

He was a little bloke and could see I'd had a gutful. He backed off, laughing nervously. 'No, no, mate. No offence. I was just pullin' yer leg, that's all.' He never mentioned it again. And, after Pearl Harbour, no one did. We all knew we would be in the thick of it soon enough.

A couple of days after the attack on Pearl Harbour we heard that the Japanese had invaded Malaya and were starting to fight their way down the peninsular towards Singapore. That, we thought, was a big mistake. Nobody could take Singapore; it was impregnable. What's more, there were Indian troops, Gurkas and the like, in Malaya. Those blokes were warriors – they *liked* to fight. We reckoned the Japs were going to get a bloody nose, especially as a lot of our troops were being diverted to Singapore to help defend it.

Shortly after Pearl Harbour I received notification from the navy board that I had been promoted to Able Seaman First Class. I was rapt. A day later, Harvey rocked up in the mess to say congratulations and to hand me a small envelope. 'What this, mate?' I quizzed him.

He shrugged. 'It's what I reckon I owe you from all the extra beers you've been buying me.'

I tore the envelope open. About twenty pounds nestled inside. 'I don't want this, Harvey,' I protested. 'Send it home to your wife and kid.' I made to hand it back. He pushed it back at me.

'You keep it, Blood. I owe you. It's from my back pay.' He walked away before I could say another word.

Harvey had been made up to Able Seaman well before the rest of us, but it had taken months for his back pay to catch up to his new status. Over the next few days I tried to return him his money but he wouldn't have it. He reckoned he owed me and that was that. And Harvey had been clever. He had made sure he had paid me on board the *Perth* where there was no chance of me buying him more beer in recompense. Harvey, like many blokes I knew on the *Perth*, was one of the best shipmates I ever had.

From early December and into January 1942, *Perth* was constantly engaged in patrols, escort duties, exercises and manoeuvres. Early in the month we were told some shocking news. *Sydney* had been sunk. No one knew the details. She had been patrolling in the Indian Ocean and had gone into action, against whom or what no one knew. So far, there were no survivors. I couldn't believe that our sister ship had gone down with all hands. It was too much to contemplate. I had gone to school with some of the blokes serving on her.

During those early weeks after Pearl Harbour we sailed into the Pacific as far west as New Caledonia, and as far north as New Guinea in the Coral Sea. Much of the time we were hunting subs. But now the mood on board was different. It was more concentrated: we moved that bit quicker, went to our duties a little more fervently, watched the cloudless blue sky more intently, monitored the waves constantly. Somewhere out there over the shimmering horizon could be a Japanese carrier group: at any time we could come under attack from Zeros and *Nakajimas*. And there was always the chance of *us* being the hunted; of being stalked by a Japanese sub. We'd been told that the Japanese navy had the best, most accurate and deadliest torpedoes in the world.

At the end of January we were back in Sydney but were scarcely there a day before we sailed east with the heavy cruiser, HMAS *Australia* and the Kiwi Light Cruiser *Leander*, a sister ship to the *Perth* and built by the British at the same time. After a few hours the *Perth* broke away from the flotilla and sailed independently to Melbourne where we refuelled at Williamstown. A day later we left Williamstown, sailing west, and Hec Waller came on the ship's PA system saying that HMAS *Perth* was heading for her home. This brought a big cheer from all the WA blokes in the crew.

We tied up in Fremantle on a Sunday, with the local lads looking forward to a spot of leave and surprising their families. But orders came through when we arrived to sail as soon as possible for Batavia in Java, so none of us got any leave, and after a few frustrating hours of being so near and yet so far while taking on fuel in Fremantle, we sailed north early the following day.

But, as so often happened in the navy, our orders were countermanded at sea and we turned around, heading back towards Freo. Naturally my mates and I were pretty pleased, especially as when we arrived we were told we had a few hours' leave. I grabbed a ship's pennant and the special half-pound box of chocolates I had been saving for Mirla.

As part of the war effort, Nestlé, the chocolate company, had been manufacturing boxes of chocolates with the name, insignia and a photo of Australian ships on the top of the box. I thought they looked very smart, so naturally I bought a box for Mirla with a picture of the *Perth* on the lid. I reckoned she and her mum would enjoy a choccie or two.

At the gangplank I ran into Harvey and offered to buy him a swift beer by way of payback for the money he had given me. He said no. He was anxious to get home and see how much his baby son had grown. It was, he reminded me, only the second time in more than six months that he had seen him. He didn't know it then, but it was also his last.

Everyone got a big surprise when I walked into our house; no one knew I was coming as wartime censorship didn't allow for ships' movements to be publicised. I spent a few hours with my parents and one of my sisters during which there was a lot of talk about how much I had filled out and how good I looked in my uniform. After that it was time to go and surprise Mirla. I took the tram to her work and waited outside. She looked like a stunned mullet when she saw me. Anyway, she was pretty pleased and gave me an enormous hug. I was always surprised how strong she was for such a little one. We caught the bus home and I gave her the pennant with HMAS *Perth* printed on it, along with the special box of chocolates. She took one look at the box and gave me another rib-crushing hug, though I noticed she didn't offer me a choccie! She put the box on a sideboard and said we'd have one later. She was, she said, in a bit of a rush. She was on duty that evening at the VAD, which stood for the Volunteer Aid Detachment, though, as it was mainly staffed by young women, we lads in the navy reckoned it stood for 'Virgins Awaiting Destruction'.

I was pretty cheesed off. I had only a few hours' leave and Mirla would be away for at least an hour and a half of it! But there was a war on and my personal feelings didn't come into it. There was no way Mirla would not turn up to do her bit, so at seven we took the bus to West Perth where I waited around in a café until she rocked up at nine. We spent the rest of the evening and well into the early hours of the morning talking. We had a lot to talk about. I think we both knew that when I left this time, I could be sailing into battle.

We didn't want to part but when, finally, we did, Mirla promised to call me on the ship's telephone hook-up the next day. It was one of the hardest partings of my life, but at last I left her and returned to the *Perth*. It was the early hours of the morning of Friday 13 February, 1942. Arriving on board, I heard that Hec Waller had postponed putting to sea until early Saturday. Our captain, like a lot of regular navy blokes, was deeply superstitious. Frustratingly, we remained in harbour throughout the day; once more so near but yet so far! I waited all evening and into the night for Mirla's phone call, but it never came. We sailed just after midnight on Saturday.

At sea a day later, we heard that Singapore had fallen to the Japanese. It was almost impossible to believe. Singapore had been the impregnable bastion of Empire in the East. Now the Japs had it and thousands of our blokes who had been sent there to defend it were either dead or captured. The land campaign in Malaya had been a disaster – nothing but reverses and retreats by our side. To me it sounded a bit like Gallipoli; damn fine troops wasted through the stupidity of a bunch of generals who didn't know what the hell was going on.

Now, we were wondering what our role would be. We had been in the process of escorting a convoy of oil tankers to the terminal at Palembang. But with Singapore gone, sooner or later Palembang was bound to fall into enemy hands. At least our blokes – the top brass in charge of the navy – had some idea of what was going on, as pretty soon the convoy was ordered to return to Fremantle while the *Perth* sailed north. Once we had received our orders the *Perth* got up speed and began steaming through the middle of the convoy which had slowed and was readying to turn back. As we sailed between the oil tankers their crews came to the railings and cheered us: crowds of merchant seamen waving us good luck as we picked up speed.

A few days later Hec Waller came on the PA system to tell us he'd received word that Darwin was being bombed. Immediately every man in the ship looked to starboard. Sailing north, we had just reached latitude twelve degrees south, on the same approximate parallel as Darwin. We stared out over the sparkling blue ocean to the distant horizon. Somewhere over there, 1300 nautical miles or 2500 kilometres east, our people were being bombed. The war was no longer on our doorstep. It was on top of us; in our laps; right in our own homes. What had been happening to other people in Europe was happening to us. And we on the *Perth* were sailing *away* from it. The knowledge that we were leaving our own people behind to suffer the bombing was disturbing and made us edgy.

Soon afterwards, somewhere to the east of Christmas Island,

the skipper again came on the PA system to tell us we could be sighting enemy ships at any time. If we sighted a ship that did not respond correctly to our recognition signals, he said he intended to 'shoot first and ask questions afterwards'. We had a bit of a grin over that. It was good to have a skipper with a bit of biff about him.

Not long after that we came in sight of Java Head before finding ourselves sailing out of the Indian Ocean and into the Pacific via the Sunda Strait, the narrow channel between Java and Sumatra. At its narrowest the Strait is no more than 30 kilometres wide: about the same distance as the island of Rottnest from Fremantle and the beaches of Perth's western suburbs. Sailing through the Strait so close to the land was like going through a narrow door into a room full of snakes, for beyond the Strait, the Java Sea was enemy waters.

Immediately after the fall of Singapore, the Japanese had turned their attention to the Dutch East Indies, which had a plentiful supply of raw materials and, most important of all, oil. We knew from naval intelligence that Jap invasion fleets were already at sea, bound for Java. Our job was to join up with a mob called ABDA, which stood for American, British, Dutch and Australian Command, and which had been ordered to defend Java. A quick look at a map showed what a hard ask *that* was. The northern coastline of Java is 700 kilometres long and no one knew exactly where the Japanese invasion fleets intended to land.

Still, the battle fleet, some assembled at Tanjong Priok, the harbour of Batavia, the others at Sourabaya, 500 kilometres east, seemed, on paper anyway, to be pretty impressive. There were seven or eight cruisers and about a dozen destroyers, though two of the cruisers and a couple of the destroyers anchored at Tanjong Priok, where we docked, were First World War vintage; pretty ancient to be an effective part of a battle fleet. I also noticed that *Perth* was the only Australian ship present, although we were joined a day or so later by another sister ship, HMAS *Hobart*.

One good thing was that the Brits were well represented, there being a fair number of Royal Navy warships anchored outside the harbour. One of them was the famous *Exeter,* the eight-inch heavy cruiser that had taken part in the sinking of the German pocket battleship *Admiral Graf Spee* at the Battle of the River Plate in 1939.

The battle fleet, which the officers were calling a 'Striking Force', was commanded by a Dutch Admiral, Rear-Admiral Doorman. None of us had ever heard of him. We wondered why a Dutchman was in charge of the fleet. One of the officers explained that as far as the Dutch were concerned, this was a last-ditch stand. Their homeland in Europe had been occupied by the Germans and now it looked like the Japanese were set to invade their colony in the East Indies. They were throwing everything they had into defending their empire. So, as this was basically a Dutch show, they were in command. Well, that made sense to us, although we hoped this admiral and the Dutch cruisers under his command knew what they were doing.

The officer told us the Dutch were a proud maritime nation. Their navy had even beaten the British a few hundred years back . . . which sounded pretty impressive until we thought about it afterwards. What our situation amounted to was that the 'Striking Force' was to be led by a navy that had not fought a battle at sea for more than two hundred years! What's more, until a few weeks earlier, no American ship had fired a shot in anger in over fifty years. That, to my mind, left just us and the Brits to do the business if or when we ran up against one of the Jap invasion fleets.

We mumbled among ourselves. Why were we being commanded by some unknown Dutch admiral? Why couldn't they put *our* skipper in charge? He had commanded a flotilla in the Med and had seen action. Or the captain of the *Exeter*, perhaps? He'd seen action and had been part of a big naval victory. All of us would have felt happier if we had been commanded by one of our own.

That afternoon we came under attack for the first time. We were in the harbour alongside an oil tanker and taking on fuel. As action stations sounded, I scrambled to put on my white canvas flash mask, gloves and tin hat. Coming in high over the ocean was a flight of nine *Mitsubishi* bombers. I leapt across the deck and heaved the first of the four-inch shells out of the hoist. Although the shells weighed about 70 pounds (that's 32 kilograms) and were at least 1.5 metres long, curiously, they seemed as light as feathers. I scuttled across to the gundeck, completely focused on getting the shell into the mechanical fuse setter and then slamming it into the gun's breech. From somewhere behind me I heard what I guessed was the whistle of dropping bombs but paid no attention. There were no explosions, so I guessed the bombers had missed. The racket from the guns was unbelievable, with the six-inch guns also firing at the bombers.

It was then I understood how well we had been trained. Without training, that ear-splitting, scalp-lifting, booming cacophony might have driven me insane. As it was, I ignored it, just as I ignored the possibility of being blown to bits at any moment.

Nothing in the world mattered – nothing at all – except getting that next shell into the breech of the gun. We in the gun crews prided ourselves on the fact that, in any single second of action, we could have twenty-five or twenty-six shells in the air. Within seconds the gundeck was littered with spent shell casings, the sun glinting on their burnished brass as I kicked them aside in my rush to feed the guns.

The action lasted several minutes, during which I heard two explosions. A couple of bombs had hit merchant ships moored ahead of us in the harbour but from what I could see later, they did little damage. Then, towards the end of the action, I noticed one of the bombers coming in to make a low-level attack on the *Perth* from dead ahead. I wasn't the only one who had seen him. Instantly every gun on the ship trained on this one aircraft. Our four-inch guns went berserk, increasing their rate of fire and unleashing such a barrage that the pilot released his bomb too early. It fell harmlessly into the waters of the harbour. As the plane turned away we saw that it had been hit – dark smoke billowing from its fuselage. Out over the ocean it began losing height. At that moment we were ordered to cease fire and all the lads let out a tremendous cheer. That's one bastard who wouldn't be making it home for tea, we reckoned.

The crew of P1 thought we were the ones who had scored the hit on the bomber, though of course the crews on all the other four-inch guns reckoned *they* were the ones who had nailed him. It didn't really matter. The bombers had come to destroy the big oil tanks on the harbour quays, yet not one tank had been hit. We had successfully defended the harbour oil terminal and seen the bombers off. And we new blokes had experienced our first action and drawn blood.

The following morning three Zeros swept in low over in the ocean, strafing the oil tanks and the decks of the warships. Once more, we went into action. A squadron of bombers followed the Zeros in, again aiming for the oil tanks. Though none of the big tanks were hit, one bomb did hit the tanker moored alongside and refuelling HMAS *Hobart*, which forced *Hobart* to move out of the inner harbour and into the anchorage to complete her refuelling.

As soon as the air raid was over we noticed that the blast from our guns had blown down many of the rickety doors of the godowns, the small warehouses on the quayside. Inside we noticed box upon box of booze stacked as high as their rattan ceilings. As fast as rats up a drainpipe, some of the lads scrambled over the side of *Perth* and invaded the godowns, forming a human chain to ferry boxes of whiskey, gin and rum, along with hundred of cartons of cigarettes, back onto the ship. Once the officers got wind of what was happening they ordered all the stolen alcohol and cigarettes to be deposited on the quarterdeck. But in many instances they were too late. A lot of the lads had already squirreled their ill-gotten gains below decks and nowhere near as much booze and cigarettes appeared on the quarterdeck as had been liberated from the godowns.

Shortly after midday we were ordered to sail east. A large Japanese invasion force had been sighted approaching the east coast of Java and we were expected to engage it and, if we could, destroy it. We set sail for Sourabaya on the afternoon of Wednesday

25 February. We were going into battle and, as if to celebrate, below decks a lot of the lads were having themselves a little party.

Mirla's Story

You could have knocked me over with a feather when I saw Arthur standing there, outside my office. He looked the bee's knees in his uniform. It was the first time I had seen him in his *Perth* cap. I could have hugged him to death. He had bought me a ship's pennant and a lovely box of chocolates with a picture of HMAS *Perth* on its lid. By this time we had been at war for over two-and-a-half years and chocolates were something none of us civilians had seen in a long time. Chocolate was so scarce I hugged the box almost as much as I hugged Arthur.

Yet, although I was over the moon at seeing him, I was also disappointed. That evening I was on duty at the VAD. Happily, Arthur said he would wait for me, so after I had done my stint in West Perth, we took the bus together back to Subiaco where we went for a long walk before going back to my house to spend the rest of the evening, and well into the night, talking and loving. Of course it wasn't the kind of loving young people do nowadays; we weren't intimate, even though we kissed and cuddled almost all night. Some of the time I just clung to Arthur and let the tears roll down my cheeks. We both had a feeling that, this time, when he left, he could be sailing into harm's way. When we finally parted and he went back to his ship, I promised to telephone him before he sailed.

The next day I made arrangements to make the call. One of my friend's parents owned a greengrocer's shop with a telephone, and they said I could use it. That afternoon I rushed home from work. I'd heard the *Perth* was still in harbour so I was excited at having a final

THE BEST AND WORST OF TIMES

chat with Arthur. But when I got home my mother told me my cousin, Joy, had received distressing news. Milton, her fiancé, who was serving with the 2nd/4th Machine Gun Battalion, had been wounded in the battle for Singapore and had lost part of his leg. Joy was distraught and my mother said we needed to go over to her house in Victoria Park to comfort her.

I hurried around to the greengrocers to make my call but the line to the telephone on the *Perth* was constantly engaged. I dialled and dialled but each time all I got was the engaged tone. I was so frustrated I was crying, but no matter how many times I dialled I couldn't get through. Meanwhile my mother was waiting for me to rush over to my cousin's house. In the end I had to abandon trying to make the call.

It was two-and-a-half years before I spoke to Arthur again.

The following day I heard that the *Perth* had sailed very early on the morning of February 14th – Valentine's Day.

Missing that last chance to speak to Arthur before he sailed made me very emotional. I was so sad, and nothing anybody said or did could get me out of it. It was as if I had had a premonition. It took me a few days to pull myself together and set myself right. When I finally got something of my old, cheery personality back, I decided to write to Arthur and tell him the truth about how I felt. This is part of that letter.

My Dearest Arthur,

 Now, don't go crook because it is over a week since I last wrote but I will tell you the reason why. I have been so miserable in the past week that every time I started to write to you, my letter was so full of misery that I wouldn't continue it to send to you. I am feeling in a better mood now so here goes

65

to write you a cheerful letter (if I can). To tell you the truth, Arthur, I have been worried. I only found out last week where you were ------- so that was the reason . . .

. . . Arthur I have never been able to pluck up enough courage to tell you this at any time but owing to the war position at present and goodness knows what will happen to you or I in the future, I want you to know that I love you and always will. Now don't go thinking that I am going in for that 'sob' stuff but I want you to know this in case anything should happen to you. I have been crazy over you for months now and haven't had the courage to tell you. Perhaps you have had just a little 'inkling' of it but when you came home . . . my heart just turned over in leaps and bounds. I was in heaven for one week.

Well, now that is off my chest, I can go about feeling a little easier, knowing that you know. Don't be too hard on me and call me a silly little fool but I mean every word I have written.

The time has come again when I must go so hoping and praying that you are safe and well and happy. I will say 'Au Revoir', Arthur.

Lots of love and xx
    From your loving
    Mirla.

Arthur never received the letter.

A couple of days later the local paper, the *West Australian*, carried the banner headline: **JAPS SINK THE *PERTH*.**

4

Every Man For Himself

They are our men in the water ahead. We are steaming at 30 knots and the skipper throws the Perth *onto the port tack so we may avoid them. But there is no notion of stopping to rescue them. Men are expendable in a battle; ships are not. That much I am learning. The men are waving their arms; we are close enough to hear their cries. Some are screaming out at the tops of their voices. The language is Dutch: foreign to my ears. Yet I need no translation. I hear the message loud and clear. The language of men abandoned in the ocean and petrified of dying is universal: 'Save me – please don't let me die,' stabs you to the heart with its tone, not its words. Yet others in the water are silent and bravely waving to us as if wishing us godspeed and good luck.*

I bend to my task, hefting another shell from the hoist, averting my eyes from the men. I straighten up and catch Lofty's glance. Guiltily, his eyes cut away from mine. I know what he is thinking; the same as me. I'm glad it's not me out there in the water. It's not a charitable thought, but this is a battle and battles do not permit the practice of charity. Another lesson I am learning.

I struggle across the deck with the shell, numbing my mind with the great anaesthetic of war – my duty – which allows for no more than a passing tinge of pity. I'm sorry for those blokes but today it's them. Tomorrow it may be me.

Returning to the hoist I see that the Java, *steaming up behind us, has not followed us around in our tack to port. If she stays on her course she could plough through the men in the water. For a moment I imagine the Dutch cruiser shoving them under her armour plate; chewing them up with her propellers. I grab the shell and hurry across the deck to ram it into the breech of the four-inch. It doesn't do to think in a battle: yet another little lesson in my continuing education. Imagination can immobilise a seaman as effectively as a serious wound. Don't think, just act, is our motto. It works. This battle, along with all the hours I have spent at action stations has turned my existence into one long continuous blur in which I have learned to eat when I can, sleep when I can, fight with as little fuss as possible and, from what I have just witnessed, to die the same way.*

These are the lessons of war.

We reached Sourabaya about noon, where I counted thirteen warships riding at anchor in the harbour. Gazing at their steel-grey hulls and abundant guns across the calm, blue waters, I thought they looked a pretty good striking force – even better now that *Perth* was on the team. Sourabaya had been hard-hit by Jap bombers: many of the oil tanks were still smouldering and we could see the anti-aircraft gunners on the other ships were closed up to their guns, like us on P1.

Two of the ships were heavy cruisers: the Royal Navy's HMS *Exeter* and the American vessel, USS *Houston*. Both were equipped with eight-inch guns and definitely looked like they meant business, though, as we steamed slowly past the *Houston,* we could see her eight-inch after turret had been damaged in action and was clearly out of commission. Still, between her and the *Exeter,* the battle fleet had twelve eight-inch guns, each one capable of hurtling 120 kilograms of high-explosive shell more than 28 kilometres. By comparison, the six-inch guns on the *Perth* could only achieve a range of 23 kilometres. But we reckoned that once we got in range we would knock the stuffing out of any Japanese invasion fleet.

Aside from the *Perth*, the other light cruisers in the battle fleet were Dutch: the *De Ruyter* and the *Java,* both of which, we noticed, were equipped pretty much like the *Perth*, with a combination of four- and six-inch guns. The *De Ruyter* was the Dutch admiral's flagship. In addition to the cruisers I counted nine destroyers: two Dutch, three British and four American. Yet, while the British destroyers were modern and the two Dutch ships reasonably up-to-date, the four American vessels looked ancient and obsolete. The fact each had four smoke stacks (called 'four-stackers'), immediately gave away their age. We guessed they'd probably been built around the end of the last war.

All of us on P1 studied the ships carefully as we cruised slowly to our appointed anchorage, noticing that *Perth* was the only Australian ship present. HMAS *Hobart* had been delayed because of the bombing of her oil tanker at Tanjong Priok and wasn't expected to arrive until the following day. It felt strange and a little unsettling to be the only Australian vessel; even stranger, now that we were actually assembled, to be part of a striking force made up of four different navies.

I wondered how everyone was going to communicate. We and the Brits could understand each other well enough and, at a stretch, we could understand the Americans, though whether they understood us Australians was a different matter. But who the hell understood Dutch? Did the admiral speak English? And how, I wondered, would the ships communicate in battle? Ships in an action at sea need to have perfect communication: I had learned that elementary fact in my first weeks at HMAS *Leeuwin* as a communications cadet. How were fourteen warships going to work it with a Dutch admiral, a different language, four different radio protocols and at least one different system of semaphore signalling? It bothered me. But I was dog-tired and reckoned that maybe I worrying without cause because I was so exhausted.

We had been at action stations for most of the time it had taken us to sail to Sourabaya: in fact, we had been pretty much at action stations since we had sailed through the Sunda Strait and even now, anchored a couple of miles off the bomb-damaged docks, we remained closed up to the guns. All of us were exhausted; the lads who had been partying below decks even more buggered than the rest of us! But we needed to stay on the alert for Jap bombers, some of which showed up not long after we anchored. They dropped their bombs, which did no damage, but veered off quickly when we and the other ships opened up on them.

Every day after sailing through the Sunda Strait we had been attacked by Japanese aircraft and each time we had beaten them off. But while we were pretty confident we could handle the air attacks, we could never relax: the sky was full of Jap aircraft . . .and *only* Jap aircraft. Since arriving off the coast of Java we had scarcely seen an Allied plane; there was no doubt among us that the skies belonged to the Japanese Imperial Navy. There had been a rumour that the Yanks were sending P40 fighters but how and where from no one knew, and there was no sign of them in Sourabaya. Without aircraft we were blind; even we ordinary seamen knew that. Japanese reconnaissance aircraft would already have reported the size and disposition of our fleet and, as soon as we left harbour, they would instantly communicate our course and speed to the invasion fleets who could then sidestep us. It was as if our side was playing football wearing blindfolds.

Not long after we had anchored, Hec went ashore to confer with Vice-Admiral Doorman and the other ships' captains. He was gone a couple of hours and when he came back on board, looked pretty grim. Marcus joked it was because he had spent all that time trying to understand double Dutch. A few hours later, at around nine that evening, we weighed anchor and cautiously steered through the minefields protecting the approaches to Sourabaya with the rest of the fleet. We headed out into the Java Sea – our mission to seek out and destroy the Japanese invasion fleet.

Clearing the minefields, we altered course to starboard, sailing eastward in battle formation, following the coastline of Madura, the big island just off Sourabaya. It was a typical tropical night with a bright moon and high humidity. The air was muggy and on the gundeck we were glad of the breeze from the steady 20 knots we were making. I presumed we weren't steaming flat-out in order to preserve fuel, but Lofty had heard a rumour that the fleet was reduced to 20 knots because *Kortenaer,* one of the Dutch destroyers, had boiler problems. Not only that, but we had noticed that if the fleet steamed at anything over 25 knots, the four American destroyers at the rear of the convoy had trouble keeping up. All of which meant that the entire fleet was sailing at the speed of the slowest vessels! I hoped Lofty was wrong about the *Kortenaer*: it was bad enough steaming into battle with four geriatric American destroyers and a third of the *Houston's* main armaments totally crook, without having another of our ships with boiler problems. I was beginning to wonder if the ABDA Striking Force, presently looking to join battle with the most powerful navy in the Pacific, was comprised of the halt, the lame and the blind.

We were stood to the guns all night, most of us dozing on our feet. As always, the cooks in the galleys kept us supplied with food, which we ate standing up. They brought it up to us in dixies. Whenever possible, what we ate at action stations was hot, though it was always food we could eat with our fingers – chips and sausages and the odd baked potato, but no steak or beans or mashed potatoes. That was the kind of tucker we'd eaten before we'd sailed through the Sunda Strait, just three days earlier. It seemed like three weeks.

Sometime in the early hours of 27 February, 1942, *Perth* steamed around 180 degrees to alter course west: now the battle fleet was sailing back the way we had come. As dawn broke we reckoned we were just about back where we had started: somewhere close to the outer entrance to Sourabaya Harbour.

No one on the gundeck said very much, but I reckon we were all thinking the same thing: the ABDA Striking Force was like a mob of headless chooks, running around in circles. We were steaming up and down a 700-kilometre coastline with no idea where the Japs were going to land their invasion troops and without the foggiest notion of where the hell their fleet was. I reckoned we would have been better off back in the harbour at Sourabaya where we might at least have been able to get a little rest. It didn't make any difference to the enemy whether we were in harbour or at sea: he knew where we were all the time.

Even before the sun had broached the horizon behind us, we heard the drone of Jap spotter planes high in the half-light sky. They were shadowing us; radioing our course and direction to their fleets. As the sun rose and the day heated up, a few solitary Jap bombers appeared. They were just specks in the sky, each one flying at high altitude from where they dropped their bombs, making no attempt to get closer. No hits were scored as we steamed west, but all morning we were expecting a concerted attack by the bombers. It never came.

In the middle of the morning the fleet made yet another 180-degree turn, heading east once more. Most of us on the gundeck guessed we were headed back to Sourabaya, Admiral Doorman having given up the hopelessly blind search for invasion fleets that could evade us with ease. All of us were hoping that once in Sourabaya we might have a chance of a few snatched hours of sleep. By early afternoon it looked as if we had guessed right: our fleet was in the Sourabaya roadstead approaching the minefields when without warning *Perth* made another about turn and steamed back out to sea with the rest of the fleet.

We knew then we weren't going to get any rest – quite the reverse. The captain came on the broadcast system to announce that an enemy convoy of over forty transport ships had been sighted about 80 miles north of our position, just to the west of Bawean Island. Protecting them was a fleet of Japanese warships.

We were going into battle.

We increased speed to 25 knots, the fastest the US ships could manage, and headed northwest. We were in line of battle with the three British destroyers, each following the other, ahead on our starboard side, the four American destroyers struggling to keep up behind, and the two Dutch destroyers off to port. *Perth* was in line behind the *Exeter* and the *Houston*, with the Admiral's flagship, *De Ruyter*, out in front, and the *Java* behind us.

Suddenly, shortly after four in the afternoon, a number of enormous water spouts erupted on either side of the *Exeter* and *Houston*. At the same time we noticed other columns of water sprouting in the vicinity of the destroyers out to our right. We were under fire. Yet even from our elevated position on the four-inch gundeck, we could see nothing. The horizon was totally clear. This was not good news. Only capital ships could fire over the horizon like that. If there were Jap battleships out there, they could stand off at over 30 kilometres, well beyond the range of our guns, and pound us to bits with their fifteen-inch guns. Our only recourse would be to close the gap until they were in range – by which time they would have got us well within their sights.

More water spouts erupted ahead as the *Perth* heeled over to starboard. A couple of minutes later the *Houston* and the *Exeter* opened up with their eight-inch guns and all of us breathed a small sigh of relief. Whatever was over the horizon was within the range of our heavy cruisers' guns . . . which suggested we were up against

Jap heavy cruisers. Sure enough, minutes later superstructures appeared over the horizon, which were quickly identified as two heavy and two light cruisers and at least a dozen destroyers. By now heavy shells were straddling all of our ships, yet *Perth*'s guns remained silent. It was frustrating, but the enemy was too far away for us to have any chance of hitting them.

The *Perth* was veering violently from port to starboard and back again, the skipper ordering her to zigzag to confuse the Jap cruisers. We had practised this manoeuvre of violently changing course in our sea trails; so much, in fact, that the captain had earned himself the nickname 'Hard-over Hector'. Hec was a superb seaman and knew exactly what he was doing; he had done it before in the Med where he had learned how to anticipate where enemy shells might land. Somehow he knew what corrections the Jap gunnery controllers would make to their fall of shot and steered the ship out of their way. Even so, there were some damn-near misses and a few times we heard the sound of shells scything through the air just above our rigging.

Before the battle I'd heard some of the old salts say that the sound of a fifteen-inch shell screaming overhead was like an express train. Well, an eight-inch shell from a Jap heavy cruiser didn't sound to me like any train. The closest I've ever heard to it was the sound of an espresso machine at full bore in an empty café. It was an ominous noise, all the same, made scarier by the fact we were standing to the guns waiting to get in range. Our skipper was weaving the *Perth* through the water like a rover on a football field, closing the gap between us and the Japs so our six-inch guns could engage. But we on the four-inch guns would have to wait a while longer before we got into action against the Jap ships: our maximum range was 15 kilometres, little more than half that of the big, eight-inch guns. Even so, there was still plenty for us to do. The Japs had spotter aircraft observing the range and fall of their shot and we opened up on them whenever they came anywhere near us.

The Japanese battle fleet was to our right and ahead on the starboard bow. Serving on the port-side gundeck, I would ordinarily have missed seeing much of the battle, but as my job was to grab the live shells from the hoist on the starboard side, I got to see quite a lot of what was going on.

Our side got on the scoreboard first. Suddenly, there was a big explosion on one of the enemy cruisers and a huge column of dark smoke rose into the air. Not long afterwards one of our ships hit another Jap cruiser and now there were two columns of smoke. Maybe to protect their cruisers, a flotilla of enemy destroyers came in to attack us with torpedoes and the surface of the ocean was combed by the wakes of multiple torpedoes. We spotted them early and our ships, manoeuvring adroitly, turned to avoid them. Throughout the battle torpedoes were a constant menace: the Japs fired scores of them. Some of the lads on P1 thought many were coming from Jap submarines on our port side.

As soon as the enemy destroyers were within range of our four-inch guns, we opened up: our guns slugging it out with theirs and once more I was racing across the deck with shells to feed the guns with only the occasional moment to look up. After a while the Jap destroyers retreated, laying a thick smokescreen over the surface of the sea behind which they disappeared.

Zigzagging through the water, we overtook the *Exeter* which for some reason had dropped out of the line. We didn't know it then, but she had taken a hit from an eight-inch shell in her boiler room, cutting her speed by over half. Hec must have known or guessed this, as now it was our turn to make smoke. In company with the American destroyers, we steamed around the *Exeter,* laying down a thick smokescreen for her to hide behind before rejoining the line to attack the enemy once more.

Up ahead there was a tremendous explosion. Dashing to the starboard to collect another shell, I saw one of our ships had been hit by a torpedo. It was the Dutch destroyer, *Kortenaer.* Within a minute she had capsized and gone under. A few seconds later she resurfaced: upside down and in two halves. The ship had, literally, been blown apart. The bow and stern sections floated for a little while before finally sinking and I heard the screams and cries of men in the water as we weaved past at 30 knots. But there was no stopping for survivors. Our orders were to engage the enemy: saving the lives of men blown out of the water was not considered a priority.

By now *Perth* was firing every gun she had: the pom-poms had opened up when someone spotted a submarine's periscope, while we on the four-inch guns were firing either at Jap destroyers or at their spotter aircraft. The noise, which shuddered the backbone and lifted the scalp, was ear-splitting; enemy shells were whooshing overhead with great spouts of water erupting on either side while, from across the water, I saw the long fiery muzzle flashes of our fleet's guns a fraction of a second before I heard the rolling sound of gunfire. Ahead and behind us were thick clouds of oily smoke, laying low over the water. It was an unbelievable sight: the biggest sea battle since Jutland in the First World War.

The Jap destroyers, realizing *Exeter* was crippled, moved in for the kill with their torpedoes. The British destroyers closed up on them and one, the *Electra*, disappeared into the smoke ahead to take them on. She never came out. Years later I learned that, somewhere beyond the smoke, she had been outnumbered, outgunned and sunk by a flotilla of Japanese destroyers.

With the two remaining British destroyers we fought off the Jap attack before sighting fresh heavy cruisers about 18 kilometres distant. Our big guns opened fire immediately while on the gundeck of P1 we waited until the captain had closed the range. *Perth's* third or fourth salvo hit one of the cruisers: there was a bright flash and suddenly the vessel was erupting like a volcano. Immediately she and the ships around her made smoke and disappeared but when the smoke cleared we saw that she was dead in the water and burning merrily. We cheered: it wasn't every day a light cruiser like *Perth* managed to severely damage a much heavier warship.

The Jap destroyers closed in again and fired more torpedoes: one of the lads said he counted at least twenty wakes but none of them hit. Considering what a single Jap torpedo had done to the *Kortenaer*, we reckoned it would only take a couple of them to sink us. From the gundeck we watched the maimed *Exeter* steering south for Sourabaya, protected by the other Dutch destroyer as the American four-stackers moved forward to fire their torpedoes at the Japs. This seemed to bother the enemy, as while none of the American torpedoes scored a hit, the Japanese ships turned and steamed away over the horizon. We were amazed. The Japs had retreated. Had they given up? We didn't reckon it was likely, for although we had scored some hits on them they had hurt us too:

the *Kortenaer* was sunk, the *Electra* had disappeared and *Exeter* was limping back to Sourabaya with another of our destroyers. We had lost 25 per cent of our ships in just over two hours; worse, we were down to only six eight-inch guns. We reckoned the Japs had three times that number.

Still in search of the Japanese invasion fleet we sailed northwest, watching the sun sink into the sea on our port beam. We were glad of the respite from battle even though once the adrenalin had dissipated, we realised how tired we were. I stared at Lofty and Marcus. Their faces were drawn and grey; like mine, I supposed. At least the lull gave us a chance to eat; the kitchen crew brought up dixies of hot chips which we wolfed down. Night fell quickly but soon a full, shiny moon was filling the sky; perfect for the Jap spotter planes we could hear droning above us. All they had to do was plot the direction of our wake to know where we were heading. At sea level our visibility was up to about 6 miles.

At about half seven we saw the dark silhouettes of warships about roughly 5 miles to port. They didn't appear to be moving so *Perth* and the *Houston* opened fire, Hec ordering the four-inch guns to fire star shells to illuminate the action. We exchanged fire for a while but then our ships changed course, looking for the invasion fleet. Soon we were sailing parallel to the north shore of Java and could see the dark shape of the land mass to port. Behind us, though we didn't know it at the time, the four American four-stacker destroyers, having fired all their torpedoes, had been ordered to peel off and return to Sourabaya to refuel. Not long after the destroyers turned back, there was a sudden explosion from somewhere aft of our stern. It was difficult to see what had happened but later some of the lads reported that *Jupiter,* the British destroyer and the last ship in the line, was sinking. She had either hit a mine or been hit by a torpedo but, as before, there was no stopping or turning back for her survivors.

About an hour later we sailed past the place where the *Kortenaer* had been sunk by the torpedo. Though it was dark we were aware that scores, maybe hundreds, of men were still in the water and our admiral must have relented in his orders not to pick up survivors as the destroyer, *Encounter,* stopped to take on survivors. The men had been in the water for about five hours. I wondered how it was possible to survive that long in the ocean.

After she had taken on the survivors, *Encounter* turned and headed towards Sourabaya, leaving just four ships out of our original fourteen to hunt down and destroy the enemy's invasion fleet. For an hour we steamed north at 30 knots until, at about eleven o'clock, our lookouts spotted two Japanese heavy cruisers on the port bow. They were just inside the range of the guns on P1, and along with the six-inch guns, we were ordered to open fire. We were dog-tired: I had been humping shells across the deck for seven hours and in the last hour each shell had seemed like it weighed a tonne. Because we were so exhausted our rate of fire was much slower than it had been in the afternoon. Our only consolation was that the Japs must have been feeling the same way; their rate of fire was, if anything, slower than ours and they were nowhere near as accurate as they had been earlier in the battle. But they had something we didn't – long-range torpedoes.

Immediately ahead of us the entire after part of the admiral's flagship, the *De Ruyter,* suddenly exploded in a massive wall of flame. The *Perth*, hard on her heels, was steering straight into her blazing stern. 'Hard-over Hec' heeled the ship over to port so steeply we had to hang on to whatever was handy to avoid being flung off the gundeck. Behind us, *Houston* was doing the same. Behind her, *Java*, the other Dutch cruiser, was also veering to port when she too erupted in a great burst of flames.

We passed within a few hundred yards of the *De Ruyter* on her starboard side. She was exploding from end to end as her ammunition blew up. We could see her crew crowding forward towards the prow to escape the flames but there was nothing we could do for them. Behind us *Java* was ablaze and settling in the water.

Two of our cruisers, 50 per cent of our fighting force, had been hit by shells and torpedoes within minutes of each other and every bloke on the *Perth* knew that was the end. We had got into a fight and, though beaten, we had given a good account of ourselves. Now it was up to Hec Waller as to whether we carried on with the battle. We all knew it would be suicide if we did: one light cruiser (unscathed and still in one piece), plus a damaged heavy cruiser against at least four Jap heavy cruisers, countless destroyers and probably a few submarines. We gazed up at the bridge, waiting for the skipper's decision. It came within a couple of minutes. To the enormous relief of everyone on the gun platform we turned away from the battle and, with the *Houston* following, steamed out of range.

Behind us the two burning Dutch cruisers were lighting up the night, intermittent explosions shooting fiery debris hundreds of feet into the air. We felt sorry for the blokes in them. Admiral Doorman and his Dutchmen had been brave. But they hadn't had battle-experience like our skipper, who, even now was tacking to port and starboard as we steamed south at high speed. Hec Waller had kept us out of harm's way even while we were scoring a good few hits on the enemy ships.

None of us felt bad about escaping the battle. We had done our best. All of us had loaded and fired, loaded and fired, until we were numb with exhaustion. Like me, a lot of the blokes, Lofty, Merv and Marcus included, had harboured premonitions about the mob we had joined up with. All of us had the notion that the ABDA Striking Force had been a makeshift, stopgap, band-aid solution to the Japanese invasion of Java: an invasion which we probably hadn't stopped by more than a few hours. The brass had thrown whatever ships they could find into an uneven battle, the outcome of which had been a bloody foregone conclusion. So we didn't think we were retreating with our tails between our legs. We had fought hard and honourably in what from the outset had been a defeat waiting to happen. Now all we wanted was to go home.

Sailing out of the battle zone, we were stood down to a lesser degree of readiness and I had a chance to get reacquainted with my hammock in the forward mess. This was my home; this and my small metal locker, bolted against the bulkhead a few feet away. The sense of security that together they provided was amazing. Here, I felt secure. I was worn-down and weary, yet even so, I tried thinking about the battle and the events of the four days since the *Perth* had sailed into the Java Sea. My exhausted brain couldn't cope. Everything in my life had merged into a blur and all I could do was sleep.

Woken after only an hour, at first I thought we were sailing back to Sourabaya, but as the hours passed I realised we were steaming southwest, towards Tamjong Priok. We arrived at about midday. It was Saturday, 28 February. We had left Tamjong Priok four days earlier and as we and the *Houston* tied up at the dockside, it was obvious that during those four days the Japanese bombers had been busy. The port and its facilities had taken a pounding. Oil storage tanks, which four days earlier had been full and intact, were now smoking hulks. Many of the dockside warehouses were piles of rubble and splintered wood. I stared at the destruction and wondered about Darwin. Is this what Darwin looked like now?

The port was strangely deserted. The obsolete warships we had seen on our arrival had gone. Where to, no one was saying. We heard that the Dutch were getting ready to destroy as much of the port as they could before the Japanese invasion fleet appeared over the horizon. The captain went ashore to confer with the brass and to see about fuel and ammunition: we were dangerously low on both. While he was away we started taking on stores marked for Singapore and, ominously, also embarked a whole lot of wooden life rafts which we were ordered to lash to the deck. Not long after the skipper returned to the ship an oil hose was connected to one of the dockside's remaining storage tanks and we started taking on fuel. It didn't pump for long: our fuel tanks would have been only half full when the hose was disconnected. The rumour was that the Dutch were saving most of what little fuel was left at Tamjong Priok for their own navy. Madness, we told each other. Didn't they realise that most of the Dutch navy was at the bottom of the Java Sea? We reckoned that the *Perth* and *Houston* deserved to get every available ounce of fuel so we could escape to fight again another day.

Ammunition was another problem. The Dutch gave us what they had but much of the ammunition stored at the port was for Dutch warships and the calibre of their guns was different to ours. All of this meant that when we and the *Houston* cast off at about seven that evening, both ships had no more than half-full fuel tanks and the blokes on the six-inch guns were saying they had only about twenty rounds left for each of their guns.

Perth led the way out of the harbour, despite *Houston's* damaged rear turret, which meant Hec was in charge. We felt good about that. Soon after leaving port he came on the PA system to say that we were making for the Sunda Strait. All of us on the gundeck glanced at each other and grinned: Sunda Strait was the fastest way home. All except Lofty, who, as usual, saw the problem in the situation. 'Sunda Strait is a like a narrow doorway leading to the Indian Ocean,' he murmured. 'Let's hope the Japs haven't already closed the door behind us.'

Hec's next words over the broadcast system dispelled Lofty's worries. Dutch air reconnaissance, the skipper told us, reported that the Strait was free of enemy ships. We laughed. What Dutch air reconnaissance? We had scarcely seen a Dutch plane all the time we had been in the Java Sea. But we knew Hec wouldn't lie to us. If he said there were no Jap ships in the Strait, then there were no Japs there. At the speed we were making we reckoned we would be through the Strait and out into the Indian Ocean by dawn.

It was another perfect, tropical night. The sea was calm and the air still; there was a clear sky with a full moon and visibility was about seven miles. For about four hours we hugged the coastline, sailing inshore of a number of the islands lying off the northwest shore of Java with *Houston* about half a mile astern. Most of the crew was stood down at the second degree of readiness and I was looking forward to a hot supper which I had been told was my favourite – sausages.

At about eleven, as we were sailing across the mouth of Bantam Bay, prior to turning 90 degrees southwest into the Strait, our lookouts sighted a ship about 5 miles ahead. At first they thought she might be one of our corvettes patrolling the Strait, but as they were trying to get her to respond to *Perth's* recognition signals, the ship made smoke and disappeared into it. She was a Jap destroyer. Action stations was sounded just as I was about to get stuck into my plate of sausages. I felt definitely jacked as I abandoned them to dash across the deck to grab a shell for loading. Just then our forward six-inch guns opened fire. For maybe five minutes or so, we hoped that what we had sighted was a solitary Jap destroyer, patrolling the mouth of the Strait. Sighting one enemy warship didn't mean to say there would be others.

It was wishful thinking.

Across the moonlit waters we watched the dark profiles of ship after ship appearing on the horizon. Enemy warships: some of the dark, silhouetted superstructures big enough to be heavy cruisers. We cursed Dutch air reconnaissance. Far from being clear of enemy ships, the Sunda Strait and surrounding water was crawling with Japanese.

Within minutes we were surrounded by enemy cruisers and destroyers while, further inside the bay, we could make out scores of Jap transport ships. *Perth* and *Houston* had sailed into the heart of the Japanese force landing on the western part of the island and

God only knew how many Jap warships were in and around the Strait protecting it.

Perth immediately increased speed and 'Hard-over Hector' began the violent and repeated alterations of course that had kept us out of harm's way twenty-four hours earlier. Behind us, *Houston* did the same. With the *Perth* weaving from tack to tack the ship's guns were split so we could take on individual targets independently. There were enough of them for both us and the *Houston*. In fact, more than enough: I counted up to a dozen destroyers and three or four cruisers, two of them heavy cruisers. Some of the destroyers came dangerously close to fire their torpedoes. We beat them off with shellfire from our four-inch guns and scored several hits. We also fired torpedoes: mainly at the transport ships sheltering in the bay. From the number of explosions we heard, I reckon we hit quite a few.

By now both the *Perth* and *Houston* were fighting independently, though a few times I noticed we circled around behind the *Houston*, presumably to provide some protection for her damaged eight-inch after-turret. Yet, despite being outnumbered and massively outgunned, miraculously *Perth* fought for more than half an hour before she was hit. Then, with a jaw-dropping explosion, a shell hit our forward funnel. A couple of minutes later we took two more shells, one exploding on the flag deck, the other somewhere amidships. At each explosion the ship seemed to falter for a moment and then carry on like a boxer taking a couple of punches. None of the hits seemed to have done us much damage. We were maintaining our speed and violently tacking while still firing with all our guns. But we were using up precious fuel and, far worse, were down to our last few live shells. All of us on P1 were acutely aware that very soon we would be out of ammunition.

A petty officer came scampering up to the gundeck with orders that once we had run out of live shells, we were to continue firing star shells. I think that's when I knew we were not going to get out of this battle. *Perth's* luck had run out. We couldn't outrun the Japanese battle fleet: much of it was between us and the entrance to the Sunda Strait and as soon as we started firing star shells, the Japs would know we had expended all our ammunition and would close in for the kill like a pack of rabid dogs. I glanced across the water as I hefted one of our last live shells across the deck. What had forty minutes before been a calm, moonlit sea, was now a maelstrom of screaming shells and booming guns. All around me were the giant water spouts of falling shells illuminated by the lightning-like flashes of our guns, the calm, white, unwavering light of our star shells and the steely-blue beams of searchlights.

It took the Japs more than an hour to hit us with their first torpedo. There was a dull boom below the waterline and we felt the ship give an almighty shudder. Our speed slacked off immediately. I glanced at Lofty and Marcus. We didn't need to be told what had happened. Across the water one of the Jap destroyers had come so close that I could see a gun layer loading his four-inch guns. I stared at him for a moment, suddenly aware that this battle was being fought on both sides by ordinary blokes. The only difference between that Japanese sailor and me was that right now his side was winning and mine wasn't. That thought sent me racing across the deck to grab one of our useless star shells to ram home into the breech of the gun. Whatever happened, *Perth* wasn't going down without a fight to the very end. The second torpedo hit us minutes later. The ship lurched and for a moment seemed to come to a dead stop. That was the killer blow. Most of us on the gundeck knew *Perth* wouldn't survive that and, sure enough, within a couple of minutes we heard the order from Hec over the PA to 'Abandon ship, every man for himself'.

The most important thing now was to think clearly; to control the panic. I knew if I lost my head, there was a good chance I wouldn't survive. Already the ship was listing to port as I scrambled across the tilting deck towards the starboard railing. The order had been 'every man for himself', and I reckoned it would be safer to enter the water from the starboard side, even though the port-side railing was closer to the sea's surface. Most of the enemy guns were on our port side and I wanted the ship between me and their shells. Just as I was about to go into the water, I heard a tremendous explosion behind me. It came from the vicinity of P1 gundeck, the place I had been standing just a few seconds earlier.

I slid easily into the warm water, took a deep breath, put the rubber tube of my 'Mae West' life jacket between my lips and blew it up. The surface of the sea was already thickly slicked with black, pungent fuel oil, and I heard a petty officer shouting not to get it in our eyes and definitely not in our lungs or our stomachs. Thank God I'm a strong swimmer, I thought, as I struck out away from the sinking *Perth*, putting as much distance between her and me as I could. About a couple of hundred yards out I turned to look at her for the last time.

She was going down by the bows, her stern rising into the night, silhouetted against the bright searchlight of the Japanese ships. I watched her, filled with impotent emotion, thinking of my bunk and my locker and the little bit of space I'd called my own. Everything I owned was on board that ship and inside that locker: a wristwatch my mum and dad had bought me when I joined up; letters from them and my brothers and sisters and, most precious of all, letters and a special photo of Mirla taken in Kings Park a couple of days before I had left to join the *Perth*.

Everything – all of it – was sinking into the sea. I was appalled, and stupidly heard myself crying out, 'There goes my home.'

Slowly, *Perth* slid beneath the waves and suddenly the sea seemed vast, dark and very, very lonely.

Mirla's Story

I rushed around to Arthur's parents as soon as I could. His father was taking the news of *Perth*'s sinking badly. Surprisingly, although he was a big man who had worked as a builder and loved the hard physical nature of football, Harold (whom I had always called 'Grandad') was much more emotional and tearful about the news than Susan, Arthur's mother, whom I called 'Nana'. Or, at least he showed his emotions more. I suspect Nana felt just as devastated and numbed at the news as Grandad but believed she had to be strong for both of them. It was hard for them: they had two other sons, Harold, a flying officer in the RAAF; and, Les, in the AIF; both of whom would, sooner or later, be posted overseas. Now, their third and youngest son was on board a ship the Japs were boasting they had sunk.

I did my best to console them, although the truth was inside I was shaking to bits. I couldn't comprehend the fact that Arthur could have gone. I refused to believe it and, on the day after the newspaper headline, was justified in my belief when Prime Minister John Curtin came on the radio to say that the *Perth* had *not* been sunk. There had been a big naval battle in the Java Sea in which some allied ships had been sunk, he said, but the *Perth* was not one of them. At that moment I felt the vast encrusted weight of Arthur's loss lifted off me. I was as light as air. Again, I flew around to his parents' house in Subiaco, this time to celebrate the good news.

Our relief was short-lived.

Four days later, another newspaper article appeared stating *Perth* had indeed been sunk in another battle somewhere in the Java Sea. This time there was no denial from the Government or the prime minister. I dragged myself once more to the house in Subiaco Road to do my best with Arthur's parents. I don't know how much use I was to them, as by this time I too was reeling at the reversal of all our hopes.

Worse was to come. Eight days later, Arthur's parents received a telegram from the Government stating that their son was 'Missing in action as a result of enemy action'. Those nine simple words were like a burst of bullets to my heart. We learned that the next-of-kin of everyone on the *Perth*, from the captain down, had received a similar telegram. The fact was, neither the Government nor anyone else knew what had happened to the *Perth*: no one could say who was alive or who was dead. For all anyone knew the *Perth* could have gone down with all hands, just like the *Sydney*.

And so began the many long months when all I had to hang on to was the hope that Arthur was alive. Along with his parents, sisters and brothers, I believed that if anyone could survive the sinking of the *Perth*, it would be him. He was physically strong and always had a good, positive attitude. He was a born survivor. Belief in Arthur's ability to survive was all I had to keep me going; that and the loving comfort and support of my mother and of my best friend, Nancy Weedon.

For my mother, helping me through the weepy evenings and bolstering my hope must have been especially hard. She had lost the man she loved to a war, and now she was helping me cope with the possibility of the same. Holding me tight when I was upset and cheering me up when I was down would have been like opening an old wound for her. Yet she was strong and always there for me: never complaining or holding back her love while I, for my part, tried not to let her see too much of what I was feeling, nor overly impose my fears on her.

Nancy was my best friend and one of those people to whom God had given an abundance of love, compassion and empathy. Nancy not only lived near me, she worked in the same building as I did. We were as close as sisters and it was with Nancy I shared my deepest fears and poured out my soul. She understood: she had that capacity; the ability to connect with what I felt, even though her young man had not yet been called up for service. She listened to me and comforted me through the blackest times; understood when I told her that one of the hardest things for me to bear was not having Arthur to write to: not being able to look forward to his wonderful, funny, newsy letters with their talented little drawings.

The hardest time, the blackest moment – an event like a blow upon an open wound – happened about two weeks after Arthur's parents received the telegram. I arrived home from work to find a bundle of letters returned to me from the navy. Every letter I had written to Arthur since he had sailed from Fremantle on Valentines Day had been 'Returned to sender'. I stared at them, tears filling my eyes. Hardest of all was to see again the letter in which I had finally told him of my true feelings.

I gazed at it; at the words and sentences of love that he had never seen. He had gone off to war unaware of how much I loved him; he had sailed into battle never knowing that he was the only man I would ever love. I felt so thwarted . . . and so guilty. Why hadn't I told him earlier? I felt somehow as if knowing I loved him might have kept him safe.

And so the weeks became months and autumn 1942 turned into winter with still no word. For me they were the seasons of the stiff upper lip, the time that I and millions like me – mothers and fathers and wives and sisters and sweethearts and children – became truly intimate with hope. I lay down with it every night and woke up with it every morning. For much of the day, every day, it was what kept me going: what stiffened my resolve and lifted my eyes.

All I had was hope that Arthur had survived: the only thing to buttress that hope – more hope. Hope against hope. For the first time in my life I learned what that expression meant. The only thing bolstering my hope that Arthur was alive was more hope that he was alive. It was like two playing cards propping each other up. Take away one, and the other falls. Add more cards, build a pyramid of cards even, and it still only takes one card to fall for all to fall. So it was with my fervent, desperate wish that Arthur was still alive. Though I firmly believed that if anyone could survive the sinking it would be Arthur, there was no evidence to suggest that he had done so. All I had to keep me going was my hope.

Very quickly I learned that to lose one small strand of that hope was to lose it all: that my hoping was a house of cards and that the most important thing I needed to learn was how to nurture and protect it from myself: from my own doubts and fears.

This was my lesson of war.

5

The End of Liberty

The Jap guard screams in my face and jabs his bayonet at me so viciously I leap backwards. 'Whoah, what's up with you, mate?'

He screams something totally unintelligible and again pokes the bayonet at me. It takes me a while to understand that he wants me to go back to the creek. I can't understand why and frown at him, which sets him off screaming some more. The rest of the bathing party have returned to camp while this goon has singled me out. I can't say I'm happy to be alone in the company of a demented little Nip carrying a loaded rifle and bayonet, but, as I have no choice, I turn and shuffle warily down to the creek again.

Once there he indicates I should get back in the water and scrub myself. I can't understand why. I've just finished doing that. I stare at the slowly flowing water. The creek is our only source of washing. It is also the local sewer. Not that it bothers us much. When you are as filthy as we are, the chance of washing, even in a toilet, is a luxury we'd kill for. Even so, I stare balefully at a couple of Bondi cigars floating majestically past before wading in and washing myself all over again.

93

Once I have done my best to get the oil off – not that, without soap, I see any difference – I clamber out.

The little runt starts all over again, jabbing his bayonet and nodding his head at the creek. I don't get it. Bathing, even in a sewer, is a privilege. This guard is granting me extra privileges. I watch him as he lays down his rifle to make a motion of scrubbing his face and arms. The stupid bastard wants me to wash myself again. I shrug. Okay by me. I wade in and scrub away, keeping a wary eye out for the occasional flotilla of bobbing brown bowel movements. With all this practice I'm getting good at dodging them. Not surprising, really: having spent a couple of days dodging torpedoes, dodging turds comes easily.

I climb out of the creek for the third time and wait for the guard to start screaming again. Instead he stares at me malevolently for a few seconds and then shrugs. Clearly he's given me up as a lost cause. He jerks his head towards the camp and I set off with him a few steps behind.

Back at the camp I recount my experience to the others. It's Marcus who susses it. 'It's your freckles, Blood,' he laughs. 'Your face and arms are covered in them. Stupid Japanese mongrels aren't used to red hair. They don't know what freckles are. They think you're still covered in fuel oil.' He laughs again. 'I reckon you'll be bathing more than the rest of us, you lucky bugger.'

Even though the sea was calm, waves covered by fuel oil were constantly slapping my face. The oil was corrosive: it seared my skin and once into my eyes, burned like acid and blinded me. My perspective on the battle was now a worm's-eye-view from half-blinded eyes a few centimetres above the surface of the sea; quite different to the view I'd previously had 15 metres up on the gundeck of a cruiser. Although the sky continued to be lit up by star shells and searchlights, the surface of the water was inky black. Thank God, I thought, that I had learned to be a good swimmer when I was a youngster. And thank God, too, that I hadn't panicked abandoning the *Perth*. So long as I l kept my nerve . . .

About a mile or so to my left I could just about see the dark hulk of the *Houston*. She had lost headway and was moving slowly through the water. Now and again I saw muzzle flashes from her forward turrets, but either she was low on ammunition or her guns had been hit by shells and were no longer working properly. All around, from every point of the compass, I saw muzzle flashes from the guns of a dozen Japanese warships closing in on the cruiser like dingoes on a wounded sheep. *Houston* was doomed. There was nothing I could do to help her – and anyway, the last order I'd been given was to save myself.

I took stock of the situation. The most important thing was to get as far away as possible from the oil slick: if the *Houston* caught fire I would be roasted. There were a lot of dark shapes bobbing about in the water: debris from the *Perth*. I kicked off my boots and swam towards them, finding a wooden life raft that someone had so presciently lashed to *Perth's* deck and I clambered on. Using my hands I paddled it away from the *Houston* and into the darkness, thinking about what I was going to do next.

Unlike the Dutch sailors in the water the previous day, I calculated I was no more than 10 kilometres from land. I was pretty confident that I was a strong enough swimmer to make it to the dark

Javanese landmass I could just see from my half-closed, burning eyes. So, if I could swim it, I knew for sure I could paddle a life raft to it, especially as there was a strong current moving me and the raft in that direction.

Floating along, I saw heads bobbing in the water and began hauling other blokes from the *Perth* onto the raft. I was hoping one of them would be Lofty, Marcus, Merv or Harvey, but no, they were just oil-soaked, exhausted sailors like me. A pile of flotsam floated past close enough for me to see the bloke perched precariously on it was Charlie Thompson. 'G'day, Arthur,' he called out cheerily, 'I'll see you in the Shents.' Charlie was always a big joker whose favourite pub in Perth was the Shenton Park Hotel and, despite our situation, I had to allow myself a bit of a smile. The way Charlie had called out to me, we could have been coming away from a football game at Subiaco Oval.

Soon, however, the raft was crowded and the more blokes we dragged out of the water, the more unstable it became. Some of the poor buggers were wounded or said they weren't great swimmers, so I reckoned it would be better all round if a strong swimmer like me made some space. I slipped into the water and struck out for the land. I had hoped by now that we would have been out of the oil slick but, though patchy, it was still there, slapping me in the face and burning my eyes. Like *Perth*'s survivors it was being carried along by the current. As I swam I realised the night had become quiet. Sometime during my time on the float, the *Houston* had gone down.

It wasn't long before I saw the outline of a Carley float surrounded by men clinging to the ropes looped around its sides.

I swam to it and grabbed a rope. About a dozen men were in the water hanging on, while inside the float were a dozen or so blokes badly wounded by Japanese shellfire as the *Perth* went down. A few were moaning; one crying out in agony. I was grateful for the dark, which made it difficult to see. Some of the wounded looked like they had lost legs or arms; one bloke had been ripped open by shrapnel and was clutching onto what was left of his guts.

An officer clinging to the float was trying to get us organised, telling those of us in the water to attempt to steer the float towards the land. But after about an hour, and despite picking up more men who clung to the ropes, it became pretty clear that the current was sweeping us past St Nicholas Point on the western tip of Java, and directly into the Sunda Strait. It was ironic. What the *Perth* had tried to do – and failed – we, its survivors, were going to do whether we liked it or not. We were shooting the Sunda Strait.

By now there must have been more than thirty blokes outside the Carley: some were clinging onto the men clinging onto the ropes. Dawn was coming up and we could see the outline of a small island inside the Strait. We tried manoeuvring the Carley towards it, but the current was far too strong and was shooting us past it. I realised I wasn't doing a lot of good where I was, while at the same time there was a good chance I could swim to the island. I paddled around the Carley to tell the officer my plans. He told me that if I thought I could make it on my own then to give it a go. He wished me good luck.

I set off and swam for about twenty minutes before realising I had got precisely nowhere. The current was much stronger than I'd thought and, after two days of battle and four days of standing at action stations, I began to realise I was more exhausted than I had reckoned. By this time the light was quite strong and the Carley float was out of sight. I started to wonder if I had bitten off more than I could chew. I'd already kicked off my boots; now I shucked off the rest of my gear into the water; saturated with oil, it was no good to me anyway. When I was down to my football shorts I struck out once more for the island but after another half hour I was still scarcely any closer.

Things were not going well and I was wondering what I could do next when I saw a lifeboat floating down the Strait towards me. I turned and began swimming towards it. Soon I was close enough to recognise it as Japanese. Despite being exhausted and pretty close to the end of my tether, I felt a great surge of satisfaction at seeing it. If the Japs had lifeboats in the water, that meant we had sunk some of their vessels. The *Perth* had not gone down without leaving her mark.

When closer I saw the lifeboat was the kind carried by Japanese merchant vessels and that she was equipped both with oars and a mast for a sail. Even better, she was full of blokes from the *Perth*! I was elated and shouted out across the water, 'Any chance of a lift?'

They dragged me aboard. It was just as well I was still wearing my money belt as I was covered in oil and as slippery as a duck's guts. A couple of blokes grabbed the belt and my football shorts and hauled me, arse first, into the boat. There were about thirty blokes aboard: a dozen or so of them wounded and lying in the bottom of the boat. Some were in a bad way: as bad as the blokes in the Carley and the seamen were doing their best for them – not that there was much they could do. The lifeboat was equipped with provisions and rudimentary first aid, but some of those blokes had lost limbs or been ripped up by shrapnel. If they didn't get treatment quickly they were going to die. Every man on the lifeboat was covered in oil; we looked like a boatload of Al Jolson look-alikes.

A petty officer in charge told me the plan was to creep through the Strait without being seen by any Japanese destroyers. That's why he had ordered the men to row rather than set the lifeboat's sail. At the southern end of the Strait we would make landfall, do what we could for the wounded and then set sail for Christmas Island, 300 nautical miles, or 550 kilometres, south. Once there, and with some luck, we could get back to Australia. It was a good plan and I reckoned my luck had held. There was a good chance I could be back in Perth in a month!

That luck ran out only minutes later when we saw, bearing down on us at 30 knots out of the rosy pink dawn, a sleek, steel-hulled Japanese destroyer. With everyone covered in oil we nursed a faint hope that the Japs might take a quick look, think we were natives, and move on. But of course, seeing one of their own lifeboats occupied by a bunch of blokes obviously not Japanese caught their attention. The destroyer hove to close by and an officer called out to us on a loudhailer. He spoke reasonably good English, which pretty much dashed our hopes that we might be mistaken for natives. Lining the ship's rails alongside the officer were a dozen naval ratings with rifles pointed at the lifeboat. The Japs obviously meant business and we were in no position to argue. Our PO ordered us to row alongside the destroyer as a ship's ladder was lowered over the side of the afterdeck.

Once we were alongside, the Jap officer ordered us to climb.

We began organising the wounded, most of whom were not in a fit state to stand, never mind climb a ship's ladder. The Jap yelled down at us. It took me a moment to realise what he was saying. 'No wounded,' he screamed. 'Leave your wounded.' Like everyone else, I stared up at him, dumbfounded. Our PO began arguing, shouting to the Jap that we couldn't leave our wounded men. The Jap officer waved his arms and pointed to a couple of his men who were crouching behind one of the destroyer's machine guns. We heard them cock the mechanism: a menacing and terrifying sound, like the hiss of a death adder. We all knew a thirty-second blast from a heavy-calibre machine gun like that would turn us and our lifeboat into a mess of bloody flesh and matchwood. The Jap officer called down that the wounded would be rescued later, which left our bloke no alternative but to order us to climb.

I was one of the first up and stood at the top of the ladder, helping some of the walking wounded. We had got most of the lads on board when, without warning, the destroyer started moving, picking up speed rapidly. A couple of blokes were still on the ladder. The first managed to scramble up as the ship made headway but the other bloke, clinging to the bottom of the ladder, had no chance. The lightweight ladder trailed aft from the destroyer's beam as she churned the water and the poor bastard, shouting madly, was finally forced to let go. The last I saw of him was a head bobbing in the wake of the destroyer, halfway between us and the abandoned lifeboat filled with our wounded. I never knew whether the bloke in the water or any of the wounded survived. All I do know is that during the twenty-four hours we were aboard the destroyer, we never went back for them.

Word came down from the bridge that the reason the destroyer had steamed away so suddenly was because of an air-raid warning. To most of us hunkered down on her quarterdeck, it was the ultimate bloody irony. Throughout our time in the Java Sea, Allied warplanes had been as scarce as hens' teeth – *now* they were turning up to bomb the Japanese ships rescuing their own blokes? Only of course they didn't. They never showed. We saw no sign of our own planes . . . not then . . . and not later.

Some of the blokes reckoned the Jap captain had invented the air-raid warning just to get away, but from the way their blokes treated us over the next twenty-four hours, I'm not so sure. I reckon in the Jap captain's book, just as in our navy's, his ship was more important than blokes in the water, though I'm pretty sure Hec would have tried to do something for the wounded. I like to think that *someone* rescued the man in the water and our wounded. All I know is that the Jap sailors on that destroyer were okay and treated us reasonably decently, for almost as soon as we got on board, some of them came around with containers of water. We were as thirsty as hell and greedily scooped the water out of the containers with our hands.

Straight away a Jap officer came down to inspect us. We were a motley crew. Most of the lads had, like me, shucked their uniforms off in the water and were down to their shorts. None of us had boots and we were all basted in fuel oil. We were beginning to stink. Even on the breezy quarterdeck I could smell us. The Jap officer, immaculate in his whites, clearly wasn't impressed and ordered us to strip off and throw our oil-saturated clothes into the sea. I was hoping he was going to have us hosed down, but no such luck. Instead, he ordered his men to issue us with G-strings: a simple length of white cotton cloth that went between our legs and up to a thong tied around our waists, the cloth looping over the thong front and back to cover our embarrassment. I had never worn one before and was intrigued. I didn't know it then, but it was to become my only form of dress for the next two-and-a-half years. Frankly, the G-strings didn't do anything to improve our appearance. Fifty filthy men in clean loincloths were still not an awe-inspiring sight. I must have looked even more bizarre as I still had my money belt on.

Not long afterwards, the Japs organised us into lines in which we shuffled blindly forward to a couple of improvised medical stations where a medical officer and some orderlies put eye-drops in our eyes. Almost everyone had been in the water long enough to be blinded by the oil slick and the relief as the Jap medical orderly washed out my eyes was beyond belief. After hours of feeling as though my eyeballs were being burned out of my head, I could see again.

By now it was mid-morning and the sun was turning the after-deck into a furnace. The steel deck was unbearable and without boots we were hopping from foot to foot. Even if the deck had not been so crowded with blokes that it was difficult to find space to stretch out, we wouldn't have been able to lie down on it without being barbecued. Between the hot sun and the burning deck, and covered head to toe in fuel oil, we were being fried.

Suddenly, a party of Jap sailors appeared and put up an awning that shaded the whole of the afterdeck. I watched them doing it. They were mainly young blokes like us; laughing and joking as they erected the canopy. Most of them seemed to be sympathetic to our situation. Maybe they reckoned that tomorrow it could be them, just as I had a couple of nights earlier. Even the ratings with the rifles had disappeared and there was only one armed sailor up on the poop deck guarding us. He didn't look like he was expecting a mutiny.

After the canopy went up I found a length of rope coiled in a corner of the deck and lay down on it. There wasn't a lot of space and it wasn't the most comfortable place I had ever slept but I draped myself over it as best I could and slept, utterly exhausted, for twelve hours. When I awoke it was dark and Japanese sailors were moving among us with dixies of rice. We were allowed only one double-handed scoop. It wasn't much and snaffling the rice up out of my cupped hands I thought longingly of the sausages I had almost eaten as we went into action on the *Perth* twenty-four hours earlier. After wolfing the rice, I slept some more and woke just after dawn.

By then the destroyer had steamed into Bantam Bay where the Jap invasion fleet was landing their troops. In the daylight we could see the damage the *Perth* and *Houston* had inflicted on their ships. A couple had been sunk, with just their superstructures show-ing above the surface of the shallow water. Another couple were beached on their beams on the beach. The sight of these ships out of action heartened us even though there were about fifty other transports anchored in the bay while, standing out to sea, was the battle fleet the *Perth* had so fatefully run into: half-a-dozen light and heavy cruisers and more than a dozen destroyers.

I noticed our destroyer had stopped engines and was anchoring among the transports. A couple of its boats were being lowered as the Jap officer who had hailed us in the lifeboat told us we were to be transferred to one of the transports, where we would be held until we could be taken ashore. We climbed down into the boats and waited for our Jap captors to accompany us. Instead, we were ordered to row ourselves about half a mile to a transport called *Somedong Maru*. Some of the lads joked about escaping: maybe, they laughed, we could fight our way through all the warships and row to Australia.

After climbing the ship's ladder onto the *Somedong Maru* we were ordered below decks into a hold recently vacated by Japanese soldiers. A lot of our blokes were already there and throughout the day more joined us so that, in the end, there were about 250 prisoners incarcerated in the cargo hold. Most were from the *Perth,* but there were about fifty blokes from the *Houston,* some Aussie sailors off a torpedoed corvette and some Pommie seamen, too. We were a mixed bag: almost all of us smeared in fuel oil, all of us with a few days stubble and none of us bathed. The stench in the hold was gut-wrenching. The accommodation was basic: wooden pallets with no palliasse on which to sleep and nothing but vast steel bulkheads to stare at. It occurred to me that if this was all that the Jap infantry had had on their journey from Japan, then their soldiers were a lot tougher than we had been led to believe.

Like everyone else I went looking for my mates and was overjoyed to find Lofty, Marcus, Merv, Harvey and so many of the other lads from WA safe and unwounded. We shook hands vigorously before recounting our personal stories of survival. We asked about other mates. A few were sadly known to be dead: blokes had seen them killed or seen their bodies. Many more were missing and those of us who were safe and well, though prisoners, hoped they'd made it. All of us felt a much greater sense of security having our mates around.

It was in the hold of the *Somedong Maru* that I began to take some stock of my situation. Firstly, I was conscious that I was alive . . . and intensely grateful for it. Having recently seen how easily it could be snuffed out, I had definitely learned how precious life could be. But now I had to think about what to do next. It hadn't really dawned on me while on the destroyer that I was a prisoner. There, I had been too exhausted, and anyway I was a naval seaman in the presence of other naval seamen who, although they were the enemy, had much in common with me. There were duties and disciplines, officers and mateship on a naval vessel; all pretty much the same in any navy in the world. But here we were on a merchant vessel manned by merchant seamen and the difference became apparent straight away.

The crew of the *Somedong Maru* were mostly older blokes to whom we were cargo: little more than cattle. The hold was stiflingly hot and thank God they had been ordered to keep the hatches open during the time we were incarcerated, otherwise the heat would have killed us, while the stink would have been unbearable. But beyond that they did little for us. Once a day they lowered metal pots of rice from which we were allowed one double-handed scoop, eating it out of our filthy hands. They also lowered a water pannier with a ladle. Despite the heat in the hold we were only allowed one ladle of water in the morning and one in the evening. We were permitted up top on deck to use the heads – the latrines strung over the side of the vessel – but only in batches and some of the poor bastards who had swallowed oil and were continuously retching still had to wait their turn.

Pretty soon our captors found a good game with which to amuse themselves. They would drop lighted cigarettes into the hold and watch some of our blokes fighting each other for them. As a sportsman I had never smoked in my life, so it was hard for me to understand why grown men would fight each other for a drag on a fag. But fight they did; often viciously. It was demeaning and I felt ashamed to watch good Aussie blokes degrade themselves in such a fashion – the shame magnified by the laughter of the merchant crew staring down through the hatches. Our petty officers did their best to put a stop to it but some of those blokes would have killed their mothers for a smoke. Fighting among ourselves didn't auger well for the future. I was a young bloke, only twenty years old (although I felt I had aged a bit in the previous three days), yet even to me it was it was obvious that, for however long it took, we would all have to hang together, otherwise the Japs would hang each of us out to dry separately.

So, in the dim sepia light of the cargo hold of the *Somedong Maru* and surrounded by my closest mates, I began to think seriously about my situation and how I might survive it. Like everyone else I'd suffered a shock to the system which, nowadays, I suppose they'd call a trauma. Apart from the physical dangers and exertion of battle, followed by hours in the water, I now had to cope with the mental and emotional stresses of finding myself in the hands of the enemy. Like everyone else, I was a prisoner of war.

The motivation I'd felt only hours earlier to come to grips with the enemy – to engage and fight the Japanese – had been replaced by an intense feeling of uncertainty, fuelled by a nagging, anxious fear for the future. This, I was to learn, was the dominant experience of the POW: that without positive thinking the powerlessness of being a prisoner would inevitably give rise to two intense and equally destructive feelings – anxiety and frustration.

What's more, now that I had slept a little and overcome my exhaustion, I felt that I still wanted to fight. For a year I had been trained for combat: taken to the peak of my physical and mental abilities to become an efficient part of a fighting machine. But here, held in the hold like cattle, there was nowhere to channel that aggression. Maybe that's why the blokes battled each other for cigarettes. There was nothing to do, and, as they couldn't fight the enemy, they fought each other.

The question was . . . How long would I have to cope with these feelings; how long would I need to suppress my anxieties and tolerate the frustration? How long would we all be prisoners of war?

Even to me it was obvious it was going to be long war: a lot longer than we had first thought back in Australia. The battle we had just survived showed the Japanese to be a formidable and well-prepared enemy. It might take years to defeat them. Yet I knew we *would* defeat them. An old war horse like Churchill was never going to let the Japs invade Malaysia and take Singapore without moving heaven and earth to get it back. And the Americans would never forgive Pearl Harbour. 'A day of infamy', Roosevelt had called it. The Americans would wreak a terrible vengeance for that sneak attack: however many men it took, whatever powerful and devastating weapons they had, they would use them in revenge.

And, I wondered, who did the Japanese think we were? What kind of people did they think they were fighting? Did they think they could do those things to us and get away with it? That we would surrender? That we would give in and walk away from the fight? I knew we would never do that. The Japs made a big deal out of saying *they* would never surrender . . . but they would. It was our side who would never give up until the Japs had surrendered unconditionally!

And that was the key. I reckoned I could get through however long I was to be a prisoner, so long as I remembered that the Japs were idiots who had made a big mistake and taken on the wrong enemy: that sooner or later our side was going to kick them right out of the paddock. As long as I could hold on to that certainty, then I could survive being a prisoner of the Japanese.

They held us in the hot, stinking hold of the *Somedong Maru* for seven days. During the first two or three they were still unloading army trucks for the invasion but after that the ship was mainly quiet. On about the fourth day a Japanese army surgeon, along with a couple of medical orderlies, appeared in the hold and set about attending to the wounded: dressing their wounds, removing shrapnel and washing out the eyes of those of us still suffering from the oil. The Jap was assisted by *Perth's* Surgeon Lieutenant, Sam Stening, who, though he was badly hurt himself, had already been doing everything he could to help our sick and injured men.

For the entire seven days we had nothing to do except talk among ourselves. Some blokes took it hard: with nothing to do they became fractious, restless and bored. Maybe that was another reason why they fought each other for cigarettes. My mates and I did our best to fill the time with stories and guessing games and quizzes – anything to keep our minds active and off the fact that we were desperately hungry and thirsty. This was another survival technique I learned in the hold: to survive I would need to keep my mind active – to find something, no matter how trivial, to keep me occupied.

By the seventh day the *Somedong Maru* had stopped receiving survivors of the *Perth*. One of the petty officers did a count and said there were about 300 blokes from the *Perth* in the hold. We stared at each other in the gloom. The ship's complement had been 680 men. Did that mean that 380 officers and men of the crew had died in the battle or in the sea? The thought that we had lost more than half our shipmates, including our skipper, who hadn't been seen since, was too terrible to contemplate.

That day we felt the ship get underway and when we went on deck to use the heads, saw she was sailing west, around St Nicholas Point into the Sunda Strait. Later she dropped anchor and we were ordered up out of the holds and into invasion barges which ferried us to the harbour at Merak. There, we were marshalled by soldiers with fixed bayonets and ordered to climb into the back of a convoy of army lorries. It was standing-room only and we grabbed hold of each other as our driver let out the clutch and our lorry jerked forward. Whoever was driving the bloody thing had no idea how to change gear. The convoy headed east.

En route we passed squads of natives walking along the road. Many of them jeered at us; waving and shouting what sounded like insults. I couldn't understand it. We were Australians who had come to defend their islands against the Japanese invader! Standing next to me, Lofty pointed out in his serious tone that they probably thought we were Dutch. 'The Dutch have been colonising these islands for hundreds of years,' he said. 'These people are probably glad to be seeing the back of them.'

'But we're not Dutch, we're Australian,' I protested. 'We didn't colonise anyone.'

Lofty shrugged. 'Doesn't make any difference to them. We're white blokes, aren't we? They think we're all the same. They probably think the Japs are here to liberate them. They'll learn.'

Later, we passed a native walking along the side of the road. He was wearing a vest made out of a flour sack on which was stencilled the words 'Dingo Flour', along with the silhouette of a dingo. Those of us from WA let out a small cheer. The lads from over east, along with the Yanks and Poms, looked puzzled until we explained that Dingo was a famous brand of flour in Western Australia. Countless times travelling to Fremantle by bus or train I had passed the giant silo in North Fremantle on which was painted the enormous dark-red logo of a dingo 'at point'. Seeing that bloke wearing the all-so-familiar image stabbed me with such a sharp pang of homesickness it was like a cut to the heart. That was the closest I came to crying in the whole of my early time as a POW.

We arrived at the town of Serang where we were ordered off the lorries and assembled for inspection and a count of the prisoners. This was the first *tenko*, or roll call, we were forced to endure. We didn't know it then, but we would be made to suffer hundreds of these roll calls, where sick, starving men would be made to stand in the burning sun or pouring rain while the Nips counted us . . . and recounted us . . . and then counted us again – every time coming up with a different figure. Most *tenkos* lasted at least an hour; some went on for much longer. At this, our first *tenko*, I noticed our guards were now soldiers of the Imperial Japanese army, stony-faced and malevolent. Unlike the navy blokes, there was no sympathy or fellow feeling from any of these bastards.

I wondered what there was to inspect in 450 oil-stained, filthy, famished blokes, all bootless and wearing only loincloths (and in my case a money belt), until it became clear that the Japs were lining us up in order to relieve us of any possessions we might have, including spare food or medical supplies.

As the Jap soldiers and non-comms worked their way through our ranks I noticed that, though they took everything the blokes were clutching to their chests or carrying in makeshift bags, they didn't body-search anyone. It occurred to me that maybe the average Jap soldier did not like touching other blokes, especially if they were prisoners and white; even more especially because to find anything on us they would need to go scrabbling around in the crotch of our G-strings. Equally as curious was the fact that, when the Jap non-commissioned officer fronted up to me, to my great relief he ignored my money belt.

After the parade we were split up, the officers and a bunch of blokes being escorted to the town jail, while the rest of us were marched about half a mile to the local cinema. For some, marching in their bare feet on what passed for footpaths in Batavia was painful. It was less so for me, for although my feet had gone soft wearing naval issue boots, my mainly shoeless boyhood had toughened the soles of my feet sufficiently to enable me to manage the march. When we arrived at the cinema one of the lads joked about how nice it was of the Japs to take us to the pictures. Those of us close by laughed, whereupon a nearby guard jabbed the poor bloke in the ribs with his bayonet.

Conditions at the cinema turned out to be bloody atrocious; our only consolation being that conditions at the jail were said to be even worse. Our numbers had grown with more blokes from the *Houston*, a few more Poms and Dutch, and some Batavian nationals, so that there were about 500 of us sleeping on the bare boards of the cinema floor with no water for washing, no sanitation facilities and no fuel for cooking. We soon solved the fuel problem by ripping out the wooden cinema seats and using the wood for fuel.

Our diet was two scoops of rice a day, with an occasional small vegetable. I was permanently ravenous and usually on the point of serious dehydration. Drinking water was scarce. It had to be boiled twice to make it safe to drink. Cooking conditions were disgusting; the little hut that passed for the galley was filthy. Running through the middle of it was a water channel which served as a sewer. The latrine was a pit about six feet square with poles for squatting slung across it. It was next to the galley and whenever it rained, which was every afternoon, the pit flooded, with everything in it floating to the surface. The stink was indescribable: nowhere in the camp could we escape the overwhelming stench of the human excrement congesting and bubbling up in that pit.

With no facilities for washing, two weeks after arriving at what we had come to call simply 'the cinema', we were still covered in fuel oil. We did our best to maintain rudimentary hygiene but it was nearly impossible. First there was diarrhoea, then dysentery, and then, because we were plagued by mosquitoes with nothing to cover us except a loincloth, malaria set in.

From about the second week at the cinema I had continuous diarrhoea. I also suffered my first of many bouts of malaria, which allied to the inadequate diet meant that in a month I had lost about 20 kilograms in body weight. Even so, I reckoned I was better off than many of our blokes, some of whom were suffering from terrible festering wounds incurred in the sea battles. Sam Stening, our medical officer, had been incarcerated in the jail with the other officers and we didn't see him for about ten days, but once the Japs let him out he was in attendance at the cinema every day performing rudimentary operations without anaesthetic and armed only with a pair of rusty scissors, while extracting shrapnel with no more than a razor blade. At any one time at least 100 blokes out of the 500 of us at the cinema were mustering as sick.

We also had to get used to being guarded by blokes with loaded rifles and fixed bayonets who at the slightest infringement, or merely on some demented whim, would go absolutely nuts and start screaming at us. We had to learn to live with jabs from a bayonet that would draw blood, or a whack on the side of the head from a rifle butt. Some of the blokes were beaten so badly they were left unconscious on the ground. Now and again one of the guards accidentally loosed off a shot and some of the more timid blokes would throw themselves to the ground in fear.

The compound outside the cinema building was overlooked by a couple of watchtowers on which were mounted machine guns. At first we were acutely aware of their menace but, as time went on, we began to forget about them. It would have been possible to escape but the Japanese commandant had told us that any attempt to flee by one man would mean the execution of everyone. We weren't sure whether to believe his threat or not, but for the sake of our mates no one was willing to put it to the test.

Slowly, conditions began to improve. We were allowed to dig a proper pit latrine, though it was still close to our cooking area where we boiled the water, and later a couple of Japanese field kitchens turned up. Even so, a couple of blokes died of dysentery: one of them from the *Perth*.

One of our biggest problems was personal hygiene: by the third week at the camp every man stank to high heaven. Without scissors or razors our hair was growing long and we were all sprouting beards; mine was an interesting combination of ginger and red which itched like hell. Every day we tried our best to wash the fuel oil off by standing beneath the sloping eaves of the cinema's wooden roof during the afternoon rains, vigorously scrubbing ourselves with our hands or palm leafs. Yet for all that it rained, after twenty days or so none of us showed much sign of removing the oil.

When – at last – even the Japanese began to notice the stink, they marched us in batches down to a local creek to bath properly. One look told us the creek was also the local sewer. No matter, our need to get clean was much stronger than any finer feelings about bathing in a toilet. Keeping a wary eye out, we plunged in and scrubbed like hell. Finally, after a few visits to the creek, the oil began to shift, though in my case, it shifted a lot faster as I made more visits to the creek than anyone else in the camp.

Marching back with the bathing party after our first session in the creek, a Japanese guard began screaming at me. I had no idea what I had done and stood there taking his abuse until I realised he was ordering me, at bayonet-point, back to the creek. I set off with the guard behind, jumped in and scrubbed up again. Getting out, the guard immediately took up screaming where he had left off. Jabbing his bayonet, he indicated I should get back in the creek once more. When I got out for the third time, the guard took a long look at me then shrugged and marched me back to camp. I had no idea what his problem was.

It was Marcus who explained it. He told me the Japanese didn't have red-haired people so they weren't accustomed to seeing freckles, which meant they thought my face and arms were still smeared in fuel oil. He was right. During the rest of our time at the cinema I was marched back to the creek at least half-a-dozen times by different guards, none of whom could understand why the marks on my skin would not wash off.

Finally, after thirty-eight days of hell at the cinema, we were ordered to prepare to move. This was a crucial time: a time when we all had to contain our anxiety about the uncertainty of our future. Would the new place we were going to be better or worse than the cinema? *Could* it be worse than the cinema? From what we were learning about the Japanese, there was no doubt that it could.

Mirla's Story

Every morning I woke up and silently repeated my mantra: *Arthur has survived. Arthur is alive and well.* It was the start of my daily routine to combat doubt and fear. For the rest of the day, every day, I kept myself busy. Work at MacRobertson-Miller Aviation kept me occupied for five-and-a-half days a week and I threw myself into it. If I didn't have any work of my own to do, then I went looking to help someone else. Anything to keep my mind occupied.

Every week I went to have a cup of tea with Arthur's parents. Nana kept herself cheerful but the news of their missing son was taking a toll on Grandad. I did my best to encourage them both and in doing so encouraged myself. It was proof, if ever proof was needed, of the old adage that both Nancy and my mother often repeated: that the best way to heal yourself was to try to heal other people.

Outside of work and family there were also other things to divert my mind away from dark thoughts and notions of doubt. I had always been a good tennis player, but after the news that Arthur was missing, I threw myself into my game with single-minded dedication and got even better. On Saturday lunchtimes I rushed straight from work to the nets and played into the evening. I would play until I was exhausted. I entered as many tournaments as possible, and won a few. It was the same with my running. I had been a member of the Perth Athletic Club for some years and now I saw to it that I entered as many competitions as I could. When the hockey season started I threw myself into the game with the same fierce dedication as I had towards tennis.

Socially too, I was kept busy. My work at the VAD was a small contribution to the war effort and I volunteered for as many duties as possible, while on Friday nights I worked in the canteen of the Young Australia League on Murray Street in Perth. It was my good friend Nancy who had encouraged me to work in the canteen, insisting that I did not cut myself off from social life. Every Friday night the YAL held a dance thronged by every available young woman in Perth and by servicemen: sailors mainly, mostly from the eastern states but also increasingly Americans.

Nancy was right: the dances were good fun; they kept my spirits up. In fact, Nancy and I would sometimes make up a foursome with a couple of the young servicemen to go to the pictures or a Saturday-night dance. In this I didn't feel I was betraying Arthur. There was no suggestion of romance or intimacy in the dates, and the men with whom I went out – boys, really – were, in the main, very respectful.

It is not a great thing to admit, but I must confess whenever I went out with a young serviceman I immediately started making comparisons with Arthur. Without exception, after every date I realised how right he was for me; how suited we were. Perhaps, almost seventy years on, that sounds callous, but it was a war and most of us were ships passing in the night. All of us, men and women, knew it wasn't a good idea to get too close.

Not long after Arthur had joined HMAS *Perth*, I had gone out with a young sailor who had later been posted missing on the *Sydney*. It saddened me to think that such a nice young boy might possibly be at the bottom of the ocean. But having Arthur missing was enough emotional stress for me to contend with, and so the dates Nancy and I went on were no more than a few hours of innocent fun; a pleasant way of passing the time and putting the war at the back of our minds.

So I coped by keeping busy. Every night I prayed for Arthur's safe return and every morning, without exception, I repeated my mantra.

6

On the Road to Mandalay

Sitting with my back to the sacking-covered entrance of the cell, I am staring at the best hand I have had all afternoon: three queens and an ace. I am concentrating hard, trying to work out what the others are holding.

Suddenly Merv says, 'Blood, don't move.'

I glance up. 'What?'

'For God's sake, don't move.' His tone is urgent, almost panicky. He nods his head. 'Look.'

I look down. In the narrow space between my arm and my body is a bright, shining, razor-sharp bayonet. 'Bloody hell!' I drop my cards, as alarmed as if I was sitting next to a King Brown. I leap up as the bayonet withdraws behind the sacking.

Now we're for it. None of us has heard the Korean approaching; probably the bastard has crept down the corridor so he could catch us before we can stand and make obeisance.

We leap to our feet as the guard rips back the sacking curtain. He starts yelling immediately, shouting, 'Kare, kare!' We stiffen to attention: feet splayed, fingers rigid, body straight and bow stiffly from the waist. The guard continues to scream and I get ready for a bashing. Instead he peers inside our little cell and sees the makeshift playing cards scattered on the floor. For some reason the sight of our diminutive cards seems to placate him and his tone lessens. He growls at us for a few seconds then stamps off down the corridor. I breathe a sigh of relief. That was a close shave: I was millimetres away from being stabbed.

Marcus, Lofty, Merv, Harvey and I, along with a few of the other WA blokes, were in the second batch of prisoners to be shifted from the cinema: the first batch, including those from the jail, had been moved two days before us.

Once more it was standing-room only in the back of the trucks and again our Jap driver shifted the gears as if he had never heard of a clutch. We swayed all over the place and clung to each other but the mood among the blokes was festive; at least we were leaving the detested cinema. Now and again we encountered groups of natives along the route, some of whom waved and threw bananas and coconuts into the trucks, which we ravenously divided and shared. 'Not so unpopular with this mob,' I said to Lofty.

'They're learning,' he murmured. We were heading east and for the first time since we had landed on Java we got a chance to take in the magnificent scenery: rolling hills of endlessly verdant jungle interspersed by a few paddy fields and villages. It was a long journey and our drivers made a few stops to allow us to relieve ourselves at the side of the road. Unlike at the cinema, our guards here seemed relaxed, even though we could have easily disappeared into the jungle. But what was the point? The Japs had threatened execution of everyone, and even though we doubted that even they would actually carry out such a savage, inhuman reprisal, whatever they did would be severe on all those left. And how would we survive in the jungle? By nightfall most of us would have been dead of snakebite. Either that or given up by a native, eager for a reward. The strangeness of the jungle and the inhospitality of the terrain was the best deterrent to our escaping, and the Japs knew it.

On one of our lavatory stops the drivers broke out some tins of Australian meat, which were greatly appreciated. Even a mouthful of meat, which is all each of us got, was a psychological boost, though after we had swallowed the one glorious morsel we fell to wondering how many of our food stores the Japs were holding back from us.

By now we were pretty certain we were making for Batavia. We had been close to the city when the *Perth* had moored briefly at Tanjong Priok six weeks earlier, though it seemed like six years ago; practically another lifetime. We were right about our destination. The convoy of trucks snaked its way through the city to arrive outside a military compound surrounded by a high brick wall which we learned later was the Dutch Army's 10th Military Barracks, Batavia. The barracks had been constructed to house both Dutch and native troops in a battalion of bicycle-mounted infantry.

Before the fall of Singapore we would have laughed at the idea of armed soldiers on bikes but many of the Japanese troops who'd invaded Malaysia had been mounted on bikes which had enabled them to move much faster than our blokes, often successfully cutting off their retreat. The speed of the Jap advance using bicycles had caught our side by surprise and now here we were at a bicycle barracks of the Dutch army. Needless to say, the place had immediately been christened 'Bicycle Camp'.

Just outside the barracks we were ordered off the trucks. A native was standing close to the gates spruiking fruit and drinks. A number of us still had Australian money; my money belt was full of low-denomination coins. What's more, the Australian penny was exactly the same shape and colour as the Dutch two-and-a-half-cent piece – which is what the native was charging for his wares. I dived into my money belt and fished out some pennies which I dished out to Lofty, Merv, Marcus, Harvey, and a few more shipmates. The native didn't notice he was taking Aussie money, he was too busy coining it in and certainly I didn't tell him. Maybe he didn't care, but it was my first act of deliberate larceny. I bought a bottle of soft drink which tasted like nectar.

Beyond the gates, the camp was immaculate. Bicycle Camp had brick-built accommodation huts with running water and electricity, good sanitation, excellent kitchens and even a canteen. There were 2000 men of the AIF imprisoned here, along with a few hundred Poms and some Americans. The prisoners assembled on the parade ground waiting to welcome us appeared fit and healthy. They looked smart. They were washed and shaved and even their uniforms were in reasonably good condition; a stark contrast to our mob of 500 G-stringed, oil-smeared, bootless blokes from the *Perth* and *Houston*. With our long hair and ragged beards, and with a fair number of our sick being carried in on stretchers, we must have looked like a crowd of extras from a film about John the Baptist. It wasn't our fault we had been sunk at sea and that everything we owned had gone down with the ship. The infantry had been captured with all their kit: some of those blokes had razors and scissors – even soap.

The Aussie infantry greeted us with open arms. An AIF warrant officer made a formal speech of welcome under the baleful eyes and sneering faces of the Japanese guards, telling us that at this camp we could count on three meals a day, decent washing facilities and good hygiene. As he spoke the smell of roasting meat wafted across the parade ground; it was so pungent I felt my mouth watering and for a moment thought I might faint. That evening we had a cooked meal of a couple of tinned sausages and rice. Though they weren't as good as the snags I had missed as the *Perth* went into action, the meal still counts as one of the best I've ever had.

We were assigned sleeping quarters inside one of the huts, all of which had been partitioned into cell-like cubicles. Four blokes were assigned to each cell and being close mates, Marcus, Lofty and I got one together, along with Harvey, who made up the fourth member of the 'Sandgroper' mob. Merv was with more WA blokes next door.

Harvey was different from the rest of us. Whereas Marcus, Merv, Lofty and I were big blokes and no one messed with us, Harvey was a short, quiet guy. He was older and more studied, I guess, because he was married and had a child – a son he'd only seen twice. But he was a good bloke: the kind who would pay back the money a mate had spent on standing him beers. He was definitely one of us.

Even though it was cramped, we soon made our cubicle home. To begin with we slept on the concrete floor but promptly scrounged rice sacks to serve as bedding, obtained an old orange crate to use as a table, and hung rice sacking at the entrance to give us a little privacy from the busy corridor outside. Although we were still prisoners of war and were definitely not living in luxury, compared to the cinema this place was easy street. Now and again we were able to have a shower, with soap donated by the infantry blokes, and finally washed off the last of the fuel oil. We also got haircuts from another AIF bloke and had our beards trimmed. There wasn't much point in shaving as there weren't enough razors to go around, so the best we could do was to keep our beards neat and clean.

Regular food, better sanitation and reasonable facilities turned us around and within days we could see and feel the difference in ourselves. My dysentery disappeared and the bouts of malaria that so many of us had suffered abated. Most of our sick made a rapid recovery as there was a hospital ward in the barracks and Sam Stening, who single-handedly had kept so many of the blokes alive at the cinema, was joined by other doctors who were prisoners in the camp.

Even so, none of us were at the peak of our physical fitness. The lack of vitamins in our diet, along with the ever-present mosquitoes, lice and other little tropical buggers, meant that every man in the camp had skin lesions which, after constant scratching, would become infected. Very rarely did we get a full night's sleep without waking up to curse and groan and violently scratch some intimate part of ourselves. Sanitation was always an issue. As there was no paper for the latrine, we had to keep ourselves clean by washing with water. The threat of typhus or cholera, though less here than at the cinema, never went away.

Pretty soon the Japs put us to work, forming labour parties of the fittest blokes for work at the docks at Tanjong Priok. Although the principle carved in stone in every branch of the armed services is 'Never volunteer for anything', almost all the light-fingered lads of the *Perth* put their hand up immediately. I was one of them. We sailors had nothing much beyond our G-strings: we relied on the generosity of the army blokes to supply us with the basic essentials. Up till now we'd had to improvise pretty well everything: turning tobacco tins into drinking mugs and mess tins and palm leaves into hats. Any chance of working at the docks and scrounging whatever we could find was too good to pass up.

We were escorted onto a train and herded to where we were set to work clearing up the warehouses and godowns on the wharves hardest hit by the Japanese bombers. The Japs were plundering everything: stripping it, ripping it and shipping it back to Japan.

On our first day we were paraded in front of a self-important Jap captain in polished riding boots who, after telling us what a privilege it was for us to be cleaning up the docks for the Japanese army, issued a dire warning about stealing: anyone caught with even the smallest item on him would be beaten severely. A second offence would mean execution.

I suppressed a smile. 'Clean up the docks,' the officer had said. This bloody mob would clean them *out*. The bloke was talking to Australians: for all his threats about stealing, he might as well have been telling the tides not to rise. The blokes around me were past masters at pilfering; many of the lads who had swiftly relieved the damaged godowns of so much booze and cigarettes when the *Perth* had been wharf-side were now paraded in front of the little

Hitler. Given the smallest chance, they would strip the place bare. I intended to be one of them.

It was ironic. I had started my career in the bank knowing that the first and most fundamental requirement of a banker was complete honesty. To steal was the cardinal sin. But here I was resolving to steal anything I could. Whatever wasn't nailed down I would take, and if it *was* nailed down – I'd go looking for a crowbar.

The work routine at the wharves was popular. It kept us active and helped keep us fit; we learned to dodge much of the Japanese scrutiny and we were able to supplement our lives at Bicycle Camp with stolen food and a lot of useful material. Yet it was strange, all the same, to be padding around the wharves barefoot and in a loincloth. Just weeks earlier I had watched natives in exactly the same garb working the docks. Now I was in their place. The world had turned upside down.

In our own small way our mob did our bit to bugger the enemy, especially when we were detailed to load machinery onto the ships: everything from machine tools and lathes to sewing machines and bicycles. Whenever we could we would strip a vital part off the machine and surreptitiously drop it into the water so that many of the items transhipped to Japan were useless. We were glad that a big number of new bikes arriving in Japan didn't have brakes.

In the meantime, most of what we stole was smuggled into camp in the pouches of our loincloths or, if we had them, beneath our straw hats. Before we went back to Bicycle Camp the Japs would pat us down but they were loath to get too intimate in their search, though running the gauntlet of the second search at the camp gate was always a bit tricky. Some blokes got caught there and took a hefty bashing.

One day I was in a squad detailed to clean out some wharf-side offices damaged in the bombing. A few of the blokes moaned that there wasn't much to steal from an office but I thought differently. This was my opportunity: my chance to start something that would occupy me during the long, boring hours of incarceration. I would keep a diary and, where I could, I'd sketch a record of our existence. Almost every day we were there I was able to lift a couple of pencils and a few sheets of paper which, back at the camp, I hid beneath some sacking in our cell. I knew that keeping a diary, in the eyes of the Japanese, was one of the most serious crimes a prisoner could commit but I was ready to take the chance. I had to do something to keep my mind occupied.

After lifting the pencils the first thing I did was to draw a mural on the dirty white-plaster wall of our cell. I didn't reckon drawing on the wall would be considered too heinous, even by the Japs, so I drew a picture, about 1 metre deep by 3 metres long, of a game of footy at Subiaco Oval. It kept me occupied for days. When finished, the others admired it and said it reminded them of home. A few blokes from some of the other cells came by to take a look and, although it wasn't Michelangelo, I was proud and glad I had drawn it. Gazing at it made me think of Mirla and my family; of Australia and the life to which I was determined to return.

After that I found another pastime to keep me occupied. I had noticed that a few of the AIF blokes had packs of playing cards and could while away hours playing bridge, poker and gin rummy. We navy blokes of course had nothing like that, so I decided I'd make my own pack. The obvious choice for my raw material was cigarette cards. Back then, packets of cigarettes came with a little card about 4 centimetres by eight. Usually they had pictures of sportsmen or racing cars on the front while the backs were often blank. Kids, usually boys, collected them but most smokers in Bicycle Camp threw them away. It took me a while but eventually I scrounged fifty-two cigarette cards in good condition and set to work creating a set of playing cards. The face cards took longest but it was a labour of love and when I had finished we spent many hours at the card table which, instead of green baize, was an upturned orange crate draped in hessian sacking.

Not long after we arrived at Bicycle Camp a mob of Americans turned up: 500 blokes from the Texas Battalion of 131st US Field Artillery. This unit had come to be known as the 'lost battalion' as it had been dispatched to various Pacific theatres of war only to have its orders countermanded and to be sent off somewhere else. In the end the battalion had arrived in Java just in time to be captured. Months earlier the *Perth* was one of the ships that had escorted the convoy carrying the lost battalion from Fiji to Brisbane.

The Yanks marching into the camp were entirely kitted up: they were fat and sassy and had everything with them, including not only plenty of tinned food and spare kit but, it soon transpired, thousands of dollars worth of Dutch guilders. The blokes in our hut stared at them in the manner of foxes contemplating chickens. Though we had bonded with the blokes from the *Houston* who, like us, were sailors who had lost everything when they went into the water, this new mob of Yanks was different. They were fair game.

Within days the *Perth* entrepreneurs had set up food stalls in our hut and were trading stuff stolen off the docks with the Yanks; subtly relieving them of their foodstuffs and guilders. With the sudden increase in specie, blackmarket trading with the natives beyond the camp wall flourished too, even though it was banned and punishable by the inevitable beating. But when it came to wheeling and dealing, Ali Baba and his forty thieves had nothing on the lads from the *Perth* and for a while life in the camp was tolerable.

Things began to change in May, after the Battle of the Coral Sea. Somewhere in the camp was a secret radio. None of us knew where; we didn't need to know. We guessed it was in the officers' compound but no one talked about it. Ever. All we knew was that from time to time we would be quietly fed snippets of information about what was happening in the war.

The Battle of the Coral Sea sounded to us like a draw. The Americans had lost an aircraft carrier but the Jap invasion force, bound for Port Moresby in New Guinea, had turned back. It was wonderful news and we were greatly heartened. In the Pacific theatre, the war's first round in the Java Sea had undeniably gone to the Japs, but the second round, the Coral Sea, was a draw. From now on we reckoned it would be the Japs who'd be taking the thrashing.

A few days later the Jap camp commandant assembled everyone to tell us what a great victory the Imperial Japanese navy had won in a tremendous battle in the Coral Sea. Every prisoner assembled on the parade ground stood straight-faced as the little Nip recounted how the entire American Pacific fleet had been sunk. According to him, Japan had already won the war. We knew differently, although there was no way we could tell him that. And even if we hadn't known, we could have guessed the outcome was not what the Jap claimed – because we prisoners started paying for it.

At the end of his victory speech the commandant issued new orders restricting movement around the camp, while telling us that anyone not properly bowing to or saluting the guards was going to cop a bashing. We knew that if the battle had been a victory the commandant would have been vauntingly magnanimous. Instead, the overwhelming Japanese desire to seek vengeance implied that the battle had not gone the way the commandant claimed. His threats were an augury: the more victorious the allies became – the more vicious the Japs would be towards their prisoners of war.

A few days later that commandant was replaced by a new Nip who told us the former bloke had been too soft on us. As POWs we were apparently too happy and had too many privileges, so now singing was banned in the huts and even laughing was frowned on. At the same time, our Japanese guards were replaced by Koreans.

Frankly, I didn't know much about Korea or Koreans at the time and would have had difficulty pointing to the place on a map. But I soon learned that, these blokes anyway, were complete mongrel bastards. If we had thought the Jap guards were bad, this lot were worse. Maybe it was because the Japs looked down on them as an inferior race and treated them badly that they treated us the same way. Beatings increased in frequency and intensity. No one was safe from the bashings, the reasons for which were always random and bizarre.

The Koreans had a fetish about us prisoners bowing to them in the proper manner. At the shout of 'Kare!' we were meant to snap to attention, heels together, feet out at the correct angle and fingers stiff, before bowing as lowly as possible from the waist. Curiously, it was the fingers not properly stiffened that would send the Koreans berko more than anything. Even when we followed the correct procedure we'd have one of the bastards kick us in the shins and slap us repeatedly around the face. Sometimes a bloke would cop a rifle butt to the head and be left unconscious in the dust. The most galling part was that, though the Koreans were bigger and bulkier than the Japanese, with broad, boorish, sallow faces – both vacant and cunning at the same time – we, generally speaking, were taller and heavier and could easily have given them a right bashing. But to retaliate was fatal. We were expected to make obeisance to the bastards and we just had to get on with it.

We called the Koreans 'duckshooters' as they carried their rifles, always with bayonets fixed, under their arms in the manner of blokes out hunting ducks. They looked ridiculous, not that we ever showed them what we thought. Not only were they free with bashings with their rifle butts, they were also not slow to jab blokes with their bayonets. A lot of blokes received stab wounds which turned septic.

One day Marcus, Lofty, Merv, Harvey and I were squatting on the floor of our little cell, playing poker with my homemade deck of cards. They had become our lifeline: allowing us to spend hours playing as many varieties of card games as we could. We were so focused on the game that we didn't hear the Korean guard approaching in the corridor outside. Incensed that we had not leapt up to bow to him, even though we could no more see him through the rice-sack curtain at the entrance than he could see us, the guard blindly thrust his bayonet through the sacking. It missed me by millimetres; stabbing between my arm and my rib cage. I'm sure that, if he had caught me in the back with the bayonet, he would have punctured one of my lungs.

The Japs were good at playing on our anxieties, especially when it came to worries about home. They started rumours that swept through the camp like the plague. The most pernicious was that the Jap army was getting ready to invade Western Australia; substance being added to the rumour when I and a lot of lads from WA were taken to Jap headquarters to be interrogated by one of their intelligence officers. The bloke, immaculately dressed in a white uniform, was seated in front of a huge-scale map of Western Australia. In perfect English he interrogated us about the towns, roads, railways and the general terrain of the state's northwest, though he also probed me about the port facilities in Albany and Freo.

The bloke couldn't help showing off how much he already knew about WA. Certainly his detailed knowledge was impressive; espionage no doubt supplied by Japanese naval personnel who, for years, had been going undercover as skippers and crew of pearling luggers off the northwest coast. The officer threatened us with serious reprisals should the invading troops find that the information we had supplied was false. I told him I couldn't help; said he already knew far more about the lie of the land in the Kimberley and the Pilbara than I did, and that the only two places in WA I knew intimately were Scarborough Beach and Subiaco Oval. He had a guard kick me out.

Even so, a lot of us were worried about what might happen if the Japs invaded WA. It took the officers a while to allay the lads' fears: to convince them that, strategically, there was no point

Arthur's parents, Harold and Suzie, married in 1910 and had seven children; Arthur was the youngest. The family moved to Subiaco in 1931 and began a long-standing association with the Subiaco Football Club.

Arthur (left) and older brother Harold, pictured in their footy gear. At the age of fourteen, Arthur was selected for the State School Boys' Football Team as half-back, and Harold played as goal sneak for Subiaco.

Arthur (far left) with older brothers Les (standing) and Harold, ready to go off to war. All three sons returned home safely.

Arthur and Mirla announced their engagement after his return from the war. Engagement rings were scarce at the time, but Arthur purchased one for Mirla with his accrued pay.

Arthur photographed at Manly in Sydney, 1941,
prior to the sailing of HMAS Perth.

The graduation class at Flinders Naval Depot, Victoria. Arthur is in the back row, second from left; his good friend Harry (Lofty) Nagle, who didn't survive the sinking of the Rakuyo Maru, *is third from left.*

Arthur's mate Marcus Clark, who was entrusted with bringing Arthur's diaries home to Australia after Arthur was shipped out on the Rakuyo Maru. *Marcus wrapped the diaries in banana leaves, buried and hid them from the Japanese until the end of the war.*

After their graduation at the Flinders Naval Depot, 1941,
Arthur and other Perth-born sailors travelled back home across the
Nullabor for a visit. Photographed in Port Pirie, South Australia,
enjoying a pint on the way, are Arthur (back row, second from right)
and mate Norm Fuller (back row, third from right). Norm also survived
the sinking of HMAS Perth and eventually returned home.

Starboard-side view of the cruiser HMAS Perth, commissioned into the Royal Australian Navy on 29 June, 1939. In this photograph, taken in 1941, she is seen in her camouflage paint, ready for action prior to her final battle at the Sunda Strait, where she was torpedoed and sunk on 1 March, 1942.

Inset: Remarkably, the Perth's bell was recovered from its wreck (minus its clapper) by an Indonesian diving team in 1974.

Mirla and her older brother Allan, 1942. Mirla is wearing her Voluteer Aid Detachment uniform and her brother is in his AIF uniform. It was through Allan's involvement with local football that Mirla met Arthur in 1936.

Entrance to the Bicycle Camp, Batavia, where HMAS Perth officers and ship's company were interned before being transported to work on the Burma–Thailand Railway.

Prisoners of War on the Burma–Thailand Railway. These HMAS Perth survivors are carrying rice bags through a jungle camp in 1943. At front left is Ernie Toovey, who later became a state cricketer for Queensland.

ABCDEFGHIJKLMNOPQRSTUVWXYZ

ABCDEFGHIJKLMNOPQRSTUVWXYZ

CLARK

EDMUND. C

WINDOW DRESSER
W.D. & H.O. WILLS
MURRAY ST
PERTH, WA

"BLOOD" MEN

ABCDEFGHIJKLMNOPQRSTUVW
XYZ

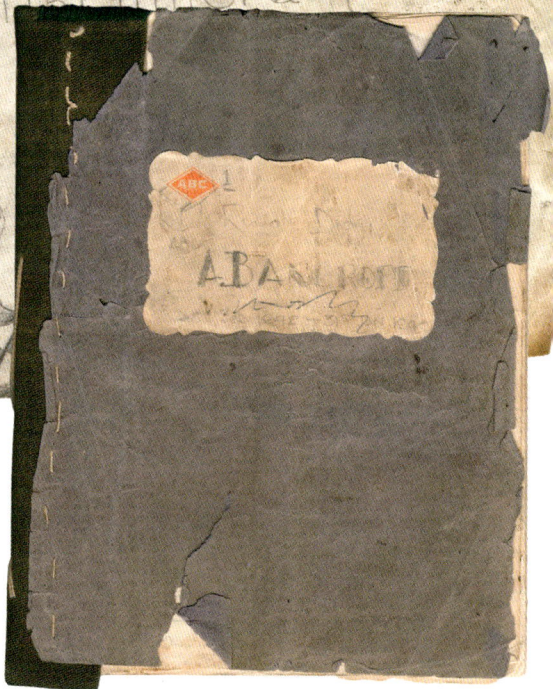

ABAN HOPE

Excerpts from Arthur's wartime diary.
Arthur kept four books while a POW,
including a daily diary, a book of poems,
and one of sketches. The fourth book
was badly water-damaged, but all books
were presented to Commander Shane
Moore for preservation and display
at the RAN Heritage Centre, Sydney,
in 2006.

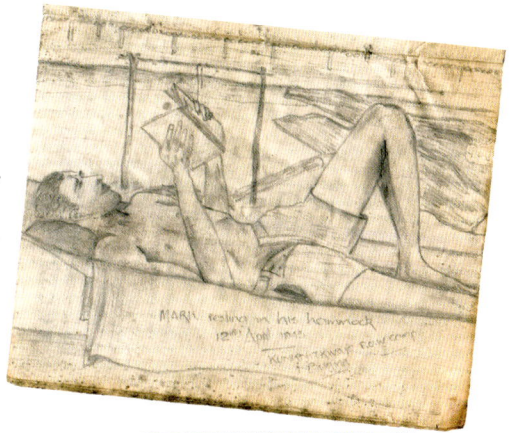

MARK resting in his hammock
12th April 1943

1942 — Had breakfast at 0500 and waited
until 0800 for train
Issued with tin of sausages and loaf
of bread each

OCTOBER 8th — About 1500 taken onto Jap.
(THURSDAY) Transport "KIN KON MARU" at TANJONG
PRIOK set sail for unknown destination
— good rice and stew meals 3 times
a day. — Half of a mug of tea 3
times a day — Conditions very
dirty and hot, salt water wash daily —
Dysentery rather bad — One man died
at sea and buried at night —
No one very thrilled at the prospect of going to
sea on a Jap ship but I guess they're the boss

OCTOBER 11th — Arrived off SINGAPORE ISLAND
(Sunday) during afternoon. spent night at
anchor —

OCTOBER 12th — Landed and transported to
(Monday) huge ALLIED PRISON CAMP at "CHANGI"
BARRACKS — A great number of
AUSTRALIAN Troops, SCOTCH, and
ENGLISH — Very good conditions —
On the whole SINGAPORE not so
damaged by bombs as I expected —

- TO MY SWEET AUSSIE GIRL -

It's only a "two by two" photo,
Encased in a small leather frame
And it's not of a world renowned heiress
Or of any titled Dame.
But just the sweetheart of a Digger
Who heeded his country's call
And went forth to do his duty
Leaving his loved ones and all
And that face in that tiny photo
Of that sweet Australian girl
Means more to that far off Digger
Than anything else in the world.
And when he opens that photo
To gaze on his darling's face
He knows he would give his life gladly
To save it from disgrace
And as he gazes on it
He hears her once more say
I know I can trust you laddie
And each night for you I pray
And with a sigh, that spell is over,
The photo put back in its frame.
And he said as he kisses it gently
"Yes, dear, I'll play the game."

Poems recorded by Arthur in his diary
were from memory or composed by
fellow POWs. Even under extreme
hardship, Arthur still kept his sense
of humour, as seen in his 'It's
moments like these you need
Minties' sketch (right).

— THE 'PERTH'S' LAST STAND —

By AB. L.J.Golding R.A.N

We had a 'six inch' Cruiser, the "H.M.A.S. PERTH"
She was built to be a fighter – and always proved her worth.
But we lost her in the finish, up against the Yellow foe.
And you'll know the inside story if you read the tale below.
The Japs were in Manilla, Malaya and Hong Kong
And the day they'd be in the N.E.I's they said would not belong.
So up to Tandjong Priok we went at utmost speed
To lend the Dutch a helping hand they were our friends in need.
The Dutch said they were eager to defend these Eastern Isles,
And they greeted us with handshakes & the friendliest of smiles.
But when the Jap 'planes raided us the Dutch went right to earth
And left the whole damn shooting match to the "EXETER" & "PERTH".
We shot two Nippon bombers down – to the Dutch that wasn't good
They said, that to retaliate the Japs most surely would.
So down to SOURABAYA we went, the "EXETER" and "PERTH"
Escorted by the "JUPITER" – much to the Dutchman's mirth.
There we joined the JAVA FLEET and went to sea that night
To find the Jap Invasion Fleet and against them have a fight.
We all were glad to have a chance of fighting Nippon's pride
But we didn't know the Javanese were all on Nippon's side.
"DE REUTER" was our Flagship, with a Dutchman in Command
No one knows why he was picked to lead that gallant band.
For when we met the Nippon Fleet his tactics were all wrong
And he kept us bunched together while the range was far too long

P.T.O.

Survivors of the sunken Rakuyo Maru *cling to ropes on their oil-soaked raft. Arthur spent six days covered in oil, surviving the hot sun and the onslaught of rough seas. He was the last of his group to be rescued by the USS* Queenfish, *September 1944, just before a typhoon descended.*

Following his return to Australia, Arthur was invited to meet the Governor-General, the Duke of Gloucester and his wife, in Melbourne. Arthur declined, as he was on honeymoon with Mirla in Mandurah, and didn't want to leave his new bride, so their meeting occurred at a later date at HMAS Leeuwin *in Fremantle, WA.*

Arthur and Mirla were married
on 10 March, 1945. Bridal gowns
were rare, but Mirla was able to
purchase her fabric with her aunt's
clothing coupons. The bridal party,
from left: Bob Scott, Nancy Scott
(née Weedon), Bob Collins
(fellow POW), Mirla and Arthur,
June Syme (née Ledger).

A family portrait at son Colin's
wedding in 1982. Back row,
left to right: Dianne, Colin
and Vicki. Front row, left to
right: Mirla, Arthur and Toni.
(Photo courtesy of Richard
Syme.)

Arthur on Father's Day, 2009, at age eighty-seven, photographed by Abigail Harman.

Arthur and Mirla pictured at Subiaco Oval in May, 2008, on the occasion of its centenary. (Photo courtesy of the West Australian.)

in invading our state and that tactically, now the Japs had been stopped from invading New Guinea, there wasn't much chance they could invade Australia. I'm not sure that the officers actually believed it themselves, but gradually the anxiety among the WA lads abated a little.

Next, the Japs came up with a directive ordering every one of us to sign what amounted to an oath of allegiance to the Japanese army. Among other things it contained a solemn promise not to try to escape. Orders immediately came down from the senior officer at Bicycle Camp, Brigadier Blackburn VC, that, as the oath was against the Geneva Convention, no one was to sign. Though we didn't know much about the Geneva Convention we knew enough not to sign anything the Japs put in front of us. We treated the directive with disdain, agreeing that if we were given such a piece of paper to sign we would find good use for it in the latrines.

But things turned nasty. The guards went on a rampage of brutal beatings; turning up at our huts in the middle of the night to bash us at random, especially the officers. Brigadier Blackburn came in for some terrific beatings, as did Lieutenant-Colonel Jack Williams of the 2/2 Pioneers. All privileges were restricted, which pissed off the Yanks no end, as they were getting ready to celebrate Independence Day. All outside working parties were curtailed and, finally, our rice ration was cut in half. Hungry men were now on the point of starving.

After three days of this, orders came down from our superiors that we were to sign. Many of us were mumbling 'Stuff that', and were getting ready to disobey our own officers when the explanation came that the Jap injunction was meaningless. We were being forced to sign under duress, which made the edict legally null and void. Any piece of paper signed under those conditions would have less standing in a court than if we had used it in the latrines.

Even so, three officers from the infantry and one of our own *Perth* blokes still refused to sign. The Koreans forced them to kneel in the sun all day, beating them unmercifully when they collapsed. These four only signed after they were given a direct order by Brigadier Blackburn himself.

Our officers were good blokes and looked out for us. They mixed with us ordinary blokes in the other ranks a lot, even though they had their own billet and an officers' mess in a corner of the compound. This area was ringed by a simple wire fence but as there was no gate, other ranks kept wandering into the area. To prevent this, a bloke was assigned to stand at the gap in the fence to head off any wanderers. It wasn't guard duty as such: we didn't stand to attention or anything like that, just stood there for a few hours and kept watch.

One day, early in my imprisonment, I pulled the duty and was watching a scruffy infantry bloke in an old pair of shorts crouching down and working at the small vegetable garden inside the officers' compound. 'Why don't you let them do that, mate?' I said. 'They're the officers' vegetables. You're not going to eat them, so let the officers look after them.'

He looked up. 'No,' he said, 'I like doing it.'

I shrugged. 'Fair enough.'

A couple of days later we were ordered to parade for an inspection by the senior AIF officer now in overall command of us blokes from the *Perth*. Standing to attention in my G-string under the hot sun, I watched in horror as the bloke I had spoken to in the vegetable garden came marching onto the parade ground in full uniform. The scruffy bugger was Lieutenant-Colonel Williams! My blood ran cold. Oh hell, I thought, now I'm for it. But as he passed through the ranks he stopped at me for a moment and I'm sure I saw a faint hint of a smile.

In early August the camp commandant was changed yet again, with the new bloke, Lieutenant Susuki, proving to be more humane than his predecessor. He instituted rest days every tenth day, a few camp concerts, and even some organised sports. The centre of the compound was turned into a court and we took the Americans on at volleyball, which they only narrowly won against a RAN team. We did better in the boxing, which surprised the Americans as they rated themselves as good boxers and had on their team a bloke called Frank Pistole, the Golden Gloves champion of their Asiatic Fleet. Our bloke was a half-Aboriginal digger, Ted (Jesse) James. The bout was even for the first few rounds until, suddenly, Jesse unleashed a furious flurry of punches that put the American on the deck for the count of ten. The American audience was stunned, though not as stunned as their Golden Gloves champion who was flat on his back, his eyes dancing with stars. Later we asked Jesse what had prompted his sudden attack. 'Bastard called me a name,' he said simply.

Among our numbers at the camp was a war correspondent, Rohan Rivett. After months of persuading he finally got the Japs to agree to him going on Jap radio to broadcast an account of the Battle of the Sunda Strait. Of course the Japs insisted he emphasise the defeat of the *Perth* and *Houston* but that was okay, he was still able to tell the world what a great fight we had put up and, most importantly, that a few hundred of our blokes and of the *Houston's* crew had survived. Everyone congratulated Rohan on conning the Japs. They thought it was a great propaganda broadcast, whereas what he had really done was to bring hope to a lot of families in Australia and the United States.

Despite the Korean guards, life at Bicycle Camp had become tolerable again and by the southern spring the twin demons of anxiety and frustration had all but disappeared. A few men had died in the camp, mainly of wounds, but the rest of us, though not pictures of health, were surviving. All that changed in early October, when rumours started circulating that we were to be moved – to where no one knew.

The anxiety levels shot up. We had been held prisoner for six months, unable to do what we wanted when we wanted, yet any change to our circumstances was instantly viewed as a potential threat. We overcame the anxiety with a lot humorous speculation: Marcus reckoned the Japs were taking us on a world cruise, or even that they were shipping us back to Australia in time for the Melbourne Cup. Mostly, the speculation centred on Japan. Some thought the Japs were taking us there: getting us out of harm's way as, sooner or later, our blokes and the Americans would be taking Java back.

Shortly after the start of the rumours everyone in the camp was ordered to parade with their kit which, for the majority of us blokes from the *Perth* and *Houston*, was pretty much all we stood up in, plus in my case, a small Dutch Army shoulder bag containing my fabricated mess tin, a mug and a few other bit and pieces. It was a special *tenko* as the Koreans searched us for contraband, grabbing our kit off us, rifling through it and then kicking it around at our feet. I had hidden my diary in the pouch of my G-string. Finally the guards ordered us back to our huts, telling us the parade was a big mistake. The guards did this a couple of times, I guess mainly to unsettle us, although by now we had discovered through the medium of the abominable, detested *tenkos* that the Japanese were hopeless organisers of men. When it came to the great dictum of armed services everywhere – 'Hurry up and wait' – the Japanese army led the world.

At 4.00 a.m. on the morning of 8 October, 1942 we were paraded and searched once more before being told that about 1500 of us, including most of the blokes from the *Perth* and *Houston*, would be leaving immediately under the command of Lieutenant-Colonel Williams. But not *everyone* from the *Perth* was going. Harvey was not in our number; for some reason he was to be shipped out with another mob a couple of days later. I never found out why Harvey, who had messed with us, sharing the same tiny cell as Marcus, Lofty and me for the past six months, was separated. We had only seconds to say good bye, all of us promising we would mess together again when we got to the other end – wherever that might be. Harvey's parting words to me were, 'Save me a good bunk, Blood. I'll be seein' ya.'

But he never did see me again. Nor I him.

They herded us to the station and onto trains which took us to the docks at Tanjong Priok, where we boarded an old, certifiably unseaworthy rust bucket called the *Kinkon Maru*. Then they ordered us down into the hold of the ship. As the crew of the *Perth* already knew about life in the hold of a Jap transport, we invited the army blokes to go first so they were in the lower levels. It was like an inferno down there and it was massively overcrowded. For some reason dysentery had broken out again and a lot of blokes, including me, were suffering. The stench in the boiling-hot hold as the ship groaned and rattled during the three-day voyage was unimaginable. One bloke died and was buried at sea. Finally, on the afternoon of the fourth day, we heard the ship drop anchor. By now the old salts knew exactly where we were. We were riding at anchor in Singapore Harbour.

We came up from the hold, squinting into bright sunshine, early the next morning. With guards screaming and swinging rifle butts at us we took our first look at Singapore. The Japanese flag, the red circle on the white background, fluttered everywhere, while the docks were a hive of activity, with native workers and many of our blokes in slouch hats loading transports with looted supplies and heavy machinery – even civilians' personal possessions.

Singapore itself was a surprise. Crowded into the back of army trucks and driven east through the city we could see scarcely any sign of resistance; hardly a bomb crater or shelled building. It looked to us like Singapore had given up and rolled over without a fight! Life in the city looked to be perfectly normal, with civilians shopping and going about their business as usual. It was disconcerting and disappointing to think that the 'impregnable fortress' had given up like a sick dog.

We were ferried to Changi Prison, where, forced to remain standing in the trucks in the blazing sun, Marcus, Lofty, Merv and I contemplated its grim, ominous façade. It looked like a real hellhole and each of us was praying that we weren't going to be incarcerated there. Our guards and the prison officers were engaged in a terrific argument which, thank God, the prison officers must have won as, after an hour or so, our driver slammed in the clutch and jerked the truck away from the prison. Instead, we were driven the short distance to the POW camp.

Changi Prisoner of War Camp was another surprise. It was actually at Selerang, the former barracks of the British garrison, and comprised a few square miles of three-storied brick buildings, surrounded by lawns and coconut palms and an abundance of sports fields. Fifty thousand allied personnel were POWs here, the place being run with all the precision and spit and polish of the British Army. There was scarcely a Jap to be seen. All the prisoners were in uniform, well fed and fit. Compared to even Bicycle Camp, this place was a holiday resort! In comparison to these blokes, the crews of the *Perth* and *Houston*, even after six months at Bicycle Camp, looked like a bunch of tropical swagmen.

For that reason the officers at Changi started calling us 'the rabble from Java', a nickname that always stung. I would have understood if the jibe had come from the Brits, but in fact it came from one of our own; a senior officer in the AIF. I resented the label. We on the *Perth* had gone down against a superior force with all guns blazing; a lot of these blokes, even though they outnumbered the Japs, had put their hands up without firing a shot. Our entire army in Singapore had *surrendered* to the Japs. We hadn't. So who were they to be calling us names?

However, we were well treated at Changi, where the 'Java rabble' was adopted by a British regiment who straight away gave us a great meal of bully beef and biscuits. We were also able to have a good wash and, for the first time in months, actually sleep on a bunk bed.

Because we were so badly kitted out, Colonel Williams immediately arranged for an issue of clothing from the stores at Changi, for which we were all very grateful. Our gratitude was short-lived as the same AIF commander who had called us a 'rabble' ordered the return of the clothing and we never saw a stitch of it. He obviously had it in for us. Even so, we were lucky in one respect. A Swedish Red Cross ship had just docked at Singapore and we had arrived in time to get a distribution of tinned foodstuffs, cocoa, sugar and cigarettes. Among my little haul was a tin of condensed milk which I thought I'd save for a rainy day.

Just two days after arriving at Changi we had orders to move. All of us were bitterly disappointed, believing that, in this place, we could survive the war with ease – not knowing what a hell on earth Changi was to later become as the Japanese began to lose the war.

A few minutes before we were to leave the camp a marvellous thing happened. An orderly appeared with a bundle of Red Cross letter cards. We were given five minutes to write no more than twenty words to the folks at home. It was as if a weight on my heart had been lifted. Finally, my parents and Mirla would know I was alive. I just hoped the card would reach home before Christmas.

We were taken back to the docks and shoved into the hold of yet another rust bucket, the *Maebasi Maru*. This was the worst voyage we had endured. For two days we lay at anchor in Singapore Harbour, sweltering in the hold without a breath of wind. We had six buckets of water between 600 blokes and the food was inedible:

the Japs were giving us soup made of rotten meat floating on dirty water, which forced us to resort to the rations we had been given by the Red Cross. Soon, most of us became smeared with lime, which had been the ship's previous cargo and that had not been properly cleaned out of the hold. It burned the skin, though at least it got rid of all the lice and other bugs inhabiting us.

At last, when the ship finally got underway, we got a trickle of fresh air into the hold. But now we had new problems. We were incarcerated in a hold 15 metres below the waterline, without lifebelts, in an unmarked Japanese merchant ship in a war. We knew from our secret radio that British and American subs were doing a lot of damage to the Jap shipping around Singapore. All we could do was hope that no Allied subs were lurking beneath the waves on this trip.

For the entire journey our tongues were swollen by the lack of water while our bodies streamed with perspiration from the heat and humidity of the holds. We were so cramped we practically lay on top of each other: blokes with dysentery cheek by jowl with blokes not yet afflicted. Though the Japs let us up to the heads once a day, for the blokes with dysentery it wasn't enough. The stench became indescribable and out of a total of 1800 men split into three holds, fourteen died and were buried at sea.

From our trips to the heads, we could tell we were sailing north, up the west coat of the Malay Peninsular. It was difficult to work out where we might be going: obviously it wasn't Japan. Rangoon seemed about the only other obvious choice – though why there was anybody's guess. There was a rumour that the Japs were building a railway to India but it was difficult to believe and, anyway, what would that have to do with us? Though we were still a hundred miles from land, confirmation that Rangoon was our destination began to jell when we noticed the sea turning muddy . . . discharge from the many mouths of the Irrawaddy River.

On my daily trips to the heads I had noticed a big Dutchman, which was not surprising as there were a lot of Dutch troops on the ship. But what made this joker different was that he was carrying *two* Dutch Army-issue water bottles, slung across his Dutch army greens. I sidled up to him. 'What would you trade for one of your water bottles?' I asked.

'What have you got?'

'Tin of condensed milk.'

He thought about it for a moment but I was pretty sure he was going to say yes, as I had seen his eyes momentarily light up. 'Yeah, okay.'

We made the exchange on our next trip topside. It was the best deal I did in the whole of the war. That water bottle was going to save my life.

On the afternoon of the fifth day of the hellish trip we heard the anchor dropping into what we guessed were the muddy waters of the Irrawaddy where the *Maebasi Maru* stayed until noon the following day. No one was allowed on deck, even though it was the hottest day of the trip. At noon the vessel upped its anchor and steamed slowly into Rangoon Harbour. That evening, after more than thirty hours in the hold, we were permitted up on deck from where we saw Rangoon's golden pagodas backlit by the vast orb of the setting sun. They looked as if they were on fire.

Our guards disembarked us the following morning: 1800 men, less our dead, with tongues swollen by dehydration and with at least half our number debilitated by dysentery. From the docks Rangoon looked extinct, the modern concrete and steel docks heavily bombed (we hoped by our side), the entire area no more than acres of twisted metal and mountains of rubble. There were no people around and no traffic. We called it 'the City of the Dead'.

We were marched along the docks to a small steamer called the *Yamagata Maru* and put on board. We sailed immediately. This time we were not ordered down into the holds but allowed, most of the time, to remain on deck. The best thing about the *Yamagata Maru* was that it had plenty of water for drinking and running water in the latrines. During the day we were given three meals of biscuits: a blessed relief from the constant diet of rice. The worst thing about the vessel was that the trip only lasted a day. We were sailing east across the Gulf of Martaban, the whole Gulf as far as the eye could see, muddy from the Irrawaddy and now the Salween. Behind us glittered the pagodas, ahead the dense green jungle.

We steamed into the mouth of the Salween and up-river for about 12 miles until finally we anchored off Moulmein at about nine in the evening. We were not there long before several big barges, towed by tugs, came alongside to unload us and carry us further up-river. Disembarking, we were ordered to march to Moulmein Jail which we reached at about three in the morning. The only other occupants of the jail were a group of about forty lepers. We were too sick and starving to care, and threw ourselves onto the floor to sleep. But the parasites in Moulmein Jail had other ideas.

We thought we knew all about tropical bugs from our time in Java, but those we encountered literally coming out of the woodwork of the jail were of a different order; especially the mosquitoes,

143

which were bigger and hungrier than any we had come across before. None of us slept much.

The next day, breakfast, such as it was, took three hours, thanks to the Jap lack of organisation in counting us – and then constantly re-counting us – at *tenko*. The rest of the day was spent getting enough water for 1800 men from one minor well with one small bucket.

I was working on this detail when I suddenly realised where I was. The jail lay in the shadow of a great pagoda, its huge, golden dome glittering in the sunshine as brightly as the sun itself. With a shock I realised I was staring at the pagoda made famous by Rudyard Kipling in his poem and later the song, 'On the Road to Mandalay': *'By the old Moulmein Pagoda, lookin' eastward to the sea . . .'*

In fact, the pagoda looked *westward* to the sea, not that it made much difference to me. Though I was in Burma I wasn't going to be taking any road to Mandalay. I was beginning to realise that I was here to build a railway.

Mirla's Story

It was a fine, sunny morning in early October just like any other. I caught the bus to work early and was already busy when the phone rang at nine o'clock; the first call of the day.

'Mirla?' It was my friend Betty from Fremantle. Betty had a brother on the *Perth*. Her voice was different; was it with happiness or grief? Had she heard something? Was she calling to tell me terrible news: the worst possible news? My heart hovered, waiting for her to go on.

'He's alive, Arthur's alive.' Betty was crying; crying for joy at my good fortune.

Even though they were the words I'd been desperately longing to hear for months, now that the moment had come I was too frightened to believe her. I could feel my tears welling up. 'How do you know?' I wailed.

'Tokyo Rose!' Betty sang. 'She announced his name this morning. He's a survivor. Arthur's alive!'

I slumped in my chair, crying like a child.

'Tokyo Rose' was the voice of Japanese propaganda in English. Broadcasting on short-wave radio across the world, she daily announced yet more stunning victories of the Imperial Japanese army and navy. Nobody believed her and most of the young servicemen I knew made terribly offensive, though extremely funny, remarks about her. But a lot of people like Betty listened to her. I would have listened myself except that she broadcast at 8 a.m. Perth time, and I was always on my way to work. Every morning Betty listened to Tokyo Rose anxious for news of her brother.

Aware that she was not getting a big listening audience, Rose had taken to reading out after each of her broadcasts a few names of men who been captured, thus forcing thousands of relatives to listen to her rubbish before she got to the day's names. That wonderful morning, while I was settling down to another ordinary day at work, Tokyo Rose had read out the name of Able Seaman Arthur Bancroft.

I thanked Betty profusely through my tears, conscious that she had yet to hear if her brother had survived. I put the phone down and turned to the girls in my office. 'Arthur's alive!' I cried.

They crowded around me with hugs and kisses, some laughing, some crying. Pretty soon word spread to the bosses' offices and Mr Gare, the office manager, appeared.

'Congratulations,' he said. 'I think you had better take the rest of the day off.'

'But aren't we busy?' I sniffed.

'Mirla, the best thing you can do today is go and tell Arthur's parents.'

I needed no second bidding. I raced from the office and down two flights of stairs to see my best friend, Nancy, who worked for an insurance company on the ground floor. Nancy was delighted and hugged me tightly, her eyes wet with tears as all the girls in her office also surrounded me with laughter and tears.

Afterwards, I ran from the building and caught a tram to Subiaco. Getting off at the tram stop I felt as though my heart would burst. I needed to tell Arthur's parents the news straightaway. Bending down, I snatched off my shoes and sprinted as fast as I possibly could all the way to their house. I don't know what people must have thought at the sight of a young girl running like the wind through the streets barefoot. But I didn't care. I had always been a good runner and had won many races at my athletic club meetings but I truly believe on that morning I ran the fastest I ever ran in my life.

I got to the door of Arthur's parents' house and began banging on it wildly. Nana finally appeared, opening the door with a shocked look. 'He's alive!' I think I may have shouted at her out of pure joy. 'Arthur's alive.'

It took her a moment to take it in: to understand what I was telling her. Then, like me, she broke down in floods of tears; all the repressed emotions of the past months flooding down her cheeks. Grandad was home and he was even more emotional. He broke down and cried for ages, pleading with me through his tears if I was absolutely sure.

Had I got it right? Had Betty heard right? I kept telling him I was sure. Arthur was alive. Their son would be coming home.

Later, I rushed home to tell my mother who also broke down. For her, the strain of Arthur being posted missing had been so reminiscent of waiting for my father to come back from a war.

That night I thanked God for his mercy in hearing my prayers and preserving my Arthur. A week later, Betty phoned to say that Tokyo Rose had read out her brother's name. He too would be coming home.

7

Where No White Man Has Been Before

'*It is a great pleasure to me to see you at this place as I am appointed chief of the war prisoners' camp obedient to the Imperial Command, issued by His Majesty the Emperor. The great East Asiatic war has broken out due to the rising of the East Asiatic nations whose hearts were burnt with the desire to live and preserve their nations on account of the intrusion of the British and Americans for the past many years.*

'*You are only a few remaining skeletons after the invasion of East Asia for the past few centuries, and are pitiful victims. It is not your fault, but until your governments do not wake up from their dreams and discontinue their resistance, all of you will not be released. However, I shall not treat you badly for the sake of humanity as you have no fighting power left at all.*

'*The Emperor's Imperial thoughts are inestimable and the Imperial favours are infinite and, as such, you should weep with gratitude at the greatness of them.*

'*We will build the railroad if we have to build it over the white man's body. It gives me great pleasure to have a fast-moving defeated nation in my power. You are merely rabble but I will not feel bad because it is the fault of your rulers. If you want anything you will have to come through me for same and there will be many of you who will not see your homes again. Work cheerfully at my command.*

'I shall strictly manage all of your going out, coming back, meeting with friends, communications. Possessions of money shall be limited, living manners, deportment, salutation and attitude shall be strictly according to the rules of the Nippon Army, because it is only possible to manage you all, who are merely rabble, by the order of military regulations.

'My biggest requirement from you is escape. The rules of escape shall naturally be severe. This rule may be quite useless and only binding to some of the war prisoners, but it is most important for all of you in the management of the camp. You should, therefore, be contented accordingly. If there is a man here who has at least 1 per cent of a chance of escape, we shall make him face the extreme penalty. If there is one foolish man who is trying to escape, he shall see big jungles towards the east which are impossible for communication. Towards the west he shall see boundless ocean and, above all, in the main points of the north, south, our Nippon armies are guarding.

'Hereafter, I shall require all of you to work as nobody is permitted to do nothing and eat at the present. In addition, the Imperial Japanese have great work to promote at the places newly occupied by them, and this is an essential and important matter. At the time of such shortness of materials your lives are preserved by the military, and all of you must award them with your labour. By the hand of the Nippon Army Railway Construction Corps to connect Thailand and Burma, the work has started to the great interest of the world.

'There are deep jungles where no man ever came to clear them by cutting the trees. There are also countless difficulties and suffering, but you shall have the honour to join in this great work which was never done before, and you shall also do your best effort. All of you shall be taken out for labour. At the same time I shall expect all of you to work earnestly and confidently. Henceforth you shall be guided by this motto.'

– Part of a speech delivered to prisoners of war by Yoshitada Nagatomo, Lieutenant Colonel, Nippon Expeditionary Force Chief No. 3 Branch Thailand POW Administration.

Tried and sentenced to death by hanging at an Australian War Crimes Trial, Singapore, September 1946. Executed for war crimes.

They marched us out of the jail early the following day. They had split us into groups of about 800: our party, which included most of the blokes from the *Perth,* was under Colonel Williams, CO of the 2nd/2nd Pioneer battalion. Also in our mob were diggers from the 2nd/4th Machine Gunners and from the 105th Transport Unit. Not surprisingly, we were known as 'Williams Force'.

There was a rumour that we would be getting a train and, sure enough, we found ourselves being marched through the town and in the direction of the railway station. En route it appeared as if the entire population had turned out to see us leave but, unlike Java, here the locals were friendly. More than friendly, in fact: they seemed entirely pro-British, darting in and out of the columns of men to dish out food and cigarettes and items of clothing – even small amounts of money. Naturally, the Jap guards set about bashing them and to impotently watch the Japs launching into these kind people with kicks and savage blows made my blood boil.

The Burmese were a small, brown, constantly smiling people; smaller even than the Japanese, and seeing our mongrel guards beat down on them with their rifle butts was almost more than I could stand. Lofty, marching beside me, murmured, 'Let it go, Blood. There's nothing you can do. This is what the Japs call liberation. Poor buggers. But they're fair dinkum all the same.' He was right. To see the way the Burmese openly defied their conquerors to be kind to us was a big boost to our spirits. If those little buggers could do it – then so could we.

At the station they herded us into cattle trucks and goods vans and we steamed south on a journey that lasted several hours before we reached a station in what amounted to little more than a small town. It was called Thanbyuzayat. None of us had ever heard of the place: I doubt whether many Burmese had – it wasn't big enough to register. But, from now on, we were to hear a lot about the town we immediately christened 'Than'.

We were marched to what was clearly a substantial POW camp, with plenty of armed guards and complete with a hospital. We came across a few hundred blokes of our draft and many others who had travelled some of the way with us from Java. A lot of rumours were flying around as we bedded down for the night; most of them centred on the fact that Than was on the railway line. Certainly the place appeared for some reason to be important to the Japanese:

there was a Jap administrative headquarters close to the camp, though exactly why this Woop Woop of a place should be so significant to the Japs we didn't discover until the following day.

Early in the morning Williams Force was marched on to a dusty parade ground with a high dais at one end where we were formed up for what we thought was yet another *tenko*. Drawn up but at ease, we were forced to wait for more than an hour in the increasingly hot sun until a Jap lieutenant colonel appeared. He was a little bloke and dapper: kitted out in his full dress uniform complete with yards of braid and acres of lace and an enormous samurai sword almost as big as he was. Even the bloke's hair looked coiffured. After he had taken a moment to awkwardly mount the high platform this short-arsed little specimen of the Jap officer class told us his name. It was Lieutenant Colonel Yoshitada Nagatomo, a name we were to come to hate and fear in the months that followed: a Jap officer whose stupendous vanity, we were to learn, was matched only by his inhumane cruelty. The little bastard was a monster, like a lot of his kind.

The previous night we had been told of the executions, or, more accurately, murder, of eight of our blokes who had been caught trying to escape from a camp at Tavoy. Their mates were forced to dig a big communal grave before the poor bastards had been marched out and shot in front of it. Soon after, three more of our blokes had been executed at Mergui, just for being outside the wire and trading with the locals.

For two hours Nagatomo kept us sweltering in the sun while he big-noted to the point of adulation the Imperial Emperor, Japan and the Imperial army. Then, in his high-pitched, sing-song voice, he told us what he thought of us. His words were translated by a Dutch prisoner who spoke both Japanese and English.

We were pitiful specimens whose lives were worthless, he announced. Life for us would be cheap, food and other essentials limited, sickness punished by half rations and attempts at escape by immediate execution. Then, finally, he announced that we would be working on a railway which, by the hand of the Imperial army, he boasted, would join Burma with Siam, or, as he called it, Thailand. Building this railway would be an honour for us; we would be working deep in the jungle where no white man had ever been before. There would be many difficulties and much suffering which we were to overcome on behalf of the Emperor. But, he warned, the railway would be finished on time, even if it meant building it over our dead bodies.

Finally, after a magnificent flourish of his arms as he told us to work cheerfully, he turned to ease himself down awkwardly from the platform. Immediately a ripple of subdued laughter went through the ranks. In the seat of Colonel Nagatomo's shiny, full-dress pants were what looked like two bullseyes. We learned later that Nagatomo was married to a Frenchwoman – in fact he spoke perfect French – and that his wife had patched his trousers where he had worn them through from horse riding. Whether she deliberately intended to make her husband look ridiculous we would never know, but if she did, she definitely succeeded. 'Struth, bastard's got eyes in his arse,' Marcus muttered. It was all I could do not to laugh out loud as Nagatomo strutted away to his staff car.

Once the little bastard had been driven away, we were hustled off the parade ground and onto the backs of about twenty trucks, where we stood waiting for the drivers to crash the gears and jerk away on the start of yet another mystery tour.

So the rumours had been right. We were here to build a railway. And not just any railway, but a railway over some of the world's most impossible terrain; so formidable in fact that the British, who had considered building a railway up the Peninsular and all the way into India, had abandoned the idea as being just too difficult. As a result, although there were independent railway networks in Siam and Burma, they were separated by about 300 miles of mountain passes, rocky gorges and impenetrable jungle; impenetrable up to now, anyway. But it was the Japs' intention to close that gap and from their point of view, I suppose it made sense.

We knew from the news passed from our secret radio that the Japanese 15th Army had crossed the Irrawaddy River and was heading towards Imphal on the Indian border. But now, with their troops virtually knocking on India's back door, supply, or more accurately, the lack of it, had become their biggest problem. At first the Japs had been supplying the army by sea: ships from Japan sailing via Singapore and the Strait of Malacca up the west coast of the Peninsular. But British submarines and bombers, based in Ceylon and India, were taking a terrible toll on their shipping, and the Japanese advance was being held up through lack of material. Clearly the alternative was to build a railway through the jungle. And we were here to do it.

I noticed that all our officers had been loaded into one of the trucks which meant they were coming with us. There had been some rumours at the camp that the officers were to be separated from the men. Apparently this had happened with some of the

British, Dutch and American contingents of prisoners. But apparently our officers refused to be separated from us. Where their men went, they went. Their attitude was whatever was going to happen to us would happen to them too.

It was the roughest ride so far: mainly because there wasn't a road; not what you could call a road anyway. We bounced and rolled and clung to each other like we were in love as the trucks, careering along the rough jungle track, followed the line of what clearly was to be the railway. Along it, every 5 kilometres or so, was a POW camp, while along the route men in slouch hats were toiling to build an embankment sufficiently substantial to take the weight of an ammunition train. Most of the blokes, mainly Australian 8th Division, had been cut off from the outside world for so long they had no idea that the navy had fought battles in the Java Sea and that Australian sailors were now prisoners of war. They were stunned to see us, especially as we scarcely looked like prize examples of the Royal Australian Navy, skinny, barefoot and in our G-strings.

Mercifully, the trucks finally shuddered to a halt at what amounted to little more than a clearing in the jungle. This, we learned, was Tanyin Camp, which because it was 35 kilometres out from the railhead at Than, was known as '35 Kilo Camp'. It basically comprised a series of abandoned, broken-down huts, each one long enough to sleep 150 men, built entirely of bamboo and standing in the middle of a clearing. The roofs of the huts were constructed of palm fronds laid side by side and bound with what we came to call 'Burma wire': strips of bark from the teak trees abounding in the jungle. In fact, the entire fabric of the huts was held together by Burma wire, with not a nail or a screw anywhere.

There was no question of living in these huts; they were places merely to sleep. Basically, they were open cupboards, with one shelf or sleeping platform about four feet off the ground with a back wall of bamboo and a palm-frond roof. Prisoners climbed up onto the bamboo shelf and slept there; if we were lucky we had some rice sacking to soften the hard ridges of the bamboo canes.

We soon got organised, fixing up the camp as best we could and getting the field kitchens going. Each of the four nationalities – the Americans, Dutch, Brits and Aussies – segregated themselves into their own huts or compounds, and the 150 or so of us from the *Perth* made sure we were all in huts close to each other. Our huts were next to those of our mates from the *Houston*, with the Poms close by and the Dutch a bit further off. The cook house, a bamboo structure with open sides, needed some work but we reckoned it wouldn't take much to make it good, while the latrines were well away from the living areas and were the usual open pit with cross bars for sitting. There was a well close by and pretty soon we had a system going for boiling water and making rice tea, while the doctors marked out a place where a small makeshift hospital could be erected. Though 35 Kilo Camp wasn't exactly the Ritz, we reckoned we could soon make it something like home.

What was surprising about the camp was the lack of Japanese. Apart from the lieutenant in command, his orderly and a quartermaster, there were no guards, although close by was a camp of Jap engineering officers, there to supervise the construction of the line. Any of us could have escaped into the jungle. But if we had seen the futility of slipping off into the jungle in Java, here it was magnified ten times. The Burmese jungle was far denser than its

Javanese equivalent. This was real jungle: thick and threatening. Maybe we felt that way because we were living in the middle of it, but we reckoned there would be more venomous snakes, scorpions and things to bite, sting and slash us than ever there were in Java. What's more, we were much further from the sea and Australia. The jungle was better than any barbed-wire fence. None of us wanted to be shot for trying to escape; none of us wanted to be digging a grave for our mates to be thrown into.

The Jap engineering officers put us to work early the next day; proper organisation of the camp and repair of the sagging huts would have to be done in our own time. Reveille was at 5 a.m. local time, which, as far as our Japanese captors were concerned, was in fact 7 a.m., as the Japs had decreed that everywhere in their new Empire should be on Tokyo time.

It had been a bitterly cold night. Having arrived in Burma at the start of the hot, Dry season which went through to April we found that, although it was burning hot during the day, the temperature at night dropped to what felt like close to zero. We were frozen and, without anything to cover us, had been awake most of the night shivering with cold and scratching at the lice and other tropical livestock infesting our bodies. The cold should have killed the little buggers stone dead, but they kept warm by burrowing into us.

After a breakfast of 'pap', which was basically double-boiled rice porridge, and the inevitable *tenko*, we were detailed off in '*kumis*', the Jap equivalent of platoons, consisting of about fifty men under a '*kumick*', or an officer. Naturally, everyone in our *kumi* were blokes from the *Perth* and, as always, Marcus, Lofty and I stuck together and made sure we were in the same work squad.

Every man of Williams Force, save for the very sick, was set to building the embankment for the railway track close by. We were told our work quota. Each man was required to shift 1 cubic metre of earth per day, digging the soil out with shovels and pickaxes and shovelling it into baskets slung on long poles. Two blokes would then take each end of the pole and trudge uphill to the top of the embankment.

Most of the tools we were forced to use were made in Japan. They were bloody useless: the shovels bent and twisted, the poles snapped because they were rotten and the woven baskets leaked liked sieves. Apparently we were meant to build this railway with the kind of tools and methods last used in medieval times. The embankment we were building was substantial: in some places along the line it was 10 metres high. Marcus reckoned we were building the Great Wall of China for the Japanese in Burma.

Even so, the requirement of 1 cubic metre a man per day was pretty easy for us and by two in the afternoon we had completed it. As the place where we were working on the line was close to our camp, we were soon back there and on our way to a local jungle stream where we could bathe. It was pure luxury. With no guards around and no wire defining the perimeter of the camp, we reckoned it was safe enough to go exploring and soon discovered a few local villages where the natives, who seemed friendly enough, invited us to take some fruit, including pomelos (a citrus fruit something like an orange only bigger), pawpaws and bananas.

Building the embankment beneath the Burma sun was hot, thirsty work and I was glad of my Dutch Army water bottle. During the first few days I suffered a bad case of sunburn, although

159

there was no way I was permitted to report sick with it. But apart from the sunburn, the work was relatively easy and we reckoned the blokes in our *kumi* were always the first to reach our quota of a metre a man. Our officers, though, kept telling us to slow down, which was a first in my experience. No officer I'd ever encountered before had told me anything other to hurry up and get on with it. Now, the officers were telling us the reverse. We reckoned the sun had got to them.

One day, after about a week at 35 Kilo, I walked past a bloke from the Pioneer battalion who was resting on his shovel. 'Too hard for you?' I laughed. 'Our mob's done our quota already. You Pioneer blokes can't keep up with the navy.'

The man dropped his shovel, walked up to me and stuck his face in mine. 'Are you stupid?' he snarled.

I reared back. 'What?' He was a tough, nuggetty bloke, smaller than me but older – in his mid-thirties I'd guess, with the hard, lined face of a professional soldier. He was definitely not a bloke to mess with.

'You keep finishing your work quota halfway through the day and these bastards will make us do more. Wassamatter – you can't see that, ya bloody drongo?'

I watched him stalk away. The bloke was as cross as a frog in a sock and I had no idea why he was spitting the dummy over nothing. But then two days later, the Japs increased every man's quota to 1.2 metres a day. It was then I began to understand that being prisoners alongside a Pioneer battalion had distinct advantages. These blokes knew about digging and construction out in the open: their job was to dig trenches and dugouts for the front-line troops.

If anybody knew how to make the job easier, it would be them. And they were older than most of us. They were men. They knew how to survive in the field; how to make the best of any situation. Instead of being a smart-mouthed, know-it-all kid and jeering at them, I realised I should be listening and learning from them.

By then my hands had become badly blistered from using the bodgy Japanese shovels. Many of the blisters were turning septic and they hurt like hell; every day was agony. One day I was trying to relive the pain by shoving them under my armpits when the same Pioneer bloke came up to me.

'What's up, lad?' he asked. I showed him my ravaged hands. 'Pee on 'em,' he said.

'What?'

'Piss on them. Each time you urinate, do it over your hands. It will toughen them up double quick.'

I wondered if he was giving me a load of bull. 'Are you sure?'

He gave me a look and walked away.

Well, what had I got to lose? I tried it – and he was right. The palms of my hands were soon almost as tough as the soles of my feet. I was grateful to the bloke. He had been prepared to help me even though I was a lippy kid who had taken no heed of his warning – a warning that had turned out to be totally on-the-money.

They were all like that, the Pioneers: always prepared to help and advise us and I reckon it is largely due to them that many a young navy lad didn't end up as a small mound of earth and a make-shift bamboo cross in the Burma jungle. I'm probably one of them.

The Pioneers understood living in the open and the fundamental importance of camp hygiene. Many of them had been farmers and builders and bushmen who had joined up during the Depression. I was rapidly coming to realise that if I was going to be building a railway for the bastard Japanese in the middle of Burmese jungle, then these were the blokes I wanted to be alongside. Due to them our camp had the lowest death rate on the line, though of course we did lose blokes and there was plenty of sickness due to diet and other factors. But through them we learned to treat hygiene as the most important element in our lives.

Colonel Williams was fixated on it. The four 'Fs' were drummed into us daily. Faeces; Fingers; Food (including water); and Flies. We cleaned up after ourselves obsessively; made sure our hands were as scrupulously clean as possible; boiled the food and water until, though pretty tasteless, it was as pure as we could make it. We never tolerated a fly if we could kill it. Of course, the open latrines attracted clouds of them, which then spread to the kitchens and, if we let them, onto our food, but we killed as many of them as was humanly possible. To have poor hygiene was a serious offence and once we had witnessed Colonel Williams ripping into a man for not washing his hands properly, we followed the code religiously. I think most of us would have preferred a bashing from a Jap.

The Japs allowed us one day of rest in every ten and on one of our first days off I went exploring in the jungle, half expecting at any moment to see Tarzan swinging through the trees. First I trekked east until I found a village where I traded a handkerchief for some salt and fruit, before turning west and walking another few miles to discover more villages where I scrounged some more fruit. I must have walked about fifteen miles and somewhere along the route I cut my foot on the sole and scratched it deeply on the instep.

So far I had remained barefoot for the entire time of my captivity, though on arriving at 35 Kilo Camp I had been given a pair of moccasins made from the green untreated hide of an ox. They had not been a success and I'd reckoned I was better off without them. So far, being barefoot had not been a serious problem as the soles of my feet were like leather, but working in the jungle it was a different matter. Here there were scorpions and thorns like daggers and swathes of *alang alang* grass as sharp as open razors. I limped into camp that afternoon and bathed my foot as best I could. While I was treating my foot Lofty told me that Marcus had gone down with dengue fever – known to us as 'dingy' fever. He was in a bad way, with a vice-like pain in his muscles and a high temperature. Lofty and I sat with him and did what we could to look after him. The doctors had no treatment for 'dingy' except for the patient to rest and drink plenty of water.

By now we had been prisoners for almost ten months, during which time we had come to realise just how close to the precipice we were living. The truth was we weren't living at all – merely hanging on, clinging to the edges of existence. The most important thing we had to take care of was our health, which was always in jeopardy. Along with the subsistence diet, which consisted almost exclusively of rice, and because we had all shed kilos of body weight, those of us with nothing more than a G-string were wide open to mosquito bites, which meant malaria and dengue fever. There were also wasps, which, attracted by our sweat, stung like hell.

All of us were intensely focused on our bodies and our bodily functions; measuring and monitoring what was going on inside us daily. It was turning into a test of endurance: which would give out first . . . our health – or the Japanese war effort? It looked like it would be a close-run thing.

From time to time we heard about the war when an officer would come by and murmur some snippets of news about how things were going. We never asked how the officers knew: we reckoned the secret radio from Bicycle Camp had been smuggled into Burma, though God knows how. We couldn't even be sure if the radio was in our camp as occasionally some of our senior officers travelled between the camps and base at Than, so it could have been any-where. Wherever it was, we were grateful that someone had taken the terrible risk of smuggling it in – especially as the news was starting to get better.

Our blokes in the North African desert, the Australian 9th Division, had beaten seven bells out of the German Afrika Corps, at a place called El Alamein. It was great news: the last time we'd heard about those blokes they'd been holed up in somewhere called Tobruk and taking a terrible bashing. Now they had given Jerry a bloody nose. Even better, some more of our blokes had stopped a Japanese advance in New Guinea, at a place called Kodoka, or something like that. The war was already turning our way. The question was: Would the Japs give up before our bodies did?

Strangely, it was beginning to look as if some of our survival would depend on money – how much money we could make to spend on extra food. The Japs had said they would pay us for our work on the line. Private soldiers were to be paid ten cents a day. However, someone had convinced the Japs that able seamen were a cut above ordinary diggers, and that we should be paid at the same rate as army NCOs. The rumour going around the camp was that a bloke from the *Perth* had pointed to an anchor tattooed on his upper arm in front of a Jap engineering officer and told him that it was a mark of a superior type of sailor – a semi-petty officer. The stupid Jap had bought it and had upped the bloke's pay. Immediately the rest of us went hunting for burned bits of wood or charcoal in order to draw anchors on our biceps. The upshot of all this rapid self-elevation was that every sailor was paid fifteen cents a day.

The difference was important: over the course of a month the extra pay might purchase salt, a slab of chocolate or even a duck egg: a crucial source of protein. Almost all our money was spent with the locals on supplementing our diet with fruit, eggs or meat. The camp had a crude type of canteen with a smattering of food from trading with the local villagers and everyone kept a keen eye on what small supplementary items were available for purchase.

Of course the Japs never paid us on time, but we did eventually receive our small monthly pittance. I received the princely sum of thirty cents. The problem was that the only thing available in the canteen at the time were small Dutch cigars at one-and-a-half cents each – not much use to me. However, Marcus, Lofty and I agreed to pool all the money we made. Sharing was absolutely essential as, naturally, the Japs didn't pay anyone who was sick and as time went on at least one of us would be laid up in what was laughingly called the hospital. It was down to the other two – or sometimes even one – to share whatever money was available to supplement the sick man's diet. It was in this way that we three, and a lot of other blokes in camps all along the railway, kept each other going.

Food was all we thought about: especially how we might supplement the constant, bland, unappetising, nutrition-deficient daily diet of rice which, giving rise to a high incidence of beri-beri, could kill us just as easily as cholera. One of the Brits had written a poem that expressed everything there was to say about it:

ODE TO RICE

In prison camps in Burma conditions were not nice
And we were fed on a diet that was wholly, solely rice
Not baked rice, flaked rice, with butter, eggs and milk, not
Cooked rice, that looked nice and ate as smooth as silk; no!!
We got glued rice, unstewed rice, not fit for even dogs,
Stone cold rice, grown old rice, not fit for even hogs.
We got broken rice, unspoken rice that argued with your plate
Unpolished rice, abolished rice, some ten years out of date
We ate burnt rice that weren't nice that tasted just like
Cinders, and brittle rice, sharp little rice that tasted like bits of
    frosted windows.
We ate mauled rice, keel-hauled rice, stuff no one even called
    rice
Hard boiled rice, part spoiled rice, and kerosene drummed oil
    rice
We had hacked rice, cracked rice, the sort used at a wedding
We got smashed rice and hashed rice that weevils made their
    beds in
We had gad rice, and sad rice, that filled you with its sorrow
We had limed rice, and grimed rice and ought to have been
    crimed rice

166

We got sloshed rice and squashed rice, but never any washed
    rice
Disrupted, corrupted rice and undischarged bankrupted rice
Low caste rice, half mast rice, and lots of unglued grass rice
There was smelly rice, rake helly rice and gripe pains in the
    belly rice
Help starting rice, quick parting rice and really first class rice
We brewed rice, we stewed rice, the lucky ones they spewed
    rice
We bit rice, we spit rice and in due course we shit rice
So there was that nocturnal rice, infernal rice and bloody well
Eternal rice they gave us three times every day in the prison
    camps in Burma
However, while conditions were not nice, somehow we lived
    on because of that
Everlasting rice.

After my trek through the jungle which had resulted in the cut on
my instep, I noticed that my foot was swelling up and was becoming
more and more painful with each passing day. When the swelling
reached my ankle I went to the sick bay to have it bathed. My
problem was that it had become painful to walk on and by now
the railhead where we were building the embankment was over a
mile from the camp. I limped off to see the camp doctor who didn't
even look at my foot and certainly didn't suggest any treatment. All
he said was, 'Excused duty.'

So that was it. I was off work, which was good . . . but I was not
being paid, which wasn't so good. At least Marcus was out of the

hospital and would soon be back at work, but for the moment the load was being carried entirely by Lofty, who never once complained.

One of the officers told us that cholera had broken out in a village upstream and that from now on we would have to use well water for washing and boiling. Our one daily luxury – a bathe and a swim in the stream – was denied until further notice. The stream was off-limits. I wondered if I had caught something on my last swim there as I was getting awful earache in my right ear. Then, on top of the earache and swollen foot, I noticed a lump in my groin.

I went back to the camp doctor who took a bit more notice this time. He told me to boil water and put a hot poultice on my foot. He had a small bottle of ear drops, which he told me was very precious. He put a few in my ear.

I was still excused duty, which at least meant that I had time to write my diary. With so few Japs around it was easy enough to get away with it. I also had time for some sketching, which I did as surreptitiously as I could. I couldn't do a lot, as I needed to conserve my paper: I had no idea how long we were going to be prisoners. Much of the paper I had liberated from the office at the docks in Java was lightweight airmail paper that I reckoned would last me for a while if I kept my handwriting small and neat. Whenever I had finished I wrapped the diary and collection of drawings in some sacking and buried them in the soil directly beneath my bed in the hut. The Japs never seemed to think of searching there, and anyway there weren't enough of them to keep watch on what we were doing in our spare time.

But, as if on cue, one morning soon after I had been excused of duty, a truckload of Korean guards arrived and everything changed.

I had no idea why the Japs had sent a bunch of duck shooters to watch over us. No one had tried to escape and as camps went, ours was pretty good. Maybe it was because the war was slowly but inexorably turning against them and they expected an invasion.

As soon as they arrived the Koreans threw up a makeshift fence around the camp and then announced that anyone found outside it would be executed. Random beatings started that afternoon. The next day the work *kumis* were accompanied by Korean guards armed with old British .303 rifles and with what looked like Australian army webbing.

It was a low time. I was lying on a thin mattress of rice sacks draped over a corrugated bed of bamboo poles with excruciating earache, a painful foot and a mysterious lump in my groin. If I wanted to continue with my diary I would have to find somewhere secret to write it. In many ways I was anxious to get back to work. Lying on my bed in the camp I reckoned there was a lot more chance of contracting malaria or cholera than if I was actively engaged on a working party. I was stuck, with nothing to do and too much time to think about my maladies.

What's more, it was my twenty-first birthday.

I had awoken after a frozen, restless night to realise it was November 24 and that today I turned twenty-one years old. I was now considered a man and entitled to vote, though I had been entitled to die for my country for the past three years. My birthday presents that morning were a throbbing earache, a poisoned foot and a lump in my groin. Merv, Marcus, Lofty and few of the other lads promised that after work they would toast me with a cup of rice tea, and with luck I would get an egg with my plate of boiled rice.

The only notable event of the day was when the doctor came around to read out the numbers of our blokes in the other camps who had died of cholera. It wasn't exactly cheery twenty-first birthday celebration stuff; the only bright spot being that 35 Kilo Camp had so far not suffered one death. I suppose in many ways that actually isn't a bad birthday present: to be told that none of your closest mates have died, though at the time I'm not sure I saw it exactly like that. At dinner time I had my promised egg and the lads toasted me a happy birthday.

We also raised our mugs or makeshift drinking tins to absent friends and I thought of Harvey and wondered how he was getting on. I hoped he was still in Changi where conditions, when we'd been there anyway, had been relatively good. I hated to think of quiet, bantam-weight Harvey going through what we were going through – building a bloody railroad with bastard Koreans on our backs.

Pretty soon after my birthday my body started to mend. On the camp's day off some of the lads announced that, despite the ban, they intended going jungle to trade with the locals and get some fruit. I wasn't up for it, but was relieved when they all came back without incident, though they were careful enough to bury the fruit peel so the guards wouldn't know they had been outside the wire.

As we moved into December we noticed that, though the days were hotter, the nights were getting even colder and the three of us, along with a lot of other blokes, usually stayed up for much of the night. We would sit up into the early hours hugging a fire we had lit in a corner of the compound and play bridge or poker with my makeshift deck of cards.

By now I realised I was fit for work, which was just as well as Lofty had gone down with dysentery. I was quite anxious to get back to being active again, but an officer told me to hold off reporting fit and to stay on excused duty for as long as possible. The rumour was when we were finished at 35 Kilo Camp we were to be moved 70 kilometres southeast to another camp over the border in Thailand. That was so much further from the sea and a possible Allied invasion force. The longer we took over the present job, the more chance we had of being relieved.

Yet though there were a few blokes like me trying to hold up the Jap war effort for a day or two plus a few malingerers, the vast majority of the men reporting sick in the camp really *were* sick; some very sick. It had gotten so bad that, out of approximately 800 in the camp, 200 or so were reporting sick every day. We hadn't had a death at 35 Kilo mainly due to the Pioneers' insistence on absolute hygiene but we all knew it was only a matter of time. The Japanese attitude to sickness among the men was bound to kill many of us sooner or later.

To the Japanese military, an enemy prisoner of war was almost the lowest form of life. They believed none of us should have been alive; we should all have died gloriously in battle. We were less than human. But even lower than a POW was a *sick* POW. The Japs' attitude was that a sick POW was a criminal who deserved punishment, not treatment. Apart from quinine, almost all medical supplies were either denied the prisoners or kept in short supply. A lot of men who died would have lived if they had been allowed basic medical treatment. Even worse was the policy the Japs introduced as soon as they started falling behind schedule of making sick men work on the railway. A lot of drastically undernourished men, shuffling like walking skeletons and shaking uncontrollably with tropical disease, were sent up the line to labour under the burning sun. They were, literally, worked to death.

About the time I was recovering the Jap camp commandant announced that any man reporting sick would get only five-eighths of his normal daily food ration. So . . . sick, practically starving, men were to be given less, not more.

I went back to work the next day and found that the railhead had moved almost another mile out: it was a long march there. The embankment we were building was now about 10 metres high and the day was stinking hot. The work was hard and tiring: the soil we had to shift, burned by the sun, hard as concrete. What's more, the Jap engineering officers had increased every man's quota to 1.5 metres a day. We were working much longer days, followed by a long walk back to camp. Almost all of us were crook one way or another: my foot was playing up, my ear still wasn't right and Lofty, having partially recovered from dysentery, had now gone down with the dengue. Out of our *kumi* of forty-eight, we could only muster twenty-seven for the work detail.

We were all beginning to suffer. Every man in the camp had things in common. We all had tinea, a fungal infection caused by heat and sweat, especially prevalent around the groin and armpits but occurring anywhere on the body. It was highly contagious and impossible not to get it. Whereas at home it would have been easy to treat, in the jungle the Japs allowed no treatment for it and the fungi, first feeding on dead cells on the surface of the skin, would eat into the body, feeding on live tissue before eventually invading

172

the lungs and heart. For the majority of us tinea resulted in open, seeping, painful sores all over our bodies.

Many of us also had tropical ulcers, usually below the knee, resulting from small cuts or abrasions which, because of our mal-nourished condition, would not heal and always turned septic. The ulcers hurt like hell and some blokes had to have a leg amputated because of them. Again they would have been easy to treat if the Japs had allowed us even basic medical supplies.

In addition we all had lice, and would stand around a kerosene drum stark naked as our clothes (or in the navy's case, our G-strings) were boiled for an hour or so to kill the little buggers. But no mat-ter how often we boiled our kit they came back and kept us awake for hours, scratching.

The other thing we had in common is that all of us, officers and men, from time to time would shit ourselves. This ultimate degrada-tion was commonplace: diarrhoea was endemic and wasn't even a reason to report sick. Often it led to dysentery, but even men with dysentery were forced to work and frequently without warning a man's bowels would open up on him. At first we were all ashamed of ourselves, but the Burma Railway did not permit personal shame. A man's mates might look away when it happened out of respect for his feelings, but there was no shock or moral judgement. We were all in the shit together and if a man was too weak to clean himself up, then his mates would help him do it.

The Japs and their Korean mongrel attack dogs disregarded all this. Their high command was pushing for the railway to be completed on time and for that to happen, sick men worked the line. Every morning one of the Korean guards toured the hospital, ordering blokes who were on their last legs out to work. Our doctors, men trained in all the latest in Western medicine, would have stand-up, dragged-out screaming matches with some guard who didn't know his arse from a hole in the road. Some of those doctors took some terrible beatings as a result, but I never saw them give up on a bloke. Not once.

Just before Christmas, on one of our days off, twenty of our men got caught outside the wire in the jungle and nearby villages. A couple of them were officers, which maybe helped, as no reprisals were taken against them – though we were told afterwards that the guards now had orders to shoot on sight anyone seen outside the wire. But a lot of our blokes, especially in the Pioneers, were good bushmen and defied the order. The Koreans never saw them either going out or coming back.

Just before Christmas we received our pay. I had two rupees, worth about fifty-five cents, while between us, Lofty, Marcus and I had just over eight rupees: about two dollars fifty. The trouble was there was nothing in the canteen to buy. A couple of days later Lofty was carted off to the hospital at Than with a bad case of tinea. It didn't look like it was going to be much of a Christmas, especially as I remembered that at that time the previous year we had been on the *Perth* steaming south along the east coast to Sydney and looking forward to a big feed and presents from home. Christmas was a great time for thinking of home and of loved ones – but not in this place. To permit myself to start thinking excessively about Mirla, Mum, Dad and my brothers and sisters and everybody else I missed would wreck me. It did no good to get nostalgic about the past. I just had to be grateful I was still alive.

Two days before Christmas the Japs told us they were bringing some pigs into camp that we could slaughter and eat. But, they said, we would have to pay for them out of our meagre income! The price the Japs wanted was extortionate: even with the officers kicking in as much as they could, we could only afford a couple for the whole camp. So every man's meal on Christmas Day consisted of the usual burnt rice along with a smattering of watery pork stew and a small mandarin sent up from base camp at Than. We made the most of it. There were a couple of 'two-up' games going that took the edge off the paucity of the celebrations and made us feel more like Aussies. But the next day we were back at work, with the Japs putting the screws on us to keep up the schedule.

When Lofty got back from Than he told us that they were averaging a death a day there – dysentery and jungle fever mainly – but also murder: blokes were being shot on a regular basis. While he was there three Dutchmen had been killed allegedly for trying to escape. There was no doubt that the Jap and their Korean stooges were putting increasing pressure on us and relations were getting very strained. There had been a few incidents at our camp where some bloke had stood up to a Korean's intolerable cruelty and had been laid low for it. A few times there had almost been a mutiny and it had taken all the effort of our officers to avert what would have been a bloodbath. Our blood. Not that the officers were wimps. Colonel Williams faced up to the Japs every time there was trouble: face to face and toe to toe, he wouldn't back down and he took some unmerciful beatings and extraordinarily cruel punishments. There wasn't a bloke in 35 Kilo Camp, Aussie, Yank Brit or Dutch, who wouldn't have followed that man into the jaws of hell.

But all we could do in the face of the increasing cruelty and inhumanity was wait and remember: grit our teeth and bide our time until it was our turn. A few of our blokes kept themselves alive on thoughts of personal vengeance; for them an Allied victory would be their day of bloody retribution. Some of our Jap and Korean guards were dead men walking, and none of them was likely to get back home without a bashing. Not if we had our way.

New Year arrived with all of us in a sombre mood, wondering what 1943 was going to bring. It was foolish, not to say depressing, to speculate about the future; the only way to survive was to take it day by day while thinking positively that we would survive. But at this time of year we couldn't help thinking about what was to come: a future that didn't bear much thinking about.

The only bright spot was that – at last – after ten months in captivity, a few of the blokes got some mail from home; one of our *Perth* boys receiving a letter telling him he had a new baby daughter. Lofty also got a letter and so did Merv, and though Marcus and I were pleased for them, we were wondering where the hell our letters were! Unlike the Pioneers and other army blokes, captured with all their kit and belongings, none of us from the *Perth* still had any of the letters loved ones had sent us. I had watched every letter from Mirla and my folks disappearing forever that night the *Perth* went down.

A couple of days later there was even more excitement when we were given a Red Cross card to write home. I wrote mine in pencil by the light of the camp fire, hoping that I had made it legible enough for my parents and Mirla to understand.

The thought of letters from home cheered us all immensely.

News from our families; simple accounts of daily life and doings, the reassurance that we had not been forgotten and abandoned was a small, bright hope in an increasingly dark and sombre landscape.

Mirla's Story

About two weeks after Betty called me with the wonderful news, Arthur's parents received an official notification from the navy saying that he was a prisoner of the Japanese. Of course we didn't know if he was wounded or anything, and we had no idea where he was. All we knew was that his ship had gone down in the Sunda Strait. So where had they taken him? Was he a prisoner somewhere on Java, or had they taken him to Japan?

My mother told me that wherever he was, he would be all right. There were special rules governing the treatment of prisoners of war: they had to be properly looked after and have medical attention and be adequately fed. So, I have to admit that in some ways I was a little relieved that Arthur was out of the firing line. Instead of being aboard a warship preparing to go into battle, he was relatively safe in a POW camp. Still, it was hard not knowing where or how he was. It was easier for the loved ones of our boys captured in the Western Desert. They'd been informed their lads had been taken to Germany; some even knew roughly where they were. The Red Cross was delivering parcels of food and clothing to them regularly and though the post was erratic and infrequent, letters were getting through to them. Not so with us. The Red Cross was having an impossible time getting into any camps run by the Japanese and we had no idea where we could write or send food parcels. It was frustrating.

I composed a couple of letters to Arthur anyway, ready to send when I knew where. As my letter telling him how much I loved him had been returned, it took me a while to compose them. I needed to let him know how I felt about him and that I was here waiting for him to come home. I also told him as many of the little facets of life as I could think of that might cheer him up. I couldn't tell him what was happening at work, as much of what I did (organising bigwigs to fly up and down WA) was classified. So, I told him about what I did at the VAD and what was going on in Perth. I didn't tell him we'd had a couple of air-raid warnings when, at the sound of the eerie, wailing sirens, the entire city had come to a standstill and everybody in our office had trooped downstairs to a sandbagged basement car park converted to a bomb shelter.

Because of my work at the VAD I'd been put in charge of first aid for everybody who worked in the offices at Pastoral House, though how much use I'd have been if anyone was hurt in a bombing raid was open to question. Thank God the air-raid warnings were false. Someone had spotted what they thought was a Japanese reconnaissance plane south of Geraldton, and the entire city had gone into lock-down. But as the warnings occurred at the height of summer and the bomb shelter was very hot and stuffy, all I'd had to do was take care of a couple of people who became dehydrated and to help calm one of our girls who had started panicking at the thought of bombs.

Finally, an advertisement appeared in the local paper informing the relatives of navy personnel captured by the Japanese that they could write to the men care of the Red Cross in Melbourne. It was great news, immediately tempered by the instruction that all we were allowed to write was twenty-five words every two weeks. I stared at the advertisement. Twenty-five words every two weeks! What could

I possibly say in that? The advertisement was quite specific. One word more and the letter would be rejected: whether by the Red Cross or the Japanese censors, it didn't say

I sat down to wrack my brains. How much of what I felt for Arthur could I express in twenty-five words? Should I just hint at what I felt or tell him outright that I loved him and be done with it? What would Arthur want to read about? What would cheer him up? And then it came to me. Football scores. I would tell him how his beloved Subiaco had got on in the season and finish with 'Love, Mirla'.

8

The Meaning of Mates

'Bancroft, isn't it?'

I look up from my bamboo pallet in the camp sick bay. I am recovering from my worst bout of malaria so far. Standing by my pallet is an AIF officer I know slightly. 'Yessir.'

'There's a bloke coming into sick bay. The guards caught him walking out of the gate. They've beaten the poor bastard practically to pulp. Now there's talk they'll shoot him for trying to escape. The thing is . . . he may try again. He keeps talking about it. The CO will try to persuade the camp commandant not to shoot the poor sod, but if he does try again, they'll definitely execute him. So we need him watched. That's down to you, Bancroft. Don't let him wander. If you do, the Japs will take it out on you. It could be you they shoot.'

'Thank you very much, sir.'

The officer catches my tone and gives me a sideways look. 'He's your baby, now,' he says, 'your digger. Don't muck it up, son. Otherwise it'll be your arse as much as his.'

They carry the bloke in a few minutes later and place him on the

181

bamboo pallet next to me. The mongrel guards have done a real job on him: I reckon they've broken his arm, his cheekbone and at least a couple of his ribs. His scalp is lacerated and his face puffed up with bruising. He's mumbling. It takes me a while to understand him; his lips are split and he's lost a few teeth. 'Dawn,' he murmurs, 'I must see Dawn. I have to get home to Dawn.'

'You can see the dawn here, mate. At least when it stops bloody raining.'

'I have to see Dawn. I want my little girl. I must get home to her.' He struggles to get up. I ease him down as gently as I can.

'You'll see her, mate. As soon as Wavyell gets here, we'll all be going home. You'll see her then.'

'I need to see her. I must hold her; hug my little girl.'

I hold him down again, watch a couple of tears seeping from the corner of his bruised, half-closed eyes. 'Listen, mate,' I whisper. 'It's no use thinking like that. Not in this place. It'll drive you mad. You can't see your daughter. Get it into your head. They won't let you. They'll shoot you if you go outside the wire again. Try to understand.'

'No, no, I have to see her. She's my little girl.'

He struggles pathetically and I hold him down. After a while he gives up and lays back on his pallet, mumbling. The only words I can make out are 'home' and 'Dawn'.

I watch him, silently cursing all officers. This is a bastard of a duty. The bloke who's my responsibility, my digger, looks to me like he's got cerebral malaria. He's deranged, has lost his mind and probably doesn't even know where he is. Yet, despite his injuries, he seems capable of struggling up and trying to stagger out of the camp gates again.

It's likely to be a long watch, with no sleep. I take my water bottle and force a little past his swollen lips. Later, when the rice comes around, I try to feed him. It's impossible; all he does is keep mumbling 'Dawn' and clutching my arm.

Darkness falls and in the pitch blackness of the jungle I keep my eyes on the slightly blacker, small, pathetically shallow shape that once was an Australian digger. He stirs in his sleep and wakes. 'Dawn!' he wails.

I do my best to comfort him. God knows, it isn't much. 'Don't worry, mate. You'll see her. You'll see your daughter again. Just hold on.'

He falls back onto his pallet and I sit watching him, willing my eyes to stay open. If I sleep and the bloke gets up and goes for the gates, then . . . I refuse to think about it. I have to stay awake; I must not sleep.

I awake with a jerk. I'm slumped on the edge of my pallet. Hell, how long have I been asleep? A grey rainy light is creeping into the hut. Shit! I blink, staring at the pallet next to me. Nothing. Just a bundle of rags. No . . . I'm wrong. The bundle of rags is the bloke I'm supposed to be watching. I move to check him.

The eyes in the battered face are wide open and staring. I feel his arm. Cold. While I slept, my digger died.

I wonder what finally did for him. Was it the beating? Maybe – men are dying every day from beatings. Or did my digger just give up? Denied his daughter, did his poor deranged brain think it wasn't worth the struggle? I shake my head. It's no good thinking thoughts like that. The one question you don't ask in this place is 'Why?'

They come for him about an hour later. It's no big event: two other blokes have died in the sick bay overnight. Only much later do I realise that I never even knew his name.

It is an omission I am to regret all my life. I would dearly liked to have told his daughter that her digger dad's final thoughts were of her; that her father's last whispered word on this earth was her name . . . 'Dawn'.

The first day of 1943 was a Jap holiday so we had a welcome break but on the second day we were back on the line and working at the railhead, which by now had moved three miles beyond the camp. It was a long tramp and when we arrived, our *kumi*, along with some others, was ordered to start clearing the way for a new section of embankment. This was when we discovered that throwing up an embankment was easy compared to the back-breaking work of clearing virgin jungle ready for the track.

Without boots and clad only in a G-string, clearing the jungle was hell. Hundreds of trees needed to be felled and dragged away to be sawn and shaped into the piles that would support the scores of bridges we had to build. Tree stumps had to be dug up and removed and enormous clumps of bamboo with their roots deep in the earth had to be wrestled out of the soil. All of this was to be done with primitive, second-rate Japanese tools undertaken by a bunch of blokes inadequately fed and many seriously ill with dysentery, tinea, beri-beri and a host of other lethal tropical maladies. In the extremely hot and sultry conditions, the thick jungle seemed almost airless: it was like working inside a Turkish bath.

Not long after we started preparing the jungle ahead of the track, a couple of elephants appeared. They were a joy to behold. Guided by their Indian mahouts they moved slowly and majestically through the jungle, easily lifting tree trunks that would have taken at least a dozen of us to shift, while saving us days of backbreaking work by dragging away stumps and great clumps of bamboo. Working with the elephants was a favourite with all of us. One of them, an august and stately old boy had '1888', the centenary of the First Fleet, burned into his hide. It was his birth date, making him 55 years old, and whenever he lumbered past I thought of home and resolved to myself, yet again, that I would come through all this and get back home to the lucky country. I loved working close to that elephant: he was huge and enormously strong and yet somehow gentle. Even his smell – big, earthy, generous – reminded me, for some strange reason, of Australia. Working close to his great bulk made me feel secure: like working in the shadow of the harbour bridge.

In many ways, of course, the elephant was a device, a mental hook, to keep my mind fixed on home. I would use anything to keep my mind focused on surviving and returning to family and friends. Earlier I had gotten a poem off another prisoner and repeated it to myself all the time.

HOME
There is a little spot in Aussie
Each sailor has his own
It's never to be forgotten
Tho' we're far across the foam

The name itself is hallowed
'Tis ever on our mind

'Tho resting after battle
Or in the fighting line

When the fight is over
No more will I roam
So back to dear old Aussie
I'm heading straight for HOME

One day a Caterpillar bulldozer appeared, driven by an Aussie combat engineer who must have had the best job on the railway. Of course we envied him, though as none of us were qualified to handle a bulldozer we were more grateful than envious. None of the Japs were qualified to handle the bulldozer either, though that didn't stop one of their engineers jumping into the driver's seat and throwing it into gear. Fortunately, it was the wrong gear. Instead of moving forward, the bulldozer surged backwards, straight over another stupid Jap who was immediately behind the machine, gazing up at it wide-eyed.

The silly bastard died awestruck. The bulldozer ploughed him down and killed him almost instantly. Everyone rushed to gather around and stare at the dead bloke. Those of us wearing hats took them off: this mark of respect greatly impressed the Japs and even the Koreans. They were right. It *was* respect. We were staring down at the only good Jap we had ever seen. They buried the bloke by the side of the railway and every time one of us passed we would nod or doff our hat in acknowledgement that we were passing the best Japanese bloke in Burma.

With the New Year came more activity. It was obvious the Japanese army was putting pressure on the engineers to finish the railway as quickly as possible, which told us they were suffering at the front. There were more guards around, not only Koreans but Japs as well. There were more bashings of blokes the Japs thought were swinging the lead, though, in fact, most of the poor bastards were too sick to work. And of course, with more Japs came more *tenko*: more roll calls where some jumped-up officer or non-com would line us up and count us off. Not once but maybe half a dozen times. As organisers of men the Jap army was about as useful as a one-legged man at an arse-kicking contest. If the time the Japs took on *tenko* had been used on the railway it might have been finished in a fortnight.

But men were being moved from camp to camp, up and down the line as the various sections of the railway came closer to being connected and so the Japs needed to feel they were in control. So far our *kumi* of *Perth* blokes had worked solely on extending the line south and east towards Siam, but other *kumis* had been working backwards, north and west, towards the other camps working out to meet it. And as the work of one camp came to an end, the men were moved out to another camp.

One day we got an intake of blokes who were being moved up from Hlepauk, the official name of the camp at 18 Kilo. Among them were quite a few British: army blokes and some sailors, survivors of the sinking of the British capital ships *Prince of Wales* and *Repulse* early in 1942. We *Perth* and *Houston* blokes immediately adopted the sailors. Like us they had nothing, everything they possessed having gone down with their ships. We called them 'Kippers' on account of the weird English penchant for eating smoked herrings or kippers with their toast and marmalade at breakfast.

They were good blokes in the main and all of them, sailors and soldiers alike, were amazed at the standard of hygiene in our camp. Apparently hygiene in the British POW camps, and in some Australian ones too, was nowhere near up to our standard – another confirmation, if any were needed, that we had to thank our lucky stars for Colonel Williams and the Pioneers.

The Brits were also impressed with how close our officers were with the men. It wasn't as if our officers were palsy with us or anything. They kept a bit of distance and we showed them respect: mainly because they earned it. But every few hours there would be some officer in among us ordinary blokes, checking up on how things were. Apparently the British officers were much more stiff and stand-offish.

One thing the British did bring with them was a great sense of humour. It was like ours: dry and caustic. It was hard to have a laugh with the Dutch, mainly because of the language difficulties, and though we were close to our mates off the *Houston,* we all agreed that when it came to a sense of humour the Americans were on a different planet. They just didn't get it – taking so many of our jokes and witty remarks literally: screwing up their faces and trying to understand when they should have been laughing their socks off. Not so with the Kippers. They could tell a joke, and take one too, and they made a big difference to our camp concerts.

Since Bicycle Camp, the Japs had been allowing – even encouraging – camp concerts. The blokes performing put a lot into them, dressing up and even decorating the stage with materials they stole or liberated from god-knows-where. Often the concerts were the only thing we had to look forward to; practically our only light relief. There were a couple of Dutchmen who were great on the accordion and some of the Americans were good musicians too, while a lot of our blokes were talented at vaudeville and would appear on stage dressed as women, to the great delight of the rest of us.

But with the advent of the Kippers, the concerts took on a whole new dimension. Some of those blokes could have been professional scriptwriters or comedians, while many of them seemed to really enjoy dressing up as women. Well, not so much as women; more like tarts, really. We laughed ourselves silly, mainly because the skits they put on at the concerts were both hilarious and bawdy. For some reason the guards enjoyed them too. It was bizarre to sit there watching some Japanese or Korean thug laughing like a hyena while, up on the platform, a Kipper in drag was asserting that the bastard's mother copulated with camels.

So many of the Kippers were good blokes yet so many of them died. A lot of them, though my age, were smaller and skinnier than most of us Aussies. The Depression had been far worse for them than us, and what with constant grey skies and poor food, these blokes seemed prematurely wizened and stooped. They had big hearts, but I think many of them just gave up. And, except for their medical men, who were excellent, I didn't meet many British officers that I much liked.

By this time the Jap engineers had increased the daily work quotas to 1.5 cubic metres of earth a day. The workload was going up and we were going down: getting sicker and weaker. There were even more guards along the line, each armed with a thick baton of bamboo ready to bash anyone they thought was slacking. Naturally we had assigned nicknames to most of them, none of which, needless to say, was complimentary. Names like 'the Maggot', 'the Mad Mongrel', 'Boy Bastard', 'Frankenstein' and 'Peanut'.

Peanut, so-called because of the shape of his head, was an especially nasty piece of work, not to say slightly mad. He kept intimating that when the Imperial Japanese Army invaded Australia, Japanese soldiers would be having lots of *jig-jig* with our wives and girlfriends; even our mothers. We thought the bloke was off his rocker. Apart from the fact that by now we were certain that Japan was not going to invade, the bloke clearly didn't know anything about Australian women – a bloke like him trying *jig-jig* with any woman I knew would be going home with a high voice. Anyway, for all his talk about women and *jig-jig*, we noticed the bloke seemed pretty interested in our young blokes. All of us kept an eye on him.

Then we heard the news. Down at 18 Kilo Camp a Sergeant O'Connell of the AIF, who had been in a working party outside the wire, had been granted permission to go into the bushes for the same reason the rest of us went into the bushes. When the work party started back for camp, O'Connell was still in the bushes so Peanut stayed behind to accompany him back. Minutes later, en route to camp, the working party heard a succession of shots, though as the Koreans were so stupidly careless with their weapons, no one took much notice. That is, until back at camp, when O'Connell didn't front up for *tenko*. A search party was sent out which quickly found his body. When Peanut was questioned he claimed that the sergeant had been trying to escape and that he had shot O'Connell running away. No one believed his story for a moment. O'Connell had been shot from the front, from point-blank range. The poor guy had one bullet in his head, two more in his chest.

Our blokes at 18 Kilo were ropeable; one spark would have set off a bloody mutiny. The Aussie officer, Lieutenant-Colonel Anderson, made such an almighty row that Peanut had to be removed from the camp and sent to Thanbyuzayat, where apparently he was bashed by a bunch of Japanese engineers. Even they knew what had really happened was cold-blooded murder.

O'Connell was a young bloke and we reckoned Peanut had taken a fancy to him and that when O'Connell resisted, Peanut had murdered the poor bugger, either out of anger at being rejected or to stop him from reporting the incident. No one, neither Aussie nor Japanese, had any doubt that Peanut had murdered an unarmed man but, needless to say, Colonel Nagatomo did nothing and Sergeant O'Connell's death was reported as 'shot while trying to escape'.

Pretty soon Peanut returned and was back on guard duty, by which time we had re-christened the bastard 'Dillinger' after the notorious 1930s American gangster and bank robber, John Dillinger. When it was known he was coming back to our camp, Colonel Williams ordered a couple of hundred of us to be ready as a reception committee. We were strictly ordered not to say a word, nor to make any threatening gesture towards Dillinger but merely to surround him and stare at him when he came into camp.

Dillinger arrived on the back of a truck which we surrounded, silently staring at him as he got down. 'This man's Japanese name is Tiemoto,' Colonel Williams announced. His voice was icy, as cold as the artic; his tone as dead as ashes. 'I want every man here to study this man, to stare hard at him and to remember his face. This man is a murderer, and when this war ends you must be able to identify him to a court that will try and then hang him for his crime.'

We stared silently and malevolently, hating the bastard. Yet not a word was said, not a gesture made. Dillinger's stony face broke: suddenly he looked sick, like a rabbit staring into the jaws of a dingo. It was scary, that mob of silent men filled with hate, emanating so much loathing and abomination you could feel it like the heat from hot coals. As he pushed his way through men as silent and immobile as Uluru, Dillinger knew we would never forget him; knew we would never forgive him.

If ever a bloke's card was marked it was his, on that day.

A few of the Jap and Korean guards kept animals: semi-wild pups hanging around the base at Than which, when the guards were rostered there, they would entice with food before bringing them back to our camp. Yet they didn't treat them as we would have treated a pet puppy.

It seemed to us that there was something in the Jap make-up which relished being cruel to anything that couldn't resist. As prisoners we knew firsthand how sadistically barbarous they could be, and we never understood it. Never mind the rules of war and the Geneva Convention, it was inconceivable to us how men could so consistently and cold-bloodedly torture and degrade other men. Defenceless men, who were their prisoners. It definitely wasn't Australian.

But, whatever went on in the Japs' skewed psychotic brains

extended to animals too. If they caught a monkey they would torture it, while it seemed the sole reason the guards kept the dogs was to ill-treat them. They would pick them up by their ears, tie them up and leave a water bowl just out of reach; beat them unmercifully. It was almost as hard to witness a pup being beaten as it was one of your mates. Hearing a pup yelping in agony was hard to take and men would clench their fists and stare in hatred. But to intervene was suicide; on the couple of occasions when one of our blokes had stepped in, the guards had beaten him unconscious.

One evening, after returning from the work detail we were getting ready for the inevitable *tenko*, while our guard was passing the time waiting for the officer by torturing a puppy at his feet. The bastard had tied a stick between the pup's rear legs so the animal couldn't scamper about but instead had to drag itself along the ground. Then he had trapped the pup between his feet so that he could squeeze its ribcage unmercifully. The animal was whimpering; the pathetic sound getting to everyone on the parade. Finally, I couldn't stand it any longer. When the guard's back was turned, I threw a pebble at him. It missed, but on the third attempt I got him hard on the back of the head. He turned in a fury, letting the dog escape from between his feet. He was screaming fit to bust and stormed up and down the line demanding to know who had thrown the stone. We looked innocent and denied all knowledge, though if the guard picked on an innocent bloke and started beating him, I would immediately step forward to take the blame. That was the unwritten code of the camp. But until a bloke started copping it, every one of us would keep quiet. The Jap began demanding that someone tell him who had thrown the stone. Of course, that was never going to happen; the guards never learned that dobbing in another bloke was not the Australian way. But when the guard started picking on a little bloke and screaming that he tell who threw the stone, I could see that at any moment I would have to step forward and take a bashing.

Suddenly, the officer of the *tenko* appeared and demanded to know what was going on. The guard, snapping to attention and bowing, started to tell him, but it was obvious the officer didn't give a stuff about the guard's problems and dismissed him. The guard marched off, casting murderous looks at us as he went. As soon as the officer had taken the count, one of the lads freed the puppy's legs and sent it scampering off. I was lucky. I'd escaped a severe bashing by the skin of my teeth but I just couldn't stand to see the pup being tortured.

After a few weeks of clearing jungle, our *kumi* was pulled out and assigned to building bridges between our camp and Anarkwan, the camp at 45 Kilo. By now, sickness was the norm. Throughout the camp less than half of each *kumi* was reporting fit for work each day as more and more blokes were being shipped off to the so-called hospital at Than. Things were so bad that the Japanese agreed to allow another makeshift hospital to be erected at 18 Kilo to save time on transporting really sick men all the way to Than. It was now usual for three out of the four of us to be either in the hospital or excused duty. Marcus was having problems with swollen and painful feet, Merv with dysentery, while Lofty, who seemed to be suffering more than the rest of us, was in and out of the hospital either with 'dingy' fever or tinea.

I wasn't feeling so hot myself. I still had intermittent ear trouble, a sore mouth and tongue, and recurring bouts of tinea. Whereas other blokes were more susceptible to malaria, dengue fever and dysentery, I seemed to have more problems with my skin, especially with tinea leading to ulcerated feet and legs. Everyone was in a bad condition and certainly not in any shape to be building bridges. But the Japs had other ideas.

Much of the railway in Burma ran alongside the Ataran River in a narrow valley between two mountain ranges. Like any river in such mountainous country, it gave rise to scores of tributaries and ravines and dry river beds, all of which had to be traversed by the railway. At each crossing we were expected to construct two 6-metre wooden scaffolds, which, when lashed together, formed a kind of pyramid down through which we would drive the piles into the bed of the stream or river or ravine.

For the piles, we used the trunks of trees we cut down in the jungle. Where they could find them the Jap engineers selected hardwood, like teak, which was hell to saw and shape, but more often they used softwood trees that were susceptible to termites. Once the trunk had been sawn we sharpened one end to a point before fitting it with a wedge-shaped metal cap so the trunk could be driven into the ground. After that the heavy trunk was carefully hauled up by ropes between the pyramid of bamboo scaffolding to be lined up beneath the pile-driver, a block of heavy metal weighing between 300 and 500 kilograms. When the trunk and the pile driver were in line, the pile driver was continuously dropped onto the trunk until it was driven into the bed of the stream or ravine to a depth of about 3 metres.

It was a medieval method of bridge-building: the kind undertaken by people with no available stone, who knew nothing of bricks or iron smelting, who seemed never to have heard of the industrial revolution. It was the kind of building undertaken when the only materials available to the builders were wood and bamboo, the only commodity in excess was slave labour.

It was the pile driving that drove us all loopy. About thirty of us were assigned to it, fifteen on each side of the pyramid of scaffolding on a fantail of ropes connected to the main drop ropes lifting the pile driver. A Jap engineer would chant 'Ichi-ni-no-sanyo . . . one, two, three,' which we would chant back before releasing the drop ropes for the weight to hammer the wooden pile a few more centimetres into the bed. It was as monotonous as hell.

All day, from practically first light until well into the evening, it would be, 'Ichi-ni-no-sanyo' – crash – 'Ichi-ni-no-sanyo' – crash. Despite my hands having been hardened by the constant work (and the Pioneer bloke's unhygienic but very effective hardening process), yanking on the cheap Japanese hempen ropes all day was ripping them to shreds. All of us were suffering from septic sores and welts across our palms.

The worst was working in the tributaries of the river when, weak and sick, we would be forced to stand all day up to our waists in water hauling on wet rope only to find, when we finally got out, fat, black, four-inch leeches clinging to our legs and around our loins.

It was sickening to feel them on my skin; their bloated, slimy bodies filling themselves with my blood. The little buggers never let go until they were completely gorged. To pull them off was painful and dangerous – the bastards had teeth and would leave wounds that always became infected. The only way to get rid of them was to burn them off with a lit cigarette, or to rub them with salt or to moisten their suckers with tobacco juice. As we didn't have enough salt to spare, I tried to make sure I was alongside a bloke who smoked when I found myself working in the water.

After we had finished building a bridge we would go looking for termite colonies, which we would lift and carefully transport as close as possible to the softwood bridge piles in the hope that the whole bloody edifice we had worked so hard to erect would fall over in a year or so.

We got our first pay for the year at about the end of February and almost immediately a two-up game got underway. I went along to watch. I wasn't interested in gambling the money I'd earned. It was going into the pot for me, Merv, Marcus and Lofty. Merv and Lofty were sick at the time and excused of duties. But just being in the crowd and hearing the banter and the calls of the Ringy was like being back in Australia, even down to the 'cockatoos', or lookouts, posted at strategic points who were watching out, not for the cops, but for the guards. The game was banned by the guards and everybody attending would have got a bashing, but the old hands were used to keeping a sharp eye out and it was a little larrikin bit of home.

March 1 was the first anniversary of the sinking of the *Perth* and the start of our captivity. It was hard to comprehend that we had been incarcerated for a year; even harder to contemplate that we might be prisoners for another one, maybe longer. Almost every day for the past twelve months we had been slaving in a hot, humid, tropical sweatshop, almost suffocated by a jungle that seemed always to be encroaching. In all that time we'd had no sight of a horizon, no vision of a distance, no view of the blue ocean and of ships in the offing. The question of how long we might have to go before we feasted our eyes on our green-and-gold country didn't bear thinking about.

The anniversary of the *Perth*'s sinking was marked by two events at Thanbyuzayat base camp, word of which spread to the rest of *Perth*'s crew like a bushfire. Firstly, we heard that on the evening of March 1, an Allied pathfinder aircraft had flown over Than and dropped flares, lighting up the whole camp. Soon afterwards, a flight of bombers had flown over and dropped bombs on the line north of the camp. This had never happened before and was a great encouragement to all of us. It was as if someone in the high command knew about the *Perth* and was telling us that we weren't forgotten. Of course that was almost certainly not the case, but it gave us hope and was definitely the way we wished to interpret the event.

On the other hand, the bombing made us realise that there was nothing to distinguish any of the camps alongside the railway as POW camps. The officers had asked the Japs to paint the roofs of the huts with a red cross or the initials 'POW'. Typically, the Japs had refused. As the war progressed we were in danger of being bombed by our own side.

The second piece of anniversary news was the death of one of the ship's company, Stoker Stokes, who had died that day of chronic malaria and diarrhoea. Stoker was one of the great characters on the *Perth* and stories about him abounded. It was hard to think we had lost him. He seemed indestructible. But his death was a turning point. It was the start of death in higher numbers.

By the middle of March, almost all the blokes from 18 Kilo under Colonel Anderson had moved in with us at 35 Kilo and the 1500 of us were known as the Williams/Anderson Force. Among the 1500 were about 150 *Perth* survivors. The other 150 of our shipmates were scattered all over. Some had followed us to Burma from Changi in another old rust bucket, the *Moji Maru*, which had been bombed en route by a couple of Allied liberators. Two of our *Perth* lads had been badly wounded in the bombing and had died in Moulmein. The only piece of good news was that another ship in the convoy had been sunk in the same bombing raid with the loss of about 400 Jap soldiers. When I met up with a couple of the lads from the *Moji Maru*, I asked about Harvey, Jim and Egghead. None were on board the ship, which meant they were either still in Changi or somewhere on the railway, maybe even in Thailand.

At the end of March the Williams/Anderson Force was assigned a different name and new work. We were to be called Number One Mobile Force and our job would be to lay the rails and ballast the track on the already completed embankments along the length of the railway in Burma. Opinion was divided about whether this was a better job than building the embankment, or worse. Nothing, we reckoned, could be worse than a life clearing the jungle. But we were wrong.

Laying the track meant lifting seriously heavy teak sleepers off rail bogies and aligning them so that, when they were in position, we could drill holes in them with a primitive kind of hand drill called, I think, an auger. This piece of junk wasn't even as advanced as an old-fashioned ratchet brace. After the holes were drilled we hand-lifted the rails into position. No elephants here, just twenty-five men to a rail, staggering it into position on the sleepers. Then came the spiking: driving spikes through the rail brackets into the holes in the sleepers. The hammers we used for this were of the worst quality imaginable. They were far too light, – the heads flew off, often injuring some poor bloke close by, or bits of metal sheared off them, flying through the air like shrapnel and slicing into the legs or arms of any bloke in the way. Sometimes the shafts would splinter, whereupon the bloke hammering would get a bashing from a Jap or Korean for deliberately destroying the hammer.

After laying the track came the ballasting: depositing tons of shale, small stones and rocks between the sleepers using dud Japanese shovels. For those of us without boots, ballasting led to a lot of cuts and abrasions which could easily turn into tropical ulcers. We were as careful as we could be: plenty of blokes had watched their own leg being amputated because of tropical ulcers. Many of them subsequently died.

Track-laying was back-breaking work, yet it wasn't the work that made our lives even more of a nightmare. Conditions deteriorated due to the fact that we on the Mobile Force had no permanent home.

I hadn't realised how important returning to the same billet every night had become. Even when wearily trudging the 5 or 6 kilometres from the railhead or a bridge we were heading back to a home of sorts. Now we were on the move, up and down the line.

Slowly we became split up from our mates as first one and then the other would become sick and be sent to the hospital, only to be reassigned to another *kumi* when they got out.

With the increasing incident of sickness, a group of us were ordered to build another hospital at 30 Kilo. Building huts for the sick was easy work compared to anything else the Japs assigned us, and hut construction was a welcome break from the heat, dust and flies of the rail track.

And then came the Wet.

The monsoon season broke in early April. How we longed to be back in the heat and the dust, as hell got wetter. It was rain like we had never seen before: 13,000 millimetres in six months. The dirt turned into quagmires. Hauling a daily 1.5 cubic metres of earth baked as hard as concrete up an embankment had been hard work. Hauling the same load of wet sludge up a muddy embankment running with water and as slippery as ice was unbelievably harder. Only now it wasn't 1.5 cubic metres.

The Japs were desperate. The war was turning against them. First they increased the daily load to 1.8 metres, then to 2.0, and then to 2.5. Men were working twenty hours a day in the sheeting rain; rest days were cancelled; concerts were cancelled; the only way to rest was to die. Some blokes just gave up and took that route.

It never seemed to stop raining. Even trudging a few hundred metres was an effort: often we were in mud up to our knees while trudging 5 or 6 kilometres to the railway; exhausted before we had even begun work. The nights were bitter and the rain blew sideways into the huts. Soon the latrine pits were overflowing, sending rivers of excrement washing through the huts and into the kitchens.

Everything was wet all the time – what few clothes we had were soaked and our rice-sacking blankets were sodden.

The humidity of the overpowering jungle made breathing difficult and in the lashing rain the tools slipped from our hands, instantly enraging the guards who would start swinging with their batons. The only words we ever got from them now were 'Speedo, speedo'. Scarcely one of us got through a day without a beating.

For those like me with nothing but a G-string, the cold pitiless rain lashed our skin like a cat-o'-nine-tails. Many of us were wondering how long it would be before we contracted pneumonia or pleurisy.

In the Wet and under the mercilessly increased workload, our horizons contracted. We stopped wondering whether we would see tomorrow – now we wondered if we would see the end of today. Tomorrow was too far off. All that mattered was to make it through today. Even so, the worst for any of us was to be separated from our mates. We believed that as long as we stayed close to each other, we had a chance of coming through.

They ordered us to 60 Kilo Camp, which was when we discovered that a camp move was a major effort. All our gear, including tools and cooking utensils, had to be transported by us. It was all right when we were being moved by train, but the camp at 60 Kilo was about half a mile from the railway. In the monsoon, and following nothing but an overgrown elephant trail, we took an entire exhausting day to stagger with our gear along what had turned into half a mile of muddy swamp.

As soon as the AIF blokes had left 60 Kilo a few weeks earlier, the local natives had moved in. Though the huts were in a reasonable state of repair, the sanitation, as practiced by the natives, was putrid and disgusting.

On the day we arrived two natives had died of cholera and underneath one of the huts we found the rotting, stinking corpses of an adult male and two children, also dead from cholera. The Japanese had a morbid fear of the disease and ordered us to move the bodies, though not to touch them. We managed, finally, to shift them with long bamboo poles, many of us retching at the gagging, throat-clutching stink, and to get them decently buried without anyone actually handling the corpses.

Cholera was a major fear. It could kill in a matter of hours and sometimes by the time a bloke knew he had it, he was already half-dead. In the Wet we reckoned it was only a matter of time before it would be out there stalking us with all the other killers. By now there was also a rumour that smallpox had broken out in one of the British camps.

The Wet also brought the scourge of malaria, a pandemic sweeping through the camps. Though the Japs dished out quinine tablets, after they ran out there was no remedy and soon we were losing at least a couple of blokes a day. Every day someone would murmur the names of that day's dead; usually from our camp but sometimes from one of the others. Often it was just a name: a bloke I didn't know. Sometimes it was the name of a digger I'd befriended in the Pioneers or the machine gunners and I would pause to recall his face. Sometimes it was a bloke well known around the camp. And sometimes it was a shipmate from the *Perth*. That hurt the most. I and the rest of the lads would reflect on the times we'd been on duty together, the drinks we'd bought each other, the good times we'd shared on a shore leave. Now the bloke was going into the ground of a strange land wrapped in a couple of rough hessian rice sacks.

There was no wood for coffins and blankets were too precious to waste on the dead, so the corpses were sacked up in rice bags: one pulled up over the legs and tied around the waist; the other pulled down over the head and similarly tied around the waist. When the doctors could, they conducted rough autopsies to determine the cause of death after which the sacked-up body was carried by whoever was off sick on a rough bamboo bier to the burial ground outside the wire. There, a padre would say a few words while the pallbearers stood in respectful silence. A mound of earth and a rough bamboo cross: it wasn't much of an end for a bloke who had only just made a beginning of his life; he'd be lucky if anybody at the burial even knew who he was. But that's what we grew used to, what we inured ourselves against: a tragedy so quotidian it became banal.

Malaria stalked us – it was everywhere, yet it was hard for those blokes who didn't have a water bottle not to drink from jungle streams which practically guaranteed a dose of malaria, if not cholera. I thanked God for the tin of condensed milk that had brought me my water bottle in the trade with the Dutchman. Every morning I filled it with double-boiled water which I shared with Lofty, Marcus and Merv. Yet, in the end, I got malaria too. I began feeling definitely crook and went on sick parade. I fronted up to the camp doc. 'Sir, I reckon I've got malaria.'

He scarcely glanced at me. Stressed, overworked and taking constant bashing from the guards over men too sick to work, he didn't have a lot of bedside manner left. 'I'll tell you when you've got malaria,' he snapped. There was no arguing with that, so I shuffled outside to join the others for the long slog through the mud and rain to the rail line. I took about three steps and fainted.

I woke up in the camp sick bay, which was no more than an open bamboo shelter like all the others, where I shook and shivered and hallucinated for a few days before I began to recover. Lofty was just getting over a dose of dengue fever so I had a mate for a couple of days before he was fit enough for work. After that there was plenty of company as the sick bay was full to overflowing.

I had almost completely recovered when an AIF officer came into the sick bay and ordered me to watch over a poor sod of a digger who had walked out of the camp gates, insisting that he needed to get home to his daughter. The bloke had most probably cracked up, but the guards had beaten him savagely and the commandant was ranting about executing the poor bugger for trying to escape. Despite his severe injuries and a few broken bones, the deranged digger was still babbling about going home to his daughter. My job was to watch over him in the sick bay and to make sure he didn't try to walk out of the camp again. I did my best for him for a few hours as he continued murmuring about home and his daughter, but he died that night. I never knew his name.

Some time afterwards they shifted us from 60 Kilo Camp to 40 Kilo for more track-laying work. This time there was no train ride; we were ordered to walk the 20 kilometres, even though by now we were in a truly pitiful state. There were no mirrors around but we knew how we must have looked. All we had to do was glance at our mates. Merv, Marcus and Lofty were walking skeletons with stick-thin legs, gaunt faces and ribs jutting out as sharp as sabres. I knew I must look the same. There wasn't a man who wasn't sick and after we set off for 40 Kilo we found we were unused to walking very far, especially carrying all our gear, much of which was lashed to long bamboo poles. Two of us would shoulder the pole at either end, and then trudge though the jungle mud. We were exhausted after a couple of kilometres, yet to collapse was to invite a beating from one of the guards.

It took all day and well into the night to get to 40 Kilo. Crossing the Ataran's tributaries or deep gullies was the worst part of the trek as it meant using the bridges built by the POWs. Many, over 15 metres above the ground, were only half finished. We found ourselves edging along 30-centimetre wide slippery bridge timbers in the driving rain, loaded up like mules and staring down at the long drop onto rocks or into fast-flowing water.

It was bad enough in daylight, but once it grew dark it was the stuff of nightmares: nowhere else is as black as the jungle at night. We had to feel our way across the last few bridges, each lead man on a carrying pole holding onto the shirt or G-string of the tail man on the pole in front, all of us edging our way over the narrow timbers like 1500 blind, emaciated skeletons in the rain and total blackness. It was a miracle we didn't lose anyone.

We arrived at 40 Kilo after midnight; 20 kilometres had taken us close to twenty hours. The guards had tents but we had nothing, as the huts there were in a shocking state of repair, so most of us slept out in the rain. We were shouted up at daybreak to get our customary bowl of watery rice and then we were back at the railway, this time unloading ballast for the track.

The death rate was spiralling: two or three a day in our force;

deaths in the other camps even higher. In one month eight of our blokes from the *Perth* had died. I knew them all. None were close but they had been shipmates and we listened to the roll call of those who were gone with increasing sadness. Death was usually from malaria or dysentery or beri-beri or cholera – they were our four horsemen of the apocalypse.

In some ways beri-beri was the worst. You would watch a man slowly dying of it: the Japs forcing him to work every day as his body bloated out grotesquely from the legs upwards until, eventually, the bloating reached his lungs and the poor bugger drowned in his own body fluids. Men with beri-beri knew that, without medication or vitamins, they were walking corpses. If they didn't know it from observing their own slowly bloating legs, they could see the horror of it in other men's eyes.

There were no more rest days and we worked far into the night, often until midnight, the Japs erecting scores of big bamboo oil-filled torches to light the track. It was a numbing existence, the only relief the wry, laconic, Aussie humour of the *Perth* lads. Sticking together was what mattered most and whenever any of our mob of four was taken off sick to a hospital camp, the rest of us were edgy until he got back. *Perth* lads were scattered all up and down the line. Blokes disappeared and then came back weeks later with tales of other camps and other workforces. Sometimes, listening to their stories, we reckoned we were lucky to be where we were.

So we went through the Wet: trudging from 40 Kilo Camp to 55 Kilo, then back to 60 Kilo before going deeper into the country and closer to the Thai border at 95 Kilo. At one camp 200 blokes – British, Dutch, Aussie and American – suffering from cholera had been left in the open to die. We weren't allowed to go near them. The Japs had discarded them like rotting timber in the jungle.

At other camps along the line we met blokes we hadn't seen for months. It was good to see them and know they were still alive; not so good to hear of the deaths of shipmates, including Able Seaman Bevan, Telegraphist Nelson, Stoker Anderson, Able Seamen 'Horse' Nichols and Jeff Garrett. The list went on.

The rumour by now was that the Jap high command had ordered the railway finished and the two links in Burma and Thailand to be connected by the middle of August. But now it was September and the line still wasn't complete. We were behind schedule and the engineers and guards, desperate not to lose face, were now demented in their treatment of the prisoners. At one camp, which was 10 kilometres from the railway, we were forced to stay out at the line for seventy-two hours, working for twenty hours through the day and into the night before sleeping for four exposed hours without shelter in the pouring rain. Our food – the thin, anaemic rice porridge – reached us cold and slopping in rain water.

All along the line sick men either worked or were denied all food and medical attention. Sometimes, men who collapsed at the side of the line were shot. It seemed to us that Nagatomo was making good on his promise that the Burma–Thailand Railway would be built on the dead bodies of every bloke who worked the line.

There was no relief: not from the work, not from the rain, nor from the all-pervading sickness. The occasional news about the war was not encouraging. Though liberators were bombing Thanbyu-zayat now and again and the Japs had been stopped at the gates of India, there was a new bloke running the show up there and nothing much was happening. All we had was each other; all we could do was to grit our teeth and stick it out.

Mirla's Story

Like everyone else with their man away at the war, I kept myself busy by getting on with my life. Every day I prayed for Arthur's safe return and then spent the rest of the day working hard and enjoying what I could without him.

Ever since Arthur had been away I had been training hard and in the autumn of 1943 I was selected to play right half-back for the WA Women's Hockey Team. I was absolutely rapt. The state team! I couldn't wait to tell everyone and to put it in my next 25-word letter to Arthur. I wrote every two weeks, as regularly as clockwork. My letter telling him the news was posted to him in late April, shortly after my birthday. I was twenty.

In the end, the state team didn't have much of a season that year. Though we had a few games in WA, because of the war we had no interstate competition, which was disappointing. Even so, I was pleased that I had been able to make the team.

Sometimes on a Sunday I would go sailing on the river with my friend Nancy and Bob Scott, her fiancé. Bob had joined the navy and Nancy took it hard when he left to join his ship, the corvette HMAS *Horsham.* Now it was my turn to help her. Nancy had always been so supportive, especially during the blackest months when we didn't even know if Arthur was alive or dead, and I was glad of the chance to do the same for her.

We did everything together: screamed in fear when we went to see *Frankenstein Meets the Wolf Man* at the pictures – and cried buckets when we saw *The Phantom of the Opera* and *The Sullivans.* We went to dances, visited each other's families, swam at the beach. Most of all, we held each other up when the pain of missing our men got us down.

Sometime in the middle of the year Arthur's mum got a letter from him: the first since his sinking. I rushed around, desperate to see what he had to say, anxious to hold something he had recently held. It wasn't much of a letter; like us, he was limited in his words. He said he was in good health, for his mum not to worry and that he hoped everyone at home was okay. But it was the final phrase he had written that held my eye; one I read over and over again: 'Give my love to Mirla'.

Those five little words kept me going for the rest of the war.

9

The Melbourne Cup — Jungle-style

I catch sight of him shuffling his way back from the latrines. Big Merv. At six foot two, Merv is taller than I am and a big, strapping bloke. Was a big strapping bloke. Now he's stick-thin and bent over. He looks ancient; like the walking dead. It is distressing to see what this bloody, mongrel existence in the camps has done to him, and I hurry across to take his arm. 'Look a bit unsteady on your pins there, mate,' I say cheerily. 'Let's get you back to bed.'

I lay him on his bamboo pallet as gently as I can. 'There you go – you're okay now. Soon have you back on your feet.'

He gazes up at me, his eyes glassy and distant. 'I don't think I'm going to make it, Blood.' His voice is thin and croaky, with scarcely a thread of sound.

'Come on, mate, you know what we agreed. No talking like that. It's not allowed. You'll come through, no worries.'

He doesn't respond but merely closes his eyes as if even that is a great effort.

The next day I am ordered onto a work detail which is forced to *march 8 kilometres to a railway siding where we unload 2500 sacks of rice from railway cars. At home I could handle one of these sacks easily; now, two of us struggle to lift one onto the truck. Afterwards, we are marched back to unload the sacks and carry them 300 metres into the camp. It's a long, hard slog, and I don't get back to my billet until dusk.*

Lofty and Marcus are waiting for me. I notice their faces.

'What's up?' I ask.

'Merv died today,' Marcus says.

It's as if I've been bashed. I sit down on my pallet and shake my head. Merv – big, strong, ebullient Merv. The first of our gang to go. I have been so confident that we will all come out of it . . .

'Anyone get to say goodbye?' I hear my voice croaking, something strained and bitter at the back of my throat. .

They shake their heads.

I know what this means. Merv would have been buried within hours of dying. The doctors would have autopsied him to ascertain cause of death and then the burial party would have taken over. They would have treated him with respect and the padre would have said some words, but the fact is that Merv O'Donaghue has gone into the ground of an alien nation with not one of his mates to see him off.

We were at 95 Kilo Camp when we heard the news: the accursed railway line was finished . . . completed . . . joined up. There had been a ceremony somewhere in Thailand around the 150 Kilo mark where the two lines met. Apparently a whole slew of Jap bigwigs, including Nagatomo, had turned up by train to celebrate this wonderful feat of Japanese engineering that would make their Emperor proud. Now the Japs could supply their army over land, cutting thousands of miles off the journey.

Not that I reckoned they would be allowed to get away with that for long. The Allies knew about the line: our bombers were flying up and down it all the time, using it as a road map to guide them on their bombing runs to Bangkok. Once they saw Jap military trains they'd be bombing seven bells out of it – with thousands of their own blokes camped all along the railway. Not that our presence would make any difference. I had learned that on the *Perth*. Already we had lost blokes in bombing raids on Than.

The completion of the line didn't make much difference to us, except that at 95 Kilo the guards got drunk which allowed us a small respite from the work, though guards when drunk were more dangerous and brutal than when sober. But next day we were out once more, ballasting the line, which, we were told, would go on for weeks until it was sufficiently ballasted to take the heavy ammunition and supply trains. Right now, all that was running on it were light locomotives and half-empty cattle trucks.

A few days later, in the middle of October, those of us left in the Williams/Anderson Force, excluding those not in a camp hospital or dispersed along the line, were ordered up to 105 Kilo Camp, the last camp on the Burma side of the border. I wasn't especially happy about that, as our little mob was already separated. Both Marcus and Lofty were at the hospital at 50 Kilo. Merv should have been there too – he was suffering badly from malaria – and I was pretty crook myself. Neither of us relished moving further away from the others, though with the end of the monsoon season the rains were easing off and it was a slightly easier trek. 105 Kilo Camp turned out to be the biggest we had encountered, with about 4000 men under the command of AIF officers. The place was very well run, and though the camp was on short rations when we arrived, at least there were concerts.

A couple of days after we settled in, a rumour went around the place that we might get a day off on Melbourne Cup Day. It would be our first rest day in months. We'd had a bit of a Cup Day the previous year at 35 Kilo, but the thought of a full day off in which we could stage our own version of the race was a big boost to morale. Apparently some of our blokes were trying to convince the Jap commandant that the first Tuesday in November was an Australian holy day – the holiest day in the entire year, dedicated to the Patron Saint of Australia, Saint Totaliser. On that day everything came to halt for Saint Tote – the saint that stopped a nation. Finally, we heard the Japs had bought it.

It was a great day and we celebrated it in true-blue style. There was a field of twenty 'horses' and the bookies, of whom there seemed to be scores, were 12–1 the field and 4–1 a place. The bookies, who had to show the colour of their money with a minimum of twenty rupees, were licensed by the race committee, who also encouraged everyone to dress up for the day. Some of the blokes dressed as women – a few appearing as *grand dames*, others more like Toorak tarts. They made their dresses from rice bags; a couple even managed to make themselves parasols.

For days before the event the excitement was intense, with a lot of talk about which 'horse' was fancied and plenty of legal (and illegal!) betting going on. The field was eclectic: as well as some well known nags like Phar Lap, Hall Mark, Rivette, Second Wind and Shadow King, also running were White Slave, which was out of Camp by Daybreak; POW, out of Luck by Cripes; Yak, out of Jungle by Shotgun; and Eggs out of Canteen by Japanese. The 'jockeys' had made little hobby horses, just like those we used to play with as kids, and had done their best to have colours to wear for the race.

The caller was a bloke who had an encyclopaedic knowledge and memory of the Cup. Some of the lads had built a rough wooden cabinet with rice-sacking panels – a bit like a life-size, old-fashioned radio – from inside of which the bloke could call the race. At three o'clock the dusty racecourse at the camp was as thronged as Flemington Racecourse and though the race itself was a bit confused and didn't really end up as the caller had it, the call itself was so realistic it sounded *exactly* like the race coming over the radio at home. All any of us had to do was shut our eyes to believe we were actually at Flemington. It was astonishing how realistic blokes who had been prisoners for almost two years could make their own version of the Melbourne Cup.

I, along with Merv and some of the other lads, had a rupee each way on Nightmarch. We lost our money but it was worth it for the excitement. The bloke calling the race collapsed soon afterwards. Poor bugger had malaria and standing in a hot wooden box in the middle of the afternoon had just about done for him. We heard later that he recovered. The Japanese thought the whole day was great, though we could see them puzzling a little as to how anybody could call the proceedings holy.

***

Soon after arriving at 105 Kilo, we found out why food was in such short supply and goods in the canteen so exorbitantly expensive. The camp commandant was a crook. He was making big money selling off a portion of our rations to the natives and imposing a huge tax on any goods coming into the canteen. We were not surprised: experience had taught us that many officers in the Imperial Japanese Army were prize hypocrites, talking of honour on one hand while robbing starving prisoners of food on the other. But their hypocrisy was taken to new heights when November 20 was set aside by Nagatomo and the Jap high command as a day of remembrance for all those who had died on the line.

We paraded, knowing full well as we listened to our camp CO, before the padre conducted a service of remembrance, that the dead were in the ground courtesy of the Japanese. We reckoned at least 1000 blokes had died during the Wet. Out of 1500 men forming the Mobile Force at the beginning of the Wet, only 500 of us were left: 1000 men from the Force were either dead or too sick to work and out of that final 500 most of us were pretty crook. The couple of hundred or so who were still capable of work were sent into Siam to work on ballasting the line.

My twenty-second birthday came and went. Lofty and Marcus were still sick and in hospital down the line, while Merv was in the 105 Kilo hospital. I celebrated with a few mates from the ship and some good pals from the AIF and RAAF.

The Wet had finished: the days turning warmer, the nights colder. It should have been a time of recuperation – heavy work was still going on up and down the line, but we could see an end to it. However, a lot of our blokes were too far gone to come back now:

instead of easing off, the deaths were increasing. It was shocking. Every day there was news of another two, three or four blokes dying up and down the line. Towards the end of November we had word that fourteen of our Mobile Force blokes had died in just thirteen days at a camp in Thailand. There was at least a death a day at 105 Kilo. I recorded many of the dead blokes' names in my diary, usually after I had shuffled back from duty as a pall-bearer.

Through every one of our moves from camp to camp I had been able to hang on to my diary and my collection of drawings. There had been a few close shaves when the guards had searched me, but somehow I had always managed to smuggle the collection of papers that formed the diary and drawings past them. I'd even managed to keep it dry though the Wet. But sometimes I wondered why I bothered. Every day I was recording a litany of death: mates I had shipped with or blokes I had got to know in Mobile Force and in the camps. It was sickening. The reason I had started the diary, as well as my drawing and collecting some of the lads' poems, was to give me something to occupy my mind. Keeping the diary now meant occupying my mind with death.

Christmas at 105 Kilo consisted of a dish of radishes and dried peas which the cooks, through yet another miracle, managed to make palatable. This was followed by rice plum pudding – minus the plums and brandy sauce, but at least with a helping of heavily disguised shindegar – native molasses – which, before the war, the natives used to feed to their cattle. We thought it a luxury.

Around Christmas I was classified as 'light sick' by the camp doc owing to the sores all over my body. There was talk that all POWs were to be moved to different destinations according to their state of health. Slowly the Japs were closing all the camps down the line in Burma and moving everyone up to 105 before dispersal. The state of some of the blokes coming in from 50 Kilo and other camps was simply terrible. Many of them hung on long enough to make the journey to 105 Kilo and then gave up and died. Many others were close to death. The word was that the very sick would be sent to a Jap hospital in Bangkok, though from bitter experience we knew that what the Japs called a hospital was the kind of place we'd keep chooks.

The rumours disturbed me. If we were to be separated according to our state of health, then certainly Merv, who was very sick, would be sent to Bangkok, while I would go elsewhere. Meanwhile, Lofty and Marcus were still somewhere down the line, the state of their health unknown. It was getting harder and harder to hold together.

Camped so close to the Thai border, some disturbing news had been filtering through to the effect that, no matter how hard we had been doing it in Burma, the boys in Siam had suffered far worse. There was a rumour that a lot of our Aussie infantry had been forced to march all the way from base camp in Siam to the Burma border: about 300 kilometres. The story was that up to half of them had died. By now we knew that Harvey and some of the other *Perth* lads had been sent to Siam. I hoped to God they were okay.

Around Christmas I got my first mail since I'd been made a POW: three letters from Mum, all dated June 1942. They were full of news about events at home: trivial stuff mainly; things I wouldn't have taken much notice of if I had been there. But here, stuck in this place, I lapped up every morsel. I was disappointed there was nothing from Mirla but told myself that getting mail was a lottery.

Some of the lads had got nothing while an AIF captain received fourteen letters. Only he had died the week before. No one knew what to do with the letters. I heard they placed them on the bloke's grave in the camp cemetery.

They moved us just after the New Year, stuffing the sick into box cars and the rest of us onto cattle trucks. It took about forty hours to travel 200 kilometres south. En route we were dumfounded at the scale of the work the prisoners in Thailand had been made to tackle. The line went through deep gorges carved out of living rock by starving men with primitive tools. Scores of bridges had been built, crossing ravines 60 or 70 metres deep. One part of the track was tacked onto a sweeping curve of a cliff face, high up the side of a mountain. The line, jutting out over a drop of hundreds of feet to the river below, was supported by long wooden beams and trestles which looked like a shaky timber equivalent of a house of cards. No wonder the British had given up on the idea of building a railway through here. If I hadn't been riding on it, I would have thought it completely impossible that sick, weak, walking skeletons of men like us could have built this thing.

Finally, we arrived at a large town called Kanchanaburi, or Kanburi, from where we were marched to our camp, Tamarkan. The camp, close to the Menam Kwai Noi River, sat in the shadow of an enormous steel and concrete bridge. This was the *real* bridge on the River Kwai, made famous years later by the movie. The eleven-span, steel structured bridge, built by the Dutch in Java, had been transported piecemeal to Thailand by the Japanese who had forced the British POWs to rebuild it by sinking enormous concrete piers into the river bed. Six hundred of them had died doing it.

Tamarkan was a revelation. Run by the Brits, it was well organised and even bigger than 105 Kilo. In comparison to what we had
been eating, the food was excellent: added to our daily diet of rice
was meat, green vegetables – even the occasional egg. There was
a good canteen with fair prices. Small vegetable plots were scattered around the camp, and we were permitted to swim in the river.
I asked some of the old hands if all the camps in Thailand were
like this. Their laughter was hollow as they told me how bad their
camps had been. They were even worse than ours, with cholera
such a scourge that many of the dead were buried in mass graves.

Obviously Tamarkan was a cut above the rest as it had been
chosen as a staging post where the Japs could get us ready for
further slave labour. The rumour was that they intended to fatten
us up a little before shipping us to Japan.

The day after I arrived, Marcus and Lofty turned up. I was
delighted, even though neither of them looked the picture of health.
However, they were alive and walking, and though Merv was in
the camp hospital, at least our mob was together again and could
look out for each other.

I heard that some of the lads we had left in Changi fifteen
months before were in the camp and I went looking for them.
I found 'Tiger' Lyons, who gave me the awful news. Harvey was
dead. It was shocking. It took me a moment to grasp what he was
telling me. My mind shot back to the time at Kalgoorlie Station
where Harvey had been so alive, so happily drunk, as we had wet
his new nipper's head. Now he was gone. I thought of Gwen, his
wife, and of the son he had seen only twice. Despite being constantly surrounded by death, the death of a mate cut deep. It was

hard to take. It hurt more. With a heavy heart I broke the news to the others, telling Merv, who didn't appear to be making much progress in the camp hospital, as gently as I could.

The hospital was better than any we had encountered before, as was the diet and even the weather. We were out of the mountains here and the climate was beautiful: the days warm and pleasant, the nights not half as cold as Burma. With the inclusion of a few fresh vegetables in the diet even my skin problems began to clear up slightly, although all of us were still subject to continuous bouts of dysentery and malaria.

Even so, the deaths were relentless: they went on and on, and when I wasn't working I was assigned to burial details and as a pall bearer. It was an awful job, burying blokes you didn't know; even worse burying blokes you did know. The only way to handle it was to keep the mind neutral.

The camp was surrounded by anti-aircraft batteries strategically positioned to protect the bridge. Needless to say, the camp wasn't marked as a POW camp, so sooner or later we expected to be targeted by the Allied bombers that were flying over with increasing frequency. First came the reconnaissance planes, heading down the line to Bangkok, then flights of Liberators a few days later.

A couple of nights after we arrived there was a full moon. I was asleep, dreaming of the action on the *Perth,* when I awoke with a start, realising that the sound of the guns in my dream was real. The 'ack ack' batteries had opened up and were punching out a few rounds. A single plane was flying over. The problem was that the anti-aircraft guns were so placed that the shrapnel from the shells, exploding high in the night, tended to fall all over the camp.

Suddenly, sharp jagged chunks of metal were slicing through the palm-leaf roofs of the huts like bullets through butter. We erupted off our bamboo pallets and dashed outside to take what cover we could. All around the camp compound the Japanese and Korean guards were running around like frightened rabbits. It was a sight for sore eyes to see those bastards running scared. It was obvious that none of them had been under fire before.

One of the guards at the camp was Dillinger, the mongrel who had murdered Sergeant O'Connell. He recognised some of us as the blokes who had eyeballed him at 35 Kilo Camp. Immediately, he started putting it around that it wasn't him who had shot the sergeant – it was his twin brother. The bloke was a half-wit who obviously believed the rest of us were as stupid as he was. We stared at him, giving him the hard-eye. Sometimes it copped us a bashing but he knew we had his number – he knew he was going to get what was coming to him; knew that Aussie justice would catch up with him. Like the rest of them, he was beginning to realise that the Japs were going to lose the war.

Sometime in the middle of the previous year we'd heard via the secret radio of a major sea battle close to some Pacific island called Midway. No one had any idea where that was, but according to the reports, the Americans had inflicted a terrible defeat on the Japanese, sinking four of their aircraft carriers. Some of the officers who understood military strategy explained that if the reports were accurate, then the Japs were bound to lose the war. They couldn't keep up with the Yanks in producing new ships, which meant their navy would continue to take a pasting and be defeated every time. And if Japan lost the war at sea, she would eventually lose it on land.

The possibility of losing appeared to be slowly dawning on our captors. There was just a little less of the imperious, disdainful 'We-are-the-chosen-people' attitude. They strutted less and sulked more: were surlier, sour, and sometimes downright gloomy. All of which made them even more dangerous. They were bad losers to whom, sooner or later, the unthinkable was going to happen – they would be defeated. It couldn't happen soon enough for us. All we had to do was survive their vengeful cruelty as the news for them got steadily worse.

Much of the work we were doing was restoring the camp. Sometimes I was assigned to help rebuild some of the huts. My dad would have laughed to know I was working as a builder's labourer. But the best job in the camp was to be sent on a barge down river to collect stores from a local town. Here we saw people in civilian dress for the first time in years – the women looking especially pretty in their colourful saris. On the barge trip we were able to steal a lot of food meant for the Japs while the locals plied us with lots of bananas. A lot of the blokes on the barge were American infantry, for although the British ran Tamarkan Camp, the influx from Burma meant that the vast majority of prisoners were either Aussie or Yanks.

We had discovered that our mates from the *Houston,* along with the Americans in general were, in the main, good blokes, though a lot more serious than us. Many of them were honest, upright, God-fearing lads who thought that stealing – even stealing from the Japs – was a sin . . . a quaint notion that we Aussies were at pains to disabuse! Stealing from the Japs was a patriotic duty, we told them, and especially on that barge trip we showed them how it was done. Once they got the hang of it the Yanks soon became very good at it: one of their blokes managed to smuggle more than a dozen eggs meant for the Japanese officers past the guards.

Under the supervision of the guards a working party of British prisoners was building a big memorial to all those who had died working on the railway. The central cenotaph of the memorial was to the Japanese, while its four smaller extensions were memorials to the Australians, British, Americans and Dutch who had died. The British POWs had cannibalised four marble table tops from a NAAFI canteen as memorial plaques for the prisoners from the four Allied nations. There was no mention on the memorial of the thousands of Siamese and Burmese natives who had also died on the railway. We reckoned more of them had died than of us – even though our losses were fearful: some of our officers were reckoning that maybe 20,000 Allied prisoners had died. So how many natives had died of cholera in the camps, God alone knew.

I talked to a cockney prisoner working on the memorial. He was stripped to the waist with a cigarette rolled in what looked like newspaper hanging from the corner of his mouth. 'This heap of shit isn't going to last a f---ing year,' he growled. 'Stupid f---ing Japs have specified one part cement to ten parts sand. Come the next f---ing monsoon the f---ing thing will fall over. But when this f---ing war is over, we'll come back here and build our own memorial to the blokes that died on this f---ing railway. It'll have four f---ing sides: one for your lot, Aussie, one for our blokes, one for the Yanks and one for the Dutch. And the f---ing Japs can go f--- themselves.'

Every day we visited Merv in the hospital to share our extra rations or a banana or stolen egg. The doc was saying that he had a really bad case of fever and was taking a long time to recover and certainly, from the look of him, he was doing it tough.

One day I was ordered onto a detail that spent the day unloading rice sacks from railway cars and carrying them into the camp. It was late when I got back to the billet, where Lofty and Marcus were looking serious. When I asked what was up, they told me that Merv had died.

I sat down with the shock. He was the first of our mob to go. We talked quietly for a while, and as none of us had known that he'd died and so hadn't attended his burial, we agreed that we'd go to the grave site as soon as we could to pay our last respects.

Afterwards, sitting on the edge of my pallet, I thought about Merv's passing. No matter what the doctors wrote on their improvised death certificates concerning the cause of his death, I knew what had really killed Merv. He had given up. In the end the backbreaking work on the railway along with the constant disease had worn him down. I closed my eyes and shook my head. Poor Merv. I felt so sorry for him and his family. Yet along with my sympathy I felt a strengthening of my resolution. No matter what, I wasn't going to let that happen to me. I wasn't going to give the Japs the satisfaction of killing me. I recalled the words of the cockney builder. Yes, the Japs could go f--- themselves. They were not going to get Mrs Bancroft's baby boy.

The melancholy death toll rolled on. Sombrely, we heard of the deaths of Egghead and Harold Williamson; of Wally Johnson and Nobby Clark; of Otto Lund who, like Merv, had apparently given up and died at Hintock Road Camp. It was then I realised that out of that boisterous mob of fourteen roaring boys from Western Australia who had joined the *Perth* thirty months earlier, there were just seven of us left. And of the seven dead, not one had died in battle.

Life in Tamarkan for the rest of us limped on, which meant that first Lofty got fever and was hospitalised, then Marcus and then me. Our food ration was cut, rice was short and we were woken more and more by the 'ack ack' guns blazing away at planes they had almost no chance of hitting. The camp was strewn with shrapnel.

Marcus got a bad dose of fever just as a bunch of Jap doctors came around to test us for cholera and malaria and to classify us into 'sick', 'light sick' and 'well'. The Jap definitions were laughable; no one in the whole camp was 'well'. Everyone was sick and many were close to dying. Even so, the arbitrary definitions meant that our group, now tragically reduced to three, would be split up again. Lofty and I were marked for shipment to Japan where we were to be put to work. Marcus was to be sent to hospital in Bangkok.

Anxiety, the POW's major affliction, stalked the 750 Australians and Americans initially selected to go to Japan. Personally, I thought nothing could be worse than the hell we had lived through on the railway and that Japan might be a change, but much of the anxiety around the camp was prompted by the 'grass is greener syndrome': the men who were going wanted to stay, while the blokes staying in Thailand wanted to go.

All of us started making preparations. We knew when the time came the Japs would give us little notice of moving. Both Lofty and I were suffering from recurring bouts of fever; one attack I had was very bad but we knew the Japs would not reclassify us. If we were 'well' when the doctors came around, then we had to stay well.

The second anniversary of the sinking of the *Perth* came – and went. I was on a ration party going down river on the barge and missed the service given by the padre, though I did get to stuff myself with bananas and steal a few eggs. No bombers came over to commemorate the event, which we thought was a pity.

The camp commandant told us that we would be transhipped to Japan through Saigon, travelling through Cambodia into Vietnam. Afterwards the guards laughed at us, saying that sailing out of Saigon and across the South China Sea, we were bound to be torpedoed by American submarines or sunk by their bombers. We knew it was a distinct possibility, for, as with the POW camps where the Japs never painted the roofs to show our bombers they held POWs, the Japanese never distinguished their POW ships either.

Just over two years after the *Perth* went down I, along with the rest of the blokes earmarked to go to Japan, received my first outfit of new clothes: one pair of shorts, one pair of underpants, a shirt, a pair of boots, a pair of white socks and a Dutch Army-issue green straw hat. It felt decidedly weird to be wearing clothes after two years in a G-string; even weirder to be wearing boots. By issuing the kit the Japs were signalling that our move to Japan was imminent.

I went to see Marcus in the hospital and quietly handed him my diary and drawings. 'If we get torpedoed, I don't want this going into the drink,' I told him. 'I already lost everything when the *Perth* went down.'

'But, Blood, this is your diary,' he said.

'I know. I want you to look after it for me.'

'You sure?'

227

'Too right. The guards will be searching us on the journey and sooner or later, they'll be bound to discover it. Better you have it. It's got more chance of getting back home if you look after it. But if they shift you to Japan, bury it.'

'Okay mate, if I can, I'll bring it home for you.' He fingered the thin, airmail paper and laughed. 'Good cigarette paper, though, Blood.'

'Look mate, if you need it for a smoko, go for it. I only kept the thing to give me something to do. It's not exactly cheerful reading, though it would be good to have a record of what these bastards did.'

'I'll do my best, Blood.'

Lofty and I said goodbye to Marcus on a bright April morning a few days later. We shook hands and said we'd all meet in the Savoy where we'd buy each other a few beers. Privately, I wondered if I really would see Marcus again. After Merv's death nothing seemed quite so certain any more. That afternoon the first batch of prisoners marched out of the camp, bound for Japan. There were about 450 of us: a mixed bunch of Aussies and Yanks. Before we left we were subjected to a rigorous body search by the Japanese guards before being herding into box cars at the rail station: thirty or forty to a car. There was no room to stretch out, except for the guards, who made room for themselves next to the sliding doors. The rest of us had to sit with our knees under our chins, gasping for air inside the metal boxes which were as hot as ovens even though the guards kept the big sliding doors open. After a long and circuitous journey, we eventually reached Bangkok where we were disappointed not to see more bomb damage. With so many Liberators flying over-head, we had expected half the city to be flattened, but someone said the bombers were concentrating on the docks and ships in the roadstead.

We were in Bangkok for little more than three hours before we were once more crushed into the box cars for the journey across country to Saigon, 550 kilometres to the east. We were two days and a night in the cramped cars, watching a flat, peaceful country of rice paddies and water buffaloes sliding past the open doors. At last we reached the city of Phnom Penh, the capital of Cambodia, where we were ordered out of the cars and able, at last, to stretch our legs and straighten our hunched, aching bodies. Phnom Penh, we discovered, was the end of the line.

As the guards marched us through the city we stared in amaze-ment at the Western men and women in civilian clothes, many of the women in pretty dresses. Cambodia was a French colony and the Vichy government in France had done a deal with the Japs over their colonies. The French were still nominally running the show, but the Jap army was everywhere. The French women stared at us in great sympathy. We must have looked a bizarre and shocking sight: a few hundred emaciated, oddly kitted out, unkempt white blokes tramping along their elegant, leafy boulevards lined with beautiful French colonial buildings

We arrived at a quay on a broad, slowly flowing muddy river: the Mekong. I stared at this great waterway of South-East Asia, finding it hard to comprehend that the source was 3000 kilo-metres away, somewhere up in the Himalayas. At the quay was a big, modern river steamer that we were ordered to board. Although not designed to take 750 passengers, the accommodation on deck wasn't too cramped. It was piled with wood to feed the ferry's boilers and the more wood we shifted to the boilers the more space we had to lie down.

The leisurely twenty-four trip down the Mekong was, as far as we were concerned, a luxury cruise. We were given two meals and we had plenty of water. Some of the Americans said it was like sailing down the Mississippi and certainly there was a feel of Huckleberry Finn to the experience. Finally, after a few hours of wending its way through the innumerable channels and waterways of the Mekong Delta, the ferry tied up at a wharf in the middle of the docks at Saigon.

Our new camp, alongside the docks, was an eye-opener. It had wooden barracks with shingle roofs, concrete floors and double-tiered bunks and boasted large green mosquito nets, big enough to cover ten men. Even better, rations in the camp included meat, eggs, beans, cabbage and sweet potatoes, while the canteen was overflowing with merchandise – even soap – all at reasonable prices. None of us had seen soap in two years. Then someone discovered that the canteen sold toothbrushes and paste! To clean my teeth properly was something I had only dreamed of.

We were told the camp would be our temporary home until we were shipped to Japan. We prayed the Japs wouldn't be in any hurry. This, compared to what we had been used to, was paradise.

They put us to work immediately, building blast screens for 'ack ack' positions and unloading stores from barges: usually sacks of rice. Even the work wasn't arduous – not in comparison to building a railway – and with the improved diet, as the days turned into weeks, we began getting stronger and gained a little weight. For the first time in over two years, no one died.

There were 250 Brits in the camp; tragically all that was left of 2000 men originally sent into the jungles to work. They had a system for getting French language newspapers inside that were then translated and the news disseminated. We were greatly heartened by what was happening in the war: everywhere the Allies were victorious. Vietnam, like Cambodia, was a colony of the French and outside, on our way to work in the back of the Japanese trucks, many of the French, as well as the natives, would wave and proffer the V for victory sign.

Things changed noticeably in the middle of June, however, when we heard that British, American and Canadian troops had landed in France. Now it looked like the Vichy French government would be replaced and France would no longer be a Japanese ally. Almost immediately the number of our guards increased and security was tightened. There was also more bombing, with the Liberators, and now American Super Fortresses, attacking the docks and shipping in the harbour. In an unprotected camp next to the docks this was not good news for us and our officers suggested to the Japs that we dig slit trenches into which we could dash at the first note of the air-raid siren. The Japs said they weren't necessary.

One night we had a heavy raid. We threw ourselves out of our bunks and clung to the concrete floor, listening to the god-awful whistle of a stick of bombs hurtling towards us. The nearest bombs fell just eighty yards away, demolishing a tobacco factory. Next morning the camp was littered with shrapnel, though miraculously no one was hurt. Almost at first light the guards appeared with shovels and ordered us to start digging slit trenches, first for them and then for ourselves. Some of them were so spooked by the bombing they took a hand at the digging themselves.

It was clear that sailing out of Saigon was becoming a dangerous undertaking; a wolf pack of American submarines lurked somewhere close to the mouth of the Mekong and was taking a terrible toll on Jap shipping. So after four months in the camp the Japs decided that shipping us from Saigon was just too dangerous. Having transported us hundreds of kilometres to Saigon they now started getting ready to transport us back again! It was the ultimate manifestation of the Jap mantra, 'All men back – all one big mistake'. For once the Japanese inability to marshal men, their tedious and innumerable *tenkos*, had worked in our favour. In one way we were pleased; at least we would not be going to sea and risking the submarines. But we were sorry to be leaving Saigon. We'd had a chance to recuperate here. It was an easier place to stay alive than anywhere else we had known.

Yet the worst thing about our leaving was when we were told that the Yanks would not be coming with us. We had bonded with the crew of the *Houston*: they had gone into the water at the same time and place as we had, and their losses had been even more horrendous than ours. Like us, they had come out of the sea with nothing; like us they had laboured and died on the railway. The banter and boasting between the two sets of blokes had been fierce and funny. Now we were to be separated. It was like parting from brothers.

We left Saigon in late July, returning to Bangkok exactly the way we had come: first a luxury river cruise followed by a nightmare thirty-six hours on a densely packed, creaking train. Bangkok had changed. Allied bombers had transformed it. The railway marshalling yards had taken a pounding and much of the city had seen severe bombing. It was like a ghost town.

Further west, at Ban Pong, we turned south to rattle and screech through the Malay jungle towards Singapore. The jungle was very thick here, while the natives, after three-and-a-half years of Japanese domination, were in a pitiful condition. Whenever the train stopped for us to be fed our meagre rations, natives as thin as wraiths would appear, begging for scraps. They were so abject most of us shared what we could with them.

Reaching Singapore, which the Japs were unsuccessfully trying to rename Syonan, we were marched four miles to a POW camp close to Keppel Harbour, called River Valley Road Camp. In it were about 2000 POWs: Aussies, British, Dutch and some captured Ghurkas.

Unlike some men in the regular Indian army, who had gone over to the Japanese to fight alongside them in what was called the Indian National Army, the Ghurkas had remained intensely loyal to Britain. They were tough, nuggetty little buggers: no one in his right mind got into a scrap with a Ghurka, and they were very well disciplined. Both traits served them well in the camps, where they survived better than most. The Japs were afraid of them, even as prisoners. In the five weeks we were at River Valley Road Camp we got to know a few. I liked them a lot and felt intensely grateful that they were on my side; I wouldn't have wanted a Ghurka as an enemy.

The camp at River Valley Road was, in all respects but one, like all the other camps. There were more than a dozen long, open, bamboo huts that could sleep between 100–250 men, each with a palm-leaf roof and single sleeping deck. The huts, along with the Jap's quarters, formed a compound in addition to which was an open-sided kitchen, open latrines and open shower facilities, all surrounded by a high barbed-wire fence with a guard house and double gate. What was bizarrely different about the camp was that it was in an urban area; instead of being surrounded by jungle beyond the barbed wire, here were streets and pavements and native Singaporeans going about their business. The camp was close to 'Happy World' – the Singaporean equivalent of 'Luna Park' – and we could hear the music and all the sounds of the funfair. It was surreal.

The camp was very close to the docks and we presumed we would soon be embarked on a transport to Japan but, as usual with the Japs, nothing happened and we remained at River Valley Road for weeks. Though hygiene was good, the food at the camp was pretty poor, even by POW standards. Soon enough many of us were going down once more with dysentery and dingy fever. The Japs put us to work loading and unloading ships at the docks that allowed us to supplement our diet with liberated tins of fruit and other luxuries when we found them, but essentially we were back to starvation rations and losing the good health we had attained in Saigon.

After about five weeks we were on the move again, though not to the Land of the Rising Sun but down the road in a fleet of trucks to a fairly remote location at the end of Jurong Road, on the southwest tip of Singapore Island, where the Japs were building a drydock. About 300 of us were assigned as slave labour on the construction. Our camp was on a small island about a mile across the water called Pulau Damar Laut. We travelled to the dock every day by ferry. By now many of us were sick again and almost as soon as we got there I went down with my usual skin troubles, as well as yet another bout of fever. I reported sick and was put on light duties, working in the cookhouse. The bloke in charge of the cookhouse was an AIF warrant officer, Bill Smith, whom I got to know quite well. Bill slipped me a little a little extra food now and again which I shared with Lofty who was working at the dock.

Our barracks on the island had been built by Jap engineers and were pretty good, but the bloke in charge was a jumped-up, demented Korean who liked to bash prisoners for no reason. He was typical of many Korean guards in both temperament and stature, being a short, squat bloke: what the Americans called a 'five by five', while the Brits would have said he was 'built like a brick shithouse'. Because of his build we called him the 'Jeep' and, as he so loved to lord it over everyone, calling unnecessary *tenkos* where we stood for hours while he and his runty, rat-like sidekick tried to count us, we called our new home 'Jeep Island'.

Drinking water on the island was in short supply but we were allowed to bathe in the sea which, surprisingly, only tended to increase my skin problems. I noticed that when the tide went out there were many small fish and a curious type of shellfish left stranded in the coral. I and another bloke, an AIF corporal, were hungry enough to try them – raw. After chewing mine for a bit I spat it out. It didn't taste all that pukka to me. The corporal ate his. Within minutes we were both vomiting violently. Other prisoners managed to get us into the sick bay where the camp doctor, Dr Rowley Richards, was sent for as I and the corporal continued to vomit uncontrollably. The only treatment Dr Richards had for food poisoning was sea water, which he forced me to drink: a pint of it, straight off. Meanwhile, the corporal, having lapsed into unconsciousness, was starting to turn blue and no matter how hard he tried, Dr Richards couldn't get him to swallow the sea water. The corporal died within minutes while I vomited and vomited until I was sure my empty, wretched stomach was about to erupt up my throat and out of my mouth. But the seawater was a powerful emetic and it did the trick. I recovered, though I was as weak as a kitten for a couple of days. The corporal's death was the first we'd had since leaving Tamarkan. It came as a shock, and as a stark reminder that our position as prisoners of the Japanese was still precarious. Every day was potentially fatal.

In early September, after about five weeks on Jeep Island, we were shifted back to River Valley Road Camp, where we were told that, very soon, we would definitely be boarding a ship for Japan. Lofty and I shrugged fatalistically. The word 'definitely' didn't mean a damn thing.

After a couple of days back at the camp I had a marvellous surprise. I got two letters from Mirla. My heart soared. They were about a year old and, like mine, limited to twenty-five words. Both were innocuous, all about ordinary events at home and how Subiaco had done in the previous season. It was marvellous to have news of home – even better to get it from Mirla. I read and reread them, looking for any hidden meaning, trying to read between the lines. In each of them she had signed off with 'Much love'. That alone kept me going. I wondered how many letters she had written; how many were lost or destroyed or rotting in some Japanese warehouse.

Mirla's letters made me think intensely about her; even more than I already did. I could picture her easily; recall in every detail our last evening together before I had shipped out on the *Perth*. The letters put me in mind of a poem I had copied in my book of poems from one of the blokes in 35 Kilo. It seemed to fit the bill exactly.

THE GIRL I LEFT BEHIND
I sit here thinking
Of the girl I left behind
And then I come to thinking
Of what is in her mind

Is she thinking of the times
When we were young and gay
Or of the things we're going to do
When I return some day

I'll bet she's acting cheerful
Tho' her heart is full of pain
Or trying to cheer the family
For my good, once again

For all the months of misery
Of sorrow, grief and pain
I'll make it all up to her
When I go home again

There'll be no more going down the street
Or to the pictures on my own
It's the pure simple home life for me
And no more will I roam

To every man who takes it hard
Or says the treatment's rough
Remember there is one at home
Who may also take it tough

Finally, on the morning of September 6, the entire camp was marched down to the docks where we were confronted by two rust buckets: the *Rakuyo Maru* and the *Kachidoki Maru*. Both ships were in appalling condition and neither had the Red Cross painted on their sides, nor any other indication that POWs were on board. All they had was the Jap flag – the rising sun – which looked uncomfortably like a bullseye for every submarine and bomber patrolling the South China Sea. Lofty and I gave each other a glance, steeling ourselves for another God-awful sea cruise courtesy of the Japs.

Needless to say, after innumerable *tenkos*, the Japs still got it wrong. A thousand British, many from a camp at Havelock Road, were herded aboard the *Kachidoki Maru,* with the remaining 600 assigned to the *Rakuyo Maru.* Then came our turn and we Aussies were ordered aboard the *Rakuyo Maru* also, *kumi* by *kumi.* Yet again, the Japs miscounted and after herding three kumis aboard – a total of 750 men – the final *kumi* was turned back at the docks. Lofty and I looked back from the ship's deck. Some of the 150 blokes stopped on the quay were *Perth* survivors. We were being separated yet again. We hated that.

As we boarded each man was given a huge slab of rubber weighing about 36 kilos which was supposed to keep us afloat if we were torpedoed. Clutching this useless piece of rubbish along with what little kit we had, we were crammed below decks where a sign signalled that the ship could accommodate 187 steerage-class passengers. There were 1300 of us. The guards were prodding men down into the hold with their bayonets but it was impossible. Men were already fainting from the overcrowding and the heat. After a lot of intense and bitter debate between our senior officers and the Japs, 600 men were allowed to stay topside.

It was difficult to know what was worse; to be cramped below decks with the smell of 900 men along with the stink of urine, vomit and faeces, or to endure the burning sun on a deck which, as soon as night fell, turned as cold as ice while we had no more than a threadbare blanket to keep us warm. We had almost no fresh water and only one cup of rice a day with, maybe, a little watery vegetable broth.

On the basis that we had successfully done it already, we survivors of the *Perth* were ordered by our senior officers to rehearse and drill the men in procedures for abandoning ship should we be torpedoed. We moved between the hold and the deck instructing groups of men: 'Don't panic . . . leave everything behind . . . don't jump into the water from a great height . . . abandon the ship on the opposite side from where the torpedoes have hit . . . and above all,' we told them, 'don't worry. It may never happen – and if it does, you can survive it. And, oh yes, forget that useless piece of Japanese

239

rubber. You hold onto that, you'll definitely drown.' All the blokes, Brits as well as Aussies, appreciated the advice.

After almost a week at sea it began to look as if our preparations for abandoning ship were for nothing. We had left Singapore in convoy. There were four transports and two oil tankers with an escort of four destroyers which, after five days at sea and somewhere west of Manila, were joined by three more transports and another two destroyers. It was a well-protected convoy, steadily zigzagging northeast towards Japan with the destroyers forming a protective ring around the merchant ships. Some of the *Perth* lads thought that maybe six destroyers were too many for the sub wolf packs. None of us could say we were sorry: the last thing any of us wanted was to have another ship sunk under us.

The night of September 11 was as cold as all the others and I was huddled on deck beneath my threadbare blanket, trying to get some sleep. I had finally succeeded when, in the early hours of the twelfth, the night was split apart by an enormous explosion.

That was the first torpedo.

Mirla's Story

By the time I was twenty-one the world had been at war for more than four-and-a-half years. Sometimes it was difficult to remember life before the war: to recall a time when we didn't have rationing and the blackout; when we didn't worry every day about our men overseas.

By then we knew we were going to win. The Italians had given up and in Italy and Eastern Europe the Germans were being pushed back. Meanwhile, in the Pacific, the Japanese expansion had been halted by the American navy and the Americans were pushing them back, island by island. Yet victory seemed so long in coming. We yearned for peace. The war seemed as if it would drag on forever and even after the D-day landings in Normandy, on June 6, 1944, the fighting continued.

Shortly after my twenty-first birthday, I met an American sailor at the Young Australia League who was also called Arthur — Arthur Lewis. He was a New Yorker, well-mannered and respectful, though what attracted me to him was that he played the saxophone in his ship's band. My mother, who was an accomplished pianist, had once had her own small dance band. I took Arthur home to meet her. After that he came to the house at least once a week to play his saxophone while my mother accompanied him on the piano. They were fun evenings that for a few hours took our minds off the war. Though I never had any romantic feelings for Arthur, I did like him and was sorry when his ship was ordered to sail. My mother and I missed him and both hoped that he would stay safe and come through the war. I'm glad to say he did. Months later he sent me a lovely box of cosmetics from New York.

By early September 1944, I had written my Arthur fifty-two letters. Having at first kept their 25-word contents light-hearted and innocuous, those I had written over the last few months became more expressive about my feelings for him. I had decided that there was no point in hiding what I felt. I hoped that knowing I loved him would help him cope with the boredom of being a prisoner of war. Every day I wondered how much longer I would have to wait before I could see him again.

1 0

The Nick of Time

Beneath the burning sun demented men are screaming and halluci-
nating and threshing the oil-slicked water. I watch Bill and the others
swimming towards a collection of solid-looking rafts a few hundred
metres off. I glance at Lofty. 'Come on, mate. It's time we got out
of here.'

'No, you go if you want, Blood,' he croaks. 'I think it's safer here.'

I blink in surprise, the oil stinging my eyes. 'Come on, mate. You
can't think this is safe. We'll be much better off away from this mob.'

'No. You go. I'll stay here.' Maybe it's the thirst, but Lofty's voice
sounds flat and lifeless. I try to study his face: it's difficult with the
waves constantly shifting us.

'Come on Lofty, mate. This is not a good place to be. We're better
off with Bill and the others.'

'No, you go Blood. I'll stay here.'

'I can't go without you. You know that. We stick together. We've
always stuck together.'

'That's all right. You go.'

I stare at him, trying to work out what's wrong . . . What's got into him? 'Look, Lofty. See those rafts over there? There're enough to make a really good float. And six blokes pulling together have more chance than the two of us in the middle of this mob. We swim over there, we'll be travelling out of here first class.'

He shakes his head. 'No, I'll stick around here.'

'Mate, there's no future staying around here! A lot of these blokes are not going to survive. You've got more chance over there with me and the others.'

He shakes his head again. 'No. I'll stay.'

I continue to stare at him. Then I hear myself saying the words I had never thought I'd say. 'Listen, mate, if you don't come, I'm going to have to leave you. I'm sorry, but over there with those blokes we've got a chance.'

'That's okay, mate. You go.'

I watch him closely. He's gripping the float tightly with both hands, staring into the water. It's as if he's somewhere else, as if he's no longer on a makeshift float in the middle of the South China Sea. I've seen that look before. Lofty is turning his back on reality. I put my hand on his shoulder and shake him gently. I'm pleading with him. 'Come on, Lofty, come with me. You can't stay here on your own. You've got to come with me.'

He shakes my hand off his shoulder. 'No, mate. You go. It's okay.'

I gaze at him for a moment longer, then allow myself to slip into the water. 'Good luck, mate. When this is all over I'll buy you one in the Savoy.'

'Yeah, good luck, Blood.'

Swimming away from a mate is the hardest thing I've ever had to do. There's something catching in my throat and my eyes are stinging with more than the oil. I turn a couple of times to see if Lofty has changed his mind. He is sitting precariously on the raft, still staring into the water. I feel my guts churning. I'm tempted to swim back to him, even though I know that getting away from the mob is the right thing to do . . . that a few motivated blokes on a solid raft have a much better chance than two of us slipping in and out of the water. But Lofty is my mate and we have been through everything together.

Everything – up till now.

I turn one more time to look at him. Dear God, I hope he's going to be okay. In the whole of the war, this is the hardest thing I've ever had to do.

Everyone on deck sprang up and rushed to the ship's rail. One of the escorting destroyers had blown up, bursting into flames and lighting up the night as she heeled over. At once the guards pushed us below decks, jabbing us with their bayonets. Though we were crammed like sardines in the hold, no one panicked. After a couple of hours there were no more explosions, and some of us began emerging back on deck. There was a bright gibbous moon and across the dark surface of the sea we could see the escort destroyers hunting the submarine; could hear dozens of depth charges going off. I was puzzled at the lack of any further action by the wolfpack; maybe it had been a hit-and-run attack by a lone sub.

It was about an hour before dawn. The night was at its darkest with the moon paling and dropping to port, silhouetting the convoy. Suddenly, with a tremendous *crump*, the oil tanker ahead on our port bow erupted into a massive ball of fire. The *Rakuyo Maru*, rocked by the force of the explosion, heeled over. As she came back up, the second tanker blew up. The flames from both vessels turned night into day and the *Rakuyo Maru*, at the tail end of the convoy, was lit up like a singer on a stage.

The *Perth* boys knew what was coming next, and from which direction. The whispered word went out immediately, 'Move to port, move to port.' Screams from the bridge told us we were right: the Jap crew had seen the white, phosphorescent track of a torpedo slicing through the water from somewhere out in the darkness on our starboard side. The torpedo hit amidships, lifting the *Rakuyo Maru* momentarily out of the water. A second torpedo hit the bows moments later, sending a great sheet of water over the vessel and into the hold.

Immediately, the Japanese crew and guards abandoned ship, taking all the lifeboats. We watched them scuttling off the vessel – rats leaving the sinking ship – as our officers calmly gave the order for our blokes to evacuate the hold. The drills we had practised paid off – the men assembled on the deck in an orderly fashion. After checking we discovered that no one had been injured in the torpedo attack.

By then the ship had lost headway and was drifting towards the nearest burning tanker. The sea around the tanker was on fire from burning oil while explosions from both tankers blasted flames and debris hundreds of feet into the air. It was obvious that we too would have to abandon ship. The officers gave the order just as dawn was breaking and we tossed overboard any remaining rafts and wooden floats lashed to the deck along with anything else we thought might possibly float. Even the makeshift wooden latrines lashed to the ships sides were cut lose. I noticed that the big blocks of rubber the Japs had given us floated for a while and then sank.

The men were controlled and orderly and there was no panic as they slipped over the side. The drop into the water was about 8 metres; it looked a long way down in the hard light of dawn but almost everyone made it without hurting themselves. Many men had lifebelts and as we expected to be in the water a while, all of us wore shirts, shorts and a hat. Most of us had water bottles. I clung to my Dutch Army water bottle for dear life. It could make the difference between living and dying.

In all, 1317 men off the *Rakuyo Maru* – the entire complement of prisoners – went into the water safely and successfully, though some of the sick didn't last long in the sea. The doctor, Rowley Richards, along with a few other officers, managed to launch two leaky and decrepit lifeboats that the Japs had left behind into which they hauled a few of the sick. But men began dying almost as soon as we entered the water.

For an old rust bucket the *Rakuyo Maru* took a long time to go under, staying afloat for about twelve hours. For most of the day we watched her settling slowly in the water and for a while were tempted to swim back and board her. But those blokes who tried couldn't manage to haul themselves up her sides. They were too weak and their hands and bodies too slippery with fuel oil. By now all of us were covered in the oil leaking from the slowly sinking tankers.

For Lofty and me and the other *Perth* lads, life had come full circle. Once more we were floating in an oil-slicked sea, only this time we were not so close to land that we could see it. This time we were somewhere in the middle of the South China Sea: by my reckoning at least 400 miles off the coast of China and about the same off the northern tip of the Philippines. This time, swimming to land was not an option. Our only hope was to be rescued, or maybe of sailing to the mainland on a makeshift raft which, given our current situation, was a tall order.

The sea was littered with rafts and other wreckage from the three or four ships that had either sunk or were in the process of sinking. Lofty and I found a few floats about the size of small table tops and lashed them together. It was a makeshift affair and wouldn't last long, but it would have to do for the time being. There was just enough room for the two of us.

That afternoon, after we had been in the water for about ten hours, two Jap frigates appeared and began slowly moving through the debris and hundreds of bobbing heads, picking up the Jap survivors from their lifeboats. Scores of our blokes started swimming or paddling towards the frigates but the Jap crews waved them off with rifles and revolvers. Men who swam too close were fired on. After they had picked up their blokes, the frigate crews, laughing and gesturing, shouted goodbye to us. We gestured back at the bastards.

But the rescue of the Japs had at least emptied a few lifeboats that were quickly filled to overflowing by the men floating close to them. Within minutes there were forty or fifty men to a lifeboat. Lofty and I had been too far away to climb aboard. I reckoned that wasn't a bad thing. With so many men, the boats didn't look too seaworthy. I reckoned we had a much better chance of sticking together and being part of a small group.

Just before nightfall of the first day a merchant ship appeared on the horizon and for a while we thought we were saved. But a Jap frigate chased the ship away and we were abandoned to the night and floating in the darkness. Thankfully, the sea was calm, the water warm, and although the night was very cold, blokes were cheerily calling to each other. We expected the Japs would come for us the next day.

Come the dawn of the second day most of the men were still in good spirits, even though there was a fair number of dead bodies floating in the water. But as the day wore on and the hot sun beat down and we sloshed about in the oil-slicked sea, the cheeriness began to wane.

Many of the army lads had allowed the fuel oil to get into their stomachs and lungs; some were clearly in a bad way and were not going to last long if we weren't rescued promptly. All of us, to a greater or lesser extent, had got oil in our eyes and were blinded by it. Many of the men, tormented by thirst, had drunk sea water. Now, with too much salt in their systems, they were beginning to hallucinate and rave. I was so thirsty my tongue was swollen, which made talking difficult. Lofty and I shared my water bottle, taking one small sip every few hours. We were especially careful not to let it slip through our oily hands into the water.

The sun beat down mercilessly. Every so often we slipped off our tiny makeshift raft to cool down in the water. No rescue ships appeared and as the day wore on I started coming to the gut-wrenching realisation that maybe the Japs were not coming back for us. Maybe they had left us all to die.

That afternoon the lifeboats moved off: the majority heading east towards the Philippines, three heading in the opposite direction for China. It made sense for them to go; however slim, they had a chance of making it to land and there was nothing they could do for the seven or eight hundred men still in the water. But it was hard to watch them disappear over the horizon all the same. We felt even more abandoned.

The second night was especially dark and cold and for most of the night I could hear Lofty's teeth chattering above the sound of my own. From time to time we talked to each other to keep ourselves awake. Although we had lashed ourselves onto our little raft as best we could, to fall into a deep sleep might prove fatal.

That night there was much less banter, with the darkness occasionally pierced by the screams and banshee wailings of demented men. It was a haunting sound and despite the cold it raised the hairs on the back of my neck.

I noticed on the morning of the third day that most of us had stayed surprisingly close in the water; hundreds of men still well within sight of each other. But by now those who had drunk the sea water were raving: they screamed obscenities or wailed for their mothers; hallucinated with visions of sea monsters or rescue ships that weren't there. Some had become violent, threshing about and drowning each other in their dementia. It was the madness of the mob and an awful sight; worse in many ways than the camps. Although there were clumps of sanity – groups of men clinging to rafts who maintained discipline and some kind of order – too many of the blokes around us were delirious and screaming. It was causing panic. We had to get away from the herd: put distance between us and men going insane before we too became infected. It was as deadly as cholera.

I told Lofty what I thought but I'm not sure if he understood; my tongue was so thick with thirst. He mumbled something and then, after a moment, whispered, 'Blood, I need water. Let me have a drink.'

I passed him my water bottle. It was covered in fuel oil. 'Just a sip, mate.'

He grasped it, lifting a hand to take out the stopper. The bottle slipped through his oily fingers and plopped into the sea. It was gone in an instant. 'Oh hell, I'm sorry, Blood,' Lofty croaked.

I stared aghast at the place in the waves where the bottle had disappeared. It took me a moment to get a grip on myself. 'Bit late to be sorry now, mate.' My mouth was hot and dry and my tongue swollen but I guess the bitterness in my tone came through. That water bottle had seen me and my mates, including Lofty, through two-and-a-half years of hell. Without it I couldn't see us lasting two-and-a-half days.

'I'm sorry, Blood. Really sorry.'

I glanced at Lofty. There were tears in his eyes. I felt bad. He was taking it hard. 'Forget it, mate. We'll manage somehow.'

'I reckon I may have killed us.'

'Come on, mate. You know better than that. Don't talk that way.'

'I'm so sorry.' He was shaking his head. 'So sorry.'

'Lofty, forget it. Come on, we'll manage.'

He continued to shake his head, softly murmuring, 'Sorry.'

I wondered what was wrong with him. I knew he wouldn't have been drinking sea water. I worried that maybe the insanity around us was getting to him. We had to get away. But if we got away from the main group, would any Jap rescue ships find us? Would there *be* any rescue ships? It was a hard decision.

After a while Lofty stopped murmuring and shaking his head and we said nothing, staring at an empty horizon beneath a burning sun. About an hour later a small group of men floated past clinging to a collection of badly lashed rafts. I eyed them suspiciously but they seemed orderly and disciplined.

'Blood?'

I frowned at the one who had called my name, his oil-blackened face unrecognisable. It took me a moment to make out it was Bill Smith, the warrant officer from the cookhouse on Jeep Island. I didn't recognise the other three with him, though I knew they were AIF. They paddled across to us.

'Sir.'

'What are we going to do, you reckon?'

I was surprised. 'You asking me?'

'You've been through this before. You survived your last sinking. I reckon you might know how to survive this one.' He was serious, so I told him the first thing they should do was to put some distance between themselves and the delirious men causing so much panic. After that, they should look out for good-sized life rafts and lash them together properly so they had something to float on.

Bill listened closely. 'That sounds like a good plan,' he said. 'Okay, I'm putting you in charge of this little mob. Including me.'

'What? You can't do that. You're the officer.'

'Yes, I can. Being an officer doesn't count for much in the middle of the ocean. You're the bloke with the experience. So, you're in command. With you and your mate, there are six of us. What do you reckon we should do?'

For a moment I was a bit taken aback. I'd heard of promotion in the field, but never in an oil-slicked sea. 'Well, first look out for some good rafts. If we find a few we can make something a lot more seaworthy than what we've got here.'

As if on cue, within minutes we saw a bunch of solid-looking rafts. They were floating a few hundred yards away. I told Bill that we would swim out to them, lash them together with whatever rope was around and then keep our distance from the main group. He set off paddling with his blokes. 'Come on, Lofty,' I said.

But Lofty refused to come. No matter what I said, he reckoned he was better off staying where he was. I knew he wasn't. Neither of us were. Stuck in the middle of a demented mob on a couple of makeshift floats we were vulnerable. I reckoned we had almost no chance of making it. But with Bill and the others on good rafts, there was some chance of surviving until we were rescued. I told Lofty this; pleaded with him to come with me, but he refused. In the end I said I would have to leave him.

It was the hardest thing I ever did.

I swam across to where Bill and the others were clinging onto some good floats and for the rest of the day we swam around and gathered together a collection of decent rafts and wooden hatch covers. I kept glancing in Lofty's direction to see if he was okay, but after a while I lost sight of him. I wondered if I should swim back, even though I knew it was crazy. In command of this small mob of diggers I knew I was doing something positive about our survival.

By the middle of the afternoon we had managed to get two big hatch covers and a good-sized raft on top of each other, so we could be out of the water and floating above the oil. We also found a couple of one-man rafts with bamboo water tanks. Each tank had a few drops of water.

The other blokes with Bill the warrant officer were Eric, Jack and Len. Jack was a strong swimmer with good eyesight. He spotted a melon floating in the water and swam out to retrieve it. Though the skin was covered in fuel oil and the fruit saturated with salt water, we each got a good mouthful of the juicy core.

During the day I had noticed a half-knot current was carrying us north-east and that we were drifting further away from the main body of men. They were less noisy now and I supposed many of the demented had drowned. I prayed hard that Lofty was all right and that he had connected with some good blokes. I just couldn't understand why he hadn't come with me. We had stuck together through so much. Could it have been losing the water bottle? I didn't understand. Whatever it was, I couldn't get Lofty out of my thoughts.

Every so often we slipped into the water to cool down and get some relief from the burning sun. Towards the end of the afternoon, as I was going in for a cooling dip one more time, I realised for the first time in more than two-and-a-half years that I was a free man. I could slip into the sea when I wanted and get back on the raft when it suited me. There were no detested guards to scream at me, no bashings with batons. I was free. The sudden realisation was exhilarating. I pulled myself onto the raft and said to no one in particular, 'I'm a free man . . . a free man.'

'Some consolation,' one of the others said mordantly. 'At least you can die a free man.'

I shook my head. 'I don't think like that, mate. I'm not planning on dying. Not for a while yet.'

We stared out over the vast sea, empty all the way to the horizon save for a few bobbing heads and rafts in the far distance. 'Then you'd better pray for a miracle,' someone said.

The night was freezing and we cuddled as close as honeymooners to keep warm.

Dawn broke to the same empty horizon. The sea was almost empty of bobbing heads and makeshift rafts now. Those that hadn't drowned had drifted out of sight of each other. I thought about Lofty and prayed again that he was okay.

As the sun came up I thought about how my little mob should spend its day. I knew boredom was an enemy and that, without enough to do, a bloke could start thinking negatively and focusing on how thirsty he was. That could lead to drinking sea water. So, when we weren't fossicking around passing debris and rafts, I had each of the blokes take a turn at telling us the story of his life. After that, we had to make up stories; anything to occupy the time. Some of the made-up tales were pretty close to the bone but I reckoned it was better for us to be telling each other dirty stories than to be thinking too hard about our situation.

As talking was so difficult with our mouths so dry, I showed Bill and the others how to wash out their mouths with sea water. They knew that to drink seawater was fatal, but if they could resist the temptation, then washing out their mouths would bring some relief. We all took it in turns to swill the seawater around our mouths, the others watching closely to make sure we spat it out again.

Halfway though the day, a flotilla of dead bodies drifted past, their faces and exposed limbs the colour of dead fish. I had grown so used to death that I watched them almost as I might have watched the passing traffic on Hay Street. One of the bodies moved an arm. 'That man isn't dead!' someone shouted.

Two us slipped into the water and brought the bloke back to the raft. Getting him onto it was a struggle as he was delirious and very weak. Later, we learned his name was Ray Wheeler. His rescue brought our number to six, though unless we were rescued soon, saving Ray might prove to have been a waste of time. We didn't reckon he had very long.

The miracle happened that afternoon. We saw a vessel approaching. At first we couldn't make out what it was: only when it was within a couple of miles could we see it was a submarine, though whether Japanese or Allied we couldn't tell. But it was definitely stopping and picking up survivors. We stood precariously on the raft and waved and shouted until night began to fall. The sub was making slow progress in our direction and had got to within half a mile of us when it stopped. With hearts sinking and tears at the back of our eyes we watched unbelievingly as it turned away and sailed into the gathering gloom, listening to the diesel engines fading until there was nothing but the slap of the waves on the raft.

We had been given a glimpse of salvation – and then had it snatched away again.

It was a bitter feeling: my dry, burning mouth felt filled with ashes. We told each other the sub would be back; it would come again tomorrow; that more vessels would come. Now they knew where we were, it could only be a few more hours before we were rescued.

The night was freezing. Again, we cuddled as close as we could and did out best to keep Ray warm. All the following day our ravenous eyes scoured the horizon, willing the rescue ships to appear. None came. It was the hardest time. Had they not seen us? Had they given up on us; considered us not worth saving? Why didn't they come, for God's sake? We told more salacious stories to take our mind off what had happened but our hearts weren't in it. We listened to each other with half an ear, our eyes lusting for a ship on the horizon.

In the late afternoon it began to rain. Softly at first, then with increasing vigour. Those of us with hats caught the water in them, those without used rubber strips. We had a small, wooden soya bean bucket in which we managed to capture about two pints of water. Though it had an oily, salty, soya bean taste, it was very welcome. It would keep us alive for another couple of days.

I worried that the weather was worsening. For six days we had been adrift in a calm sea but now the wind was whipping up and the waves rising. After a couple of hours they were 3 to 4 metres high. I knew our raft wouldn't withstand bad weather. Pretty soon it would break up and we'd be plunged into the water where it would be only a matter of time before we drowned. We couldn't survive a storm. And a storm was coming.

I showed the blokes how to lash themselves to the raft as the waves began breaking over us. No one said anything but I think everyone guessed that this was the end.

And then we glimpsed her.

Out of the rain and squally sea we saw another sub heading straight for us. Often she disappeared as the waves buried us, only to reappear a moment later. We shouted and cheered and even risked standing up on our dangerously pitching raft.

Then, as before, she turned away from us. Strange, frenzied noises came from our parched throats. They were meant to be shouts, though there was not a chance anyone could hear us. We were close to hysterical. *Please God, not again. Don't turn away again!* The sub disappeared through the rain and the heaving sea, though we could hear her engines above the noise of the weather. It was hard to know if they were fading or getting closer.

And then we saw her, a few hundred metres away. An American sub, making directly for our raft. Oh, you beauty! We didn't know whether to laugh or cry – so most of us did both.

She got close alongside us, the sea tossing both her and our raft around like corks. She was rescuing us! Getting on board was going to be dangerous. I looked up at concerned faces staring down from the sub and realised it would be dangerous for their crew too. What I didn't realise then was that the looks of concern were for us: to the crew balancing on the heaving deck we looked scarcely human: drenched, emaciated and covered in oil, clinging to a few bits of wood that, even as they watched, were breaking up in the storm.

I tied a line to Ray Wheeler, still delirious, and they hauled him aboard. The others scrambled up the rigging lines onto the pitching deck as best they could. I saw them all up first and was the last to scramble aboard.

As my feet touched the solid, friendly deck I had an overwhelming sense of elation – I had come through. With a sudden unbelievable burst of energy I wanted to leap in the air; to hug the officer of the deck, a young lieutenant with a typical American face and the broadest grin imaginable. Instead, I saluted the ship and announced, 'HMAS *Perth*, sailor. What ship are you?'

'This is the USS *Queenfish*, buddy,' he grinned.

I noticed the captain of the sub looking down on us from the conning tower. I looked up and saluted. 'Permission to come aboard, sir.'

He laughed. 'Granted, sailor.'

I wanted to leap up the conning tower and hug him. 'I knew you bloody Yanks would rescue me!' I shouted up at him.

The captain laughed as the deck officer grasped me around the shoulders. 'Okay, buddy, let's get you below.'

And so we were saved.

If ever the phrase 'in the nick of time' applied, it applied to us on that September afternoon. It wasn't a storm coming – it was a typhoon.

After that, everything became a blur.

With the others I was lowered down the forward escape hatch into the forward torpedo room where the crew gently lowered our filthy bodies onto mattresses covered in snowy white sheets.

My first impression was of American sailors as giants. They all seemed so big. Their husky, physical presence was daunting; they filled the space, overawed their environment, seemed almost to suck out all the air. After years of diminutive Japanese and squat Koreans, and after seeing everyone around me shrink in stature and heft, men of a normal size appeared gigantic, dominating – almost oppressive.

Yet the sailors and their officers were anything but oppressive. They treated us with the tenderness of mothers towards their babies. It was hard to comprehend that big fighting men such as these could be so gentle towards us.

They were clearly shocked at our condition: not only the filthy fuel oil smearing our bodies and the effects on us of exposure to the elements – these things they had seen before – but also the emaciation of our frames, the clear evidence of malnutrition, the huge, weeping, tropical ulcers . . . these they had not seen before. Obviously they had no idea of what was happening in the Japanese POW camps.

Queenfish had rescued eighteen of us. There were fourteen Aussies and four Brits, though despite the twenty-four-hour non-stop attention of Pharmacist's Mate 'Doc' Dixon, two of the Brits died. I was the only sailor. The deck officer told me that other subs were still looking for survivors and I hoped to God Lofty had been picked up.

Each man saved had an American sailor individually assigned to look after him. My man was Artie Grandinetti from New York. He told me to call him Artie – and he called me Artie. After plying me with as much fresh water as I could drink – the first really good water I had tasted in more than thirty months – Artie handled me like a baby, gently wiping the fuel oil off my skin, being especially careful with the large areas of my body burned by the sun. After that he put me in the shower, where he gently soaped me down and washed the fuel oil out of my hair. He then sat me down and shaved off my filthy beard. For the first time in as long as I could remember, I felt clean.

'You wanna eat first or sleep?' Artie asked me.

Curiously, I didn't feel tired. 'Eat,' I whispered.

'Okay – whadaya want? Whatever it is, we gottit.'

For some reason my mind shot back to the night of the battle in the Sunda Strait and the meal I had missed on the *Perth* as we were ordered up to battle stations. 'Snags.'

'Say what?'

'Sausages.'

He stared at me. 'Artie, buddy, this here is Uncle Sam's navy. You can do a helluva lot better than sausages. You name it and you can have it – pork ribs, prime beefsteak . . .'

I shook my head. 'Sausages. I've been looking forward to sausages for over two years. That's what kept me going.'

'Okay, buddy' Artie said, 'sausages it'll be, along with mashed potatoes and followed by ice cream. How about that?'

I licked my lips. It was a meal fit for a king. Only I never got to eat it. 'Doc' Dixon said a meal like that, after the diet I'd been existing on, might kill me. So, instead of my longed-for snags I had a bowl of thin broth and some fruit juice. The only consolation was a tumbler of brandy and water. Years later I learned that the brandy had been liberated from the captain's cabin.

After that it was time to sleep. Only I couldn't.

I shut my eyes but sleep just would not come. Artie sat beside me. 'I haven't slept more than six hours in six nights.' I whined. 'In fact, I haven't slept properly since I was made a prisoner. But now I can't.'

Artie grinned and produced a pack of Philip Morris cigarettes. 'Have one of these. They'll get you to sleep.'

'I don't smoke.'

'Try.'

He lit one and gave it to me. The first drag produced a coughing fit. I tried to hand the cigarette back. Gently, Artie pushed my hand. 'Try it again.'

261

Too weak to resist, I filled my lungs with cigarette smoke – and passed out.

During the hours I was asleep the *Queenfish* kept searching for survivors. With the typhoon raging, the captain, Lieutenant-Commander Loughlin, knew there was practically no chance of finding anyone alive. He was right. The sub encountered many dead bodies, and we were the last survivors to be rescued. Even so, it was a brave thing for the American submariners to do. The sub was deep inside enemy waters.

Although not the submarine that had sunk the *Rakuyo Maru*, the *Queenfish* had been part of the wolfpack that had attacked our convoy – and sunk every merchant ship in it. Later, one of the submarines moving in to pick up what it thought were Japanese survivors of the attack had discovered they were Allied POWs. The sub had taken aboard seventy-three survivors, almost the same complement as its crew. The *Queenfish*, on its way back to base, was ordered to return 400 miles into enemy waters to search for more Allied survivors. When I awoke I knew I was among brave men.

Realising I was a sailor off the *Perth*, Lieutenant Bennett, the executive officer who had received me aboard, came to ask about the *Houston*. I told him as much as I could about the action in the Sunda Strait when the *Houston* went down. He spent hours with me, and when he saw I was tired – and I tired easily – he allowed me to rest before coming back to quiz me some more. What I didn't realise was that I was supplying the US navy with its first account of what had happened to the *Houston*. During those many hours of quiet conversation in the forward torpedo room of the *Queenfish*, John Bennett and I formed a life-long friendship.

Another lifelong friend I made in those few days on board the sub was the *Queenfish*'s Radio and Sound Operator, Charlie Levine from Tennessee.

It took us nine days to sail, sometimes on the surface, sometimes submerged, through Japanese waters to the American naval base on Saipan in the Marianas Islands. For the first few days the typhoon raged and when we were on the surface we were pitched about in the furious sea. But no amount of rough weather could detract me from nine days of sleeping on a luxurious mattress, of enjoying wonderfully hot showers, of eating the kind of delicious food about which I had only dreamed. Of course the survivors' intake of food was strictly limited in case our stomachs couldn't take it. In comparison to what the sub's crew ate, our portions were tiny, but to me they were beyond all comparison.

The naval base at Saipan was in the front line of the Pacific War. The Americans had invaded the island in late July and had at great cost wrested it from the Japanese. But even though Jap planes still appeared from time to time to bomb the facilities, the Yanks had set up a fully functioning Medical Army Surgical Hospital under canvas and almost as soon as we arrived we were transported by ambulance to the 148th M*A*S*H. Sadly, I said goodbye to Charlie Levine and John Bennett, but promised them both, as the men who had pulled me out of the water and taken such good care of me, that I would stay in touch with them.

After the Japanese hospitals I had been in, the 148th was a sight for sore eyes. It was clean, hygienic, efficient – and very busy. A lot of US marines, wounded when they had stormed the beaches, were being treated there. But the attention the American nurses and doctors lavished on us was beyond compare. We were the first escaped POWs they had seen and everyone was very interested in us.

I, for my part, was desperate to know if Lofty had been picked up. As soon as I was settled in the hospital, I made enquiries. I asked a medical officer how many of us had been pulled out of the sea. 'A hundred and fifty-two,' he said.

'That's it?'

He nodded sadly. 'I'm afraid that's all we got.'

I was shocked. Out of the 1317 men who had safely abandoned the *Rakuyo Maru*, only 152 of us had survived. Of course there was no word of the 500 or so men who had sailed away in the lifeboats, but out of the 800 men left in the water, four out of every five had died.

I asked the doctor about any sailors picked up by the subs. He didn't know so I trawled the wards, shuffling around in American pyjamas way too big for my skinny frame, until I found an orderly who had collected the names of the survivors. I asked about *Perth* survivors and he told me he would come to my cot with a list of all the names. I had just got back under the sheets when he arrived.

'Who else got out?' I asked eagerly.

'Three others,' he said.

'What, only three?' I couldn't believe it. 'You mean there are only four of us?'

'Fraid so.'

'But more than forty of us got off the *Rakuyo Maru*! They can't all have gone.'

'Sorry, buddy; four of you is all we got.'

I stared at him. The statistics were piteous. 'So who are they?' There was a catch in my throat, as if I was back in the sea and dying of thirst.

'I think one's a buddy of yours.'

My heart leapt. 'Who?'

'Able Seaman Collins.'

Bob Collins *was* a mate of mine, but his wasn't the name I was so desperate to hear. 'What about the other two?'

He looked down at his list. 'Jack Houghton and Lloyd Monroe.'

'What about Lofty? I mean Harry Nagle? Is he down there somewhere? In among the army blokes, maybe?'

The orderly checked his list then looked up, shaking his head. 'No. Was he a buddy?'

I nodded, my heart as heavy as a ship's anchor. 'You sure he's not there?'

'I'm sorry, buddy, I'm certain. There are only four of you and Nagle ain't one.' The orderly gave me a sympathetic look and left as I closed my eyes and slumped against my pillows. Lofty hadn't made it. I could scarcely believe it. Yet, I knew it had to be true. There was no chance he would appear now. If he hadn't been picked up before the typhoon, there was absolutely no possibility afterwards. I felt sick. Lofty gone. I wondered . . . Could I have saved him? Could I have *made* him come with me? I felt the tears rolling down my cheeks.

For the next couple of days I kept myself to myself. I wanted to be left alone; wanted to think about my mate Lofty Nagle. I had survived and he hadn't. I knew it could have gone the other way, but the fact that I was alive and he wasn't burdened me. I felt weighed down with a tremendous guilt.

I was in the hospital on Saipan for eight days. The American treatment of the survivors was superb and due to their care I grew stronger every day. Everything about life in the hospital was a novelty – sleeping in a warm, comfortable cot; three small but square meals a day; coming and going pretty much as I pleased; watching movies in the evening – all the things I had once taken so much for granted I now relished and appreciated. Even so, like all the others, I was in a weak condition: covered in malarial sores, an acute ulcer running from the ankle to my knee on my left leg, incipient beriberi, a swollen liver, bleeding gums, and still, even after slowly increasing my food intake, malnutrition.

But on the eighth day the army and navy brass reckoned that all Australian and British survivors were fit enough to travel and the Americans kitted us out in their naval uniforms: khaki shirt and pants with a navy baseball cap. We said goodbye to the Pommies, who were to be shipped back to the Old Dart via Pearl Harbour and then across America, before about ninety of us were shipped aboard a US minelayer to sail south via Guadalcanal to Australia. Once aboard the minelayer I wrote to my mother and father and also to Mirla: a two-page letter way in excess of the twenty-five words the Japs had allowed us.

On 18 October we anchored in Brisbane Roads, in plain sight of our longed-for country, where a RAN corvette came alongside to transfer on board Commander C R Reid, an Australian Naval Officer who at one stage had been acting commander of the *Perth*.

He had been flown from Pearl Harbour as soon as the navy heard that survivors of the *Perth* had been picked up. In the wardroom of the American minelayer he interviewed Bob Collins, 'Darby' Monroe, Jack Houghton and me about the sinking of the *Perth*.

He was anxious to know the details of the action in the Sunda Strait and though he was quite considerate and eased off whenever we got tired, keeping us going with a constant supply of tea and coffee, he was pretty insistent and interrogated us for six hours. He had a complete list of the ship's crew, asking what we knew of the fate of each man on the list. Many of the names he reeled off were those of men who had died in the camps. After a while I saw him frowning. 'Are you sure about these men?' he asked. 'It seems to me a lot of men died in the POW camps.'

It was then I realised he didn't know. *No one knew.* No one knew what the camps had been like. We were the first ones back to tell the whole bloody world.

So we told him. We could see from his eyes he scarcely believed us. 'Ask the diggers,' we said. 'Ask all the blokes on board this ship who the Japs left to drown. You'll get the same bloody story.'

We were flippant with him, bordering on insolent. But none of us were in the mood to be questioned by an officer who didn't believe what we had been through.

After Commander Reid finally left, the minelayer got under way and moved onto a quay in Brisbane Harbour. Slowly, almost tenuously, as if we didn't believe it, I and ninety other blokes shuffled down the gangplank onto the soil of Australia.

The moment I stepped onto the quay I dropped to my knees and kissed the ground of my beloved home. This was the moment we had all dreamed of, the vivid image that had kept us going through the darkest times. Around me, every survivor was on his knees, kissing the ground. Most blokes were crying like babies. I think I was one of them.

On the quayside petty officers and sergeants were yelling at us fit to bust; screaming at us to line up and stand to attention. We took no notice of them. What did they know? What could they possible do to us that had not already been done? But when, finally, they got us into some semblance of order, though the line was pretty ragged and no one was much bothered with standing to attention, they marched us off: eighty-eight diggers one way; us four naval types, the other.

They took us to the RAN headquarters in Brisbane where we stayed a day and a night, sleeping on cots in a wardroom. After the commanding officer had welcomed us, they gave us a good meal and more medical attention before handing us over to a bunch of naval officers with poker faces and sceptical eyes. The officers questioned us separately, each interrogating us about our lives in the camps from the moment we were picked up in the Sunda Strait to abandoning ship in the South China Sea. It took me a couple of hours to realise that these blokes were naval intelligence and to grasp that the one questioning me, though not unpleasant, was insistently asking me the same questions over and over again, only using different words. He was testing me. Like Commandeer Reid, he couldn't believe that life in the camps was as bad as I was making out. That made me angry.

'You don't believe me?' I told him. 'Well, you'd better believe me. There are 150 survivors of the *Rakuyo Maru*, and every single one of them will be telling the same story.' After about four hours I could see he was starting to accept what I had to say. Behind the hard façade his eyes had acquired a look of incredulous acceptance. There was something else there too – pity. Only I didn't want an officer's pity. I wanted to go home.

After twenty-four hours at Naval HQ, the commanding officer hauled us up to the captain's cabin where he informed us that, in consideration of all we had been through, if any of us wished to leave the navy immediately we would be granted an honourable discharge without delay. Bob and Jack opted for out straight away, while Darby Munro said he would stay.

I considered for a couple of minutes. Maybe, I thought, the navy could use me. I had survived two sinkings and believed I could help train blokes in how to survive in the water. Also, I thought I might be of help when more of our blokes got back from the camps. So, I put my hand up to stay in the navy.

The commander then sent for the medical officer and asked him if we were fit enough to go home. Without a moment's hesitation the medical officer said we were. Even though I was desperate to get back to WA and my family and Mirla – especially Mirla – I thought that was pretty dismissive of the navy. It was as if they were surprised at suddenly having POWs appear out of nowhere and weren't quite sure what to do with us. The AIF lads on the quay had been told they were going to an army convalescent home until they were fit enough to travel.

However, I can't say I was sorry. I was going home. Before they put me on a plane to Melbourne, the captain and one of the intelligence officers emphasised to me that under no circumstances was I to discuss or reveal what had happened to us in the camps. Not even to my family.

I spent a night in Melbourne before boarding the plane to Perth. I was as excited as a kid. I couldn't wait to see WA again. A woman plonked herself in the seat beside me. I glanced up. It was my old English teacher from Claremont High, Miss Tangney. I looked away, thinking she wouldn't remember me, but soon after take-off she said, 'Excuse me, aren't you Arthur Bancroft?' I nodded. I was surprised. The last time she had seen me I was a fifteen-year-old kid. 'Well, what are you doing here, dressed in an American uniform? I'd heard you were a prisoner of war.'

I told her I had been but that I'd got away. She wanted to know how I'd managed that, as well as what life was like as a POW. I told her the navy had ordered me not to tell anyone about it.

'Well, you can tell me. I'm a federal senator now.'

I congratulated her. I knew she had stood for the senate in 1940 before I had joined the navy. She told me she'd been elected as the country's first woman senator in 1943. 'Even so,' I said, 'I don't think the navy wants me to talk about what happened to us'.

'Arthur, I'm a member of the government, and if I say you can tell me, then you may tell me.'

I smiled. It was the same slightly imperious voice she had used in the classroom. I had always liked Miss Tangney. She was a woman who could get a bunch of boisterous teenage boys to do as exactly as they were told without ever raising her voice . . . or her fist. After what I had been through, I respected that.

So, on the long flight over the Nullarbor, I told her everything. She listened quietly. We were coming in to land just as I finished. 'Thank you, Arthur,' she said. 'I will of course respect your confidentiality, although sooner or later the Australian people must be told what their boys have been made to endure. But in the meantime, good luck to you. I'm very glad you came back to us safely.'

We shook hands. I was glad I had met her and had spent a few hours in her company. To me, Miss Tangney, with her civilised reticence and quiet, ironic sense of humour, represented so much that was good about my country. She offered me a lift home in her official car as the plane taxied towards the terminal shed at the end of the runway. I peered out of the cabin window. Then I saw them. My mother and father were waiting on the concrete outside the terminal. Seeing them so unexpectedly, I had to choke back my tears. Desperate to get off the plane, I was forced to shuffle out with the other passengers before leaping down the steps and sprinting across the tarmac into my parents' arms.

They were both shedding tears, my father unsuccessfully trying to hide his; my mother openly crying. I think I was too. I grabbed them both and pulled them in tight: all three of us hugging and kissing; my mother howling with joy.

And then my tears dried up. Suddenly I felt an overwhelming sense of exultation; of victory. It was the weirdest feeling. I felt as if I was a gift; as if I was *giving myself* as a present to my mum and dad: especially to my mum. I had come through; I had endured; I had survived for this moment. All so I could come home.

The bastard Japs hadn't got me. Instead, Mrs Bancroft had got her baby boy back.

Mirla's Story

I took the phone call at work. It was from Arthur's mother. She never called me at work and my heart raced when I heard her voice. 'Mirla, Arthur's safe,' she gabbled. She sounded as if she had been crying.

I didn't understand. It had never occurred to me he wasn't safe. 'What do you mean?'

'I mean he's safe in Allied hands. I've just got a telegram from the navy. It states his name and serial number and says he's in Allied hands.' Still I didn't understand. 'It means they're sending him home!' She was almost shrieking. 'Arthur's coming home!'

It took a few seconds for the news to sink in and then the room began to spin. I almost fainted. I couldn't believe it. My Arthur was coming home.

That evening I went straight from work to his parents' house to see the telegram for myself. The Red Cross had been in touch to say they would find out when and how he would be arriving in Perth and, if necessary, send a car and driver for Arthur's mother and father to pick him up.

About three weeks later the Red Cross contacted Arthur's parents to tell them that he would be arriving that day on a fight from Melbourne. As the car was only for immediate family, Arthur's mother told me to go to the house so that I could meet him there when they drove home. I could feel myself trembling as I walked there. I'd asked my mother to come with me. She was fond of Arthur and I needed some support. I was so excited. By then I had received a lovely letter from him, written on USO notepaper, promising to celebrate his belated twenty-first birthday with me and telling me to get my dancing shoes on, as we were going to be having some high times.

But would he like me as much when he saw me again, I wondered? Had I changed? Maybe I wasn't as pretty as he remembered me . . . Would he decide to go off me? My mother said I was being foolish and worrying needlessly, but I was twenty-one and in love with a young man who had been away to war. Would he have changed?

We got to his parent's house, where Iris, his sister, sat us down in the living room and made us a cup of tea. Suddenly we heard the sound of car drawing up, of doors banging and suddenly he was in the living room and I caught my breath. Oh, he looked so handsome. He was wearing a light tan American naval uniform and though he was very thin and his eyes shrunken, he was still my tall, handsome man. I couldn't take my eyes off him.

He gave me a kiss on my cheek and a bit of a squeeze but everyone wanted his attention and the room was filled with noise and laughter. He seemed exactly the same: still with his quick wit and sense of humour and I was speechless. I didn't know what to say or how to say it. I sat in a corner and stared at him in awe, saying nothing, worrying that he might think I was boring: terrified that he might not like me anymore. Yet, at the end of the evening, when he asked if he could walk us home, I said no. Though the streets were intensely dark in the blackout, my mother was with me and there seemed no point in Arthur walking with us. I saw his face alter as I turned down his offer and instantly regretted my decision. But then he said, 'Oh well, I'll come and see you tomorrow,' and I thought maybe there was a chance he still liked me.

He did come to see me the next day and that evening too. After our first kiss and little bit of a cuddle in almost 1000 days – 987, to be exact – I knew we would be all right. I was even more assured when, five days later, Arthur proposed to me.

It took me about a tenth of a second to think about his proposal; another tenth of a second to say yes. We set the wedding date for March the following year.

Then the navy took him away again.

11

Enduring Love

THE QUEEN AND I BID YOU A VERY WARM WELCOME HOME THROUGH ALL THE GREAT TRIALS AND SUFFERINGS WHICH YOU HAVE ENDURED WHILE IN THE HANDS OF THE JAPANESE. YOU AND YOUR COMRADES HAVE BEEN CONSTANTLY IN OUR THOUGHTS. I REALISE FROM THE ACCOUNTS WHICH YOU HAVE ALREADY GIVEN HOW HEAVY THOSE SUF-FERINGS HAVE BEEN. I KNOW TOO THAT YOU HAVE ENDURED THEM WITH THE HIGHEST COURAGE. WE HOPE WITH ALL OUR HEARTS THAT YOUR RETURN FROM CAPTIVITY MAY BRING YOU AND YOUR FAMILY A FULL MEASURE OF HAPPINESS.

GEORGE R

Telegram dated 14 November 1944, sent to the survivors of the Rakuyo Maru *by His Majesty the King, George VI.*

MY WIFE JOINS ME IN EXPRESSING OUR DEEPEST GRATITUDE TO YOU FOR YOUR COURAGE AND FORTITUDE UNDER THE MOST TRAGIC CIR-CUMSTANCES. WE WELCOME YOU BACK TO OUR HOMELAND AND JOIN

WITH YOU IN SOLEMN REMEMBRANCE OF YOUR MANY COMRADES WHO
LOST THEIR LIVES.

PRINCE HENRY, DUKE OF GLOUCESTER,
GOVERNOR-GENERAL OF AUSTRALIA

Telegram dated 14 November 1944, sent to the survivors of the Rakuyo
Maru *by HRH The Duke of Gloucester, Governor-General of Australia.*

THE MINISTER FOR THE NAVY AND THE NAVAL BOARD WISH TO CON-
VEY THEIR CONGRATULATIONS TO YOU ON YOUR SAFE AND WELCOME
RETURN.

THEY REALISE AND ENDORSE THE THANKFULNESS WHICH YOUR
FAMILY MUST FEEL AT YOUR SAFE DELIVERANCE FROM HANDS OF THE
ENEMY AND TRUST THAT MANY MORE OF YOUR COMRADES WILL BE
RELEASED IN THE NEAR FUTURE.

THEY WISH YOU A COMPLETE AND SPEEDY RECOVERY FROM THE
ORDEAL THROUGH WHICH YOU HAVE PASSED.

Telegram dated 14 November 1944, sent to the survivors of the Rakuyo
Maru *by the Royal Australian Navy.*

Mirla was sitting in a corner of our living room when the car dropped
us at home. I caught sight of her as I walked in and felt I had
been punched in my heart. I could hardly take my eyes off her
all evening. She was so beautiful she shimmered. For me she was
the prettiest girl on the planet. But she was very quiet and after
a while I wondered if she had gone off me. Maybe more than

thirty months of Japanese hospitality – of dysentery, skin lesions and tropical ulcers – had altered me so much that she found me repulsive. I worried that she had met someone else. To cap it all, when I offered to walk her and her mother home, she refused me. I tried to pass it off and said I'd see her tomorrow.

I needn't have worried. The next evening she told me that seeing me after so long had made her feel shy, though she didn't seem too shy when I kissed her and after a couple of hours alone with her I knew she was still my girl. A few days later, I proposed. One of the things I had learned, courtesy of the Imperial Japanese Army, was that life was short and there was no point in pussyfooting around when you had a chance at happiness. I think Mirla had learned that too, as the moment I proposed she said 'Yes' pretty damn quick. We set a date for March 1945.

The navy had given me a month's leave and life was sweet until *The West Australian* carried an article about me coming home after the sinking of the *Perth*. Instantly I was inundated with letters and requests for information from the wives and mothers of former shipmates. In the hospital in Saipan, when we realised we would be the first to get back home, I had agreed with Bob, Jack and Derby that we would tell the truth about what had happened to our shipmates. Now, faced with the task of having to tell people what I knew, the tragic enormity of that promise assailed me. I replied to every letter I received, telling what I knew of the enquirer's husband or son, brother or fiancé.

But there were some, the relatives of my mates, who I believed deserved to know the truth firsthand and without having to ask. Where I could, I went to see them. It was a bastard of a job, setting out to tell someone their son or husband was dead and I needed to steel myself. I freely admit that on some occasions, I took my mum with me for support.

I went to see Otto Lund's father. He had fought in the First World War and knew what war was like. He had seen death, though it was hard for him to learn that his son had survived battle only to die in Hintock Road Prison Camp. I didn't tell him, as I didn't tell any of the others, that his son's death had been unnecessary: that, in my opinion, it was murder. The old bloke took it well enough, though I saw in his eyes how much the news ravaged him. It was always hardest telling the parents. Otto's dad had expected to grow old and die and be buried by his son. Now he had no son, nor even a body to bury. It seemed to go against all the laws of nature.

I took my mum when I went to see Gwen Gilbey, Harvey's wife. She didn't believe Harvey was dead. She had just received a letter-card from him. I hated doing it but I convinced her that the letter was nearly two years old; that her husband, the father of the little boy whose head we had so happily wet in Kalgoorlie, was buried in a grave in Thailand. He had been dead for more than a year.

I went to see Harold Wikinson's fiancé and also Merv's parents. I saw the agony flare in their eyes when I told them their son was dead. I did lie to them. I told them I had been with him when he died. That seemed to bring them a small measure of comfort.

The hardest task was going to see Lofty's mother. Mum agreed to come with me and I'm glad she was there as Lofty's mother refused to accept that her son was dead. I told her it was impossible for anyone to have survived the typhoon. 'Then if he's dead, it's your fault, Arthur,' she said bitterly. 'You should have *made* him go with you. You left him alone and he died.'

I felt my guts wrench at her words and was silent on the journey home. 'You have to realise that she's lost a child,' my mother said quietly when we got off the bus. 'There's nothing more terrible in the whole world, Arthur. It's the worst possible thing that can happen to a human being. She's looking for someone to blame, trying to ease the pain. You have to forgive her.'

I mumbled something.

'Even so, she's wrong. It's not your fault he's dead.'

'But maybe it is. I *did* leave him.'

'Yes, but doesn't the navy say when you abandon ship, that it's "Every man for himself"? If you had tried to force him to go with you, the two of you could have ended up drowning each other. He made his choice and you made yours. Yours turned out to be the right one. It could have been otherwise. Anyone can see that. You have to get over this, Arthur. You cannot blame yourself for Lofty's death.'

She was right, of course. Mothers generally are. And I did get over it. Though never completely. The loss and sadness has stayed with me always.

A week later Lofty's mother arrived on our doorstep, waving a letter-card. I was wrong, she told me triumphantly. Lofty was alive. She had a letter from him. I felt sick as I told her that the letter was over a year old: that I remembered Lofty writing it at 105 Kilo Camp months before he died. She wouldn't have it. He was alive, she repeated. Thank God my mother was there. She told me to let Lofty's mother go; to let her believe what she wanted to believe.

All over the country relatives were receiving letters from men who were dead. It would take some of them years to accept that their men were not coming home; that they were lying under a shallow mound of soil with a makeshift bamboo cross somewhere in the jungle.

Most days when I had nothing to do, I would go down to the centre of the city to meet Mirla from work. Sometimes, when I was getting under mum's feet, I would go early and have a couple of pints in the Savoy on Hay Street. Occasionally I had company and one time shared a few beers with a couple of Pommie sailors. I drank them under the table, though Mirla was not totally stoked when, having missed her from work, I turned up at her house later somewhat the worse for wear.

Sitting alone at the bar one afternoon I was remembering my mates – thinking of those who would never again come swaggering into the bar with a grin on their faces and their caps on the back of their heads – when I felt an overwhelming sense of emptiness descend on me. Suddenly, I found myself *longing* to be back with them on the railway. I was shocked. Back in the camps the vision of having a beer in this bar had kept me alive. Now that I was here – when so many others never would be – how could I possibly want to be back there? The thought was crazy, obscene: it was as if I had developed a notion to take an axe and chop up my parents. It didn't make any sense. Yet the thought had definitely been there, as solid and palpable as a Jap guard's baton. It scared me. What the bloody hell was wrong with me? How could I possibly think that?

Back then we didn't have counselling for blokes like me coming back from POW camps. But we had families. I told Mirla what I'd thought and she covered my face with kisses and told me I would be all right. I talked to my mum and dad and finally worked it out.

It was quite simple, really. Now I was no longer surrounded by death, no longer threatened by the very real possibility of dying, I missed what had kept me alive. I missed my mates – missed them so much that, in my mind anyway, I could even contemplate a return to the camps. Our mateship had been so intense I was bound to miss it; to yearn for its return, though that could never be. The emptiness, the sad feeling of loss, came from realising that I would never again be quite as close to a mob of blokes as I had been in on the *Perth* and in the camps.

My leave came to an end and I reported for duty to be told I was to be shipped to a navy convalescent home in St Kilda, Melbourne. I didn't see a lot of sense in that: they were taking me from my mother's cooking and my fiancée's kisses in the quaint belief that I would recuperate faster in a navy convalescent home. Still, it beat being returned to duty, so I went along with it.

Bob, Jack and Darby were already there; Bob and Jack convalescing before their discharge from the service. Apart from attention from the nurses and visits by navy doctors, we had a teacher to bring us up to date with the progress of the war and world events. We noticed that none of the other occupants of the convalescent home spoke to us and after a few days enquired of the teacher why. Orders, he told us. The navy was worried in case we were unstable after our experience in the camps. They didn't want the others blokes exposed to unbalanced ex-POWs. We asked him if he thought we were unstable.

He said that as our sole topics of conversation were football, beer and women, in his opinion we were perfectly normal! Soon after that the other convalescents started talking to us.

They sent us home for Christmas and though there was rationing and everything was in short supply, it was a wonderful time. I relished every moment of it before being ordered back east for another stay in the convalescent home. As far as I could see, I was well on the mend and couldn't fathom why the navy thought I needed more convalescence.

I flew home at the end of February to get ready for my wedding day on 10 March. It was a marvellous day. Bob Collins had said he would be my best man and came over from New South Wales especially. Nancy, Mirla's best friend, was a bridesmaid along with June Ledger, whose great nephew, Heath, became famous as an actor before his tragic death. My mum and Mirla's mum shed buckets of tears and everyone had a marvellous time.

We went to Mandurah for our honeymoon and sometime in the second week strolled along to the open-air cinema to see an Abbott and Costello picture. In the intermission, between the 'B' movie and the big picture, we were shocked to see a message appear on the screen requesting Able Seaman Arthur Bancroft to go to the local post office. I wondered what the hell could be wrong, though it didn't spoil my night. I was on my honeymoon.

Waiting for me at the post office was a telegram from the navy ordering me to fly to Melbourne to be presented to the Duke of Gloucester, the Governor-General of Australia. Mirla was rapt. She thought it a great privilege. I didn't, not if I couldn't take her with me. So I wired back saying I would only go if Mirla could come with me, and if not, I refused to go. I was not prepared to be separated from my new wife.

Mirla was worried, especially as on our return we were staying at my parents' house while they were holidaying in Tasmania. She was expecting a couple of military policemen to turn up on the doorstep and cart me away for being discourteous to the Governor-General. Instead, a telegram arrived from the navy saying that the Duke of Gloucester quite understood and that he and the Duchess would meet us when they came to Fremantle. A few weeks later a navy staff car arrived outside the house to take Mirla and me to HMAS *Leeuwin* in Fremantle, where we were presented to the Duke and Duchess. We enjoyed the experience very much, though we were somewhat overawed. We were young and royalty was a long way outside our experience. To us it was mystical and exalted and foreign: it existed beyond our shores.

After more than a month at home the navy once more ordered me east, first to the convalescent home, where I heard the wonderful news that the war in Europe had ended, and then, after a few weeks, to HMAS *Cerberus* at Flinders.

I can't say I was happy to be back at *Cerberus;* the place held too many memories of mates I had lost, though I tried to make the most of it. But what was becoming increasingly clear was that the navy had no idea what to do with me. My naïve notion that they might use me to train young seamen in how to survive shipwreck and that I could help blokes coming back from the camps was obviously a romantic, pie-in-the sky idea. I was a square peg.

One morning I was detailed with a squad of ratings to pick up some shovels from the stores after which the petty officer marched us along to the narrow-gauge railway track running through the camp. 'Right, lads, you're going to be ballasting this track,' he told us.

I took one look at the railway, shoved my shovel into the ground and sat myself on the handle. 'Not me, chief.'

He reared back like I had hit him. 'What?'

'I'm not ballasting that track, chief. I'm done ballasting all the railway track I'm ever going to ballast.'

The PO's face turned red. I watched a vein in his neck quivering. 'You'll obey orders,' he snapped, 'or you'll find yourself on a charge bloody quick! Now, get to work!'

I shook my head calmly. 'Not me.'

Just then an officer walked past. 'What's the problem here, chief?' he asked.

'This man's refusing to obey an order, sir.'

The officer looked at me. 'Bancroft, isn't it?'

'Yessir.'

'So why are you disobeying an order?'

'I did all the ballasting I'm ever going to do in Burma, sir. I'm not ballasting track here at *Cerberus*.'

The officer nodded. 'Yes, I see. Very well, I'll handle this, chief. Come with me, Bancroft.' I followed him, leaving my shovel sticking in the ground and the chief staring daggers at my back. .

We marched into the deserted wardroom where the officer turned to me. 'You were on the Burma Railway, weren't you?'

'Yessir.'

'Well, I can understand you refusing to ballast, so I think we can overlook you giving the chief apoplexy this time. But what exactly is your problem, Bancroft?'

'Sir?'

'With the navy? It seems to me you're not very happy now you're back.'

'I thought the navy could use me, sir.'

'Really – how?'

I told him what I had hoped. The officer smiled. 'The navy isn't that clever, Bancroft. The idea of using a man to do what he might be good at would never occur to it.'

'So what am I going to do, sir?' I pleaded. 'I don't fit anymore. I mean, I did once, but it's all different now I'm back. The navy keeps ordering me to do things I don't want to do.'

He nodded. 'The navy hasn't changed, Bancroft. You have. Not surprising, given what you have been through. The fact is, the navy won't use you and it can't scare you. Nothing we could hand out by way of discipline or punishment could compare to what you've suffered. And anyway, the navy may be inept, but it isn't heartless. We don't want to be disciplining a man like you for disobeying orders.'

'So what do I do, sir?'

He thought for a moment. 'Do you have a job back in Perth you might go to?'

'Yes, sir. The general manager of my bank says they would take me back in a minute.'

'Then leave. Apply for a medical discharge. You'll be marked, "Physically Unfit for Naval Service".'

I stared at him. 'Can I do that? The navy has just spent almost the last eight months getting me well.'

'The navy would be delighted,' he said. 'Inside, you're a problem;

an embarrassment. They don't know what to do with you. Outside, they can fete you as a favourite son.'

And so I left the Royal Australian Navy, not with the big bang of a marching-out parade but with the whimper of a medical discharge. It suited me well enough. They sent me back to the convalescent home where I sat it out until the discharge came through in the middle of July.

When I got back, Mirla's mother, who knew about these things, said that as I was considered unfit for naval service, I could apply for a navy pension. I decided I didn't want to do that. I wanted to go back to playing football for Subiaco and I didn't see how I could play football with a pension.

Mirla suggested we have another honeymoon in Kalamunda, up in the hills east of Perth. As I'd enjoyed my first honeymoon so much I said yes immediately. I didn't care too much where it was; it wasn't as if we would be doing a lot of sightseeing.

The bank sent me to work at the branch in Northam. I was there only a few days when, on Monday afternoon of August 6, I heard that something called an atomic bomb had been dropped on Hiroshima in Japan. Three days later, another atomic bomb was dropped on Nagasaki and in the middle of the following week, on August 15, the announcement came over the radio that Japan had surrendered. The country went wild and people were dancing in the streets.

My mates – those who had survived – started trickling back in November of that year: Charlie Thompson, who had shouted to me from a pile of flotsam after the *Perth* had gone down that he would see me in the 'Shents'; Norm Fuller; and then, finally, Marcus. He'd been in hospital in Singapore for three months, yet he still looked thin and weak. Miraculously he had preserved almost all my diary and sketches, though he admitted to smoking February through to October 1943. I didn't care. I was rapt to see him safely home. We had a lot of beers together and told each other our experiences.

I was able to persuade Subiaco Football Club to throw open their clubhouse for a big party for all the returning sailors off the *Perth*. It was a great night: we all got gloriously drunk and shed a few tears when we toasted those of our brave mates who had not made it home. Three hundred men had survived the battle of the Sunda Strait and the sinking of the *Perth*. Out of that 300, less then 200 came home. A hundred and ten men had died needlessly in Jap captivity.

Slowly, civilian life began to take over. I couldn't say that life returned to normal. I didn't know what 'normal' was. I had left home a boy and come back a man, who very quickly became a married man, and then, when Mirla gave me the news in late August, a man who was about to become a father. In fact, adjusting to civilian life with a wife and a growing family took me, like many men who had been in the camps, a few years.

Our first daughter was born in April 1946 and over the next twelve years we had three more children. We were a blissful little family and I would like to have been able to say that we lived happily ever after. Yet, though Mirla and I have been very happy together, we've also had our share of grief.

In 1990 we lost our youngest daughter, Toni, to a malignant

brain tumour. She was only thirty-seven. Watching her die was the worst thing I have ever endured; far harder than anything I experienced in the camps. Many times during those dark, painful months I recalled the agonised faces of the parents I had told forty-six years earlier that they had had lost their sons. Now it was our turn. My mother had been right; losing a child was the most terrible thing a human being could have to endure.

Four years later Vicki, our second daughter, was also diagnosed with a brain tumour. We couldn't believe the horror was being revisited on us but, thank God, Vicki's tumour ultimately turned out to be benign. She made a full recovery. But not long after that we lost a lovely grandson to an accidental drug overdose. Again, along with our daughter and her family, we were plunged into the worst and most painful thing to befall a person. Eight months later another of our grandsons fell under a train and was badly injured.

However, throughout everything, our little family loved and supported each other, and because of that we came through. I was reminded often during those black years of the mateship I had experienced in the camps. The memory prompted me, if I needed prompting, just how much my family and I needed to look after each other in the same way we had done in the camps.

Now we are settled into old age with children and grandchildren and even great-grandchildren around us. We have a lovely fourth floor 'Mercy Village' retirement apartment where I have a grand view of the new Subiaco football stadium, much different and improved from the one I played in seventy years ago. This one has great banks of floodlights that blaze through the night and I can hear the roar of the crowds easily.

The *Perth* pennant I brought home for Mirla before we sailed north into battle now hangs in a glass case on a wall in St George's Cathedral in Perth, while the box of chocolates I brought her with the picture of the *Perth* on the front holds all our letters. I have to admit I was a bit irritated when I returned from the camps to find she'd eaten all the chocolates. I'd only been away two-and-a-half years. She might have saved me one!

Some years ago, while attending a navy function, a middle-aged man approached me. He had deliberately sought me out, he said, as I had been in the war with his dad. When I asked who he was he said he was Harvey's son; that little nipper whose entry into the world we had celebrated all those years before! He was a fine man and had done well for himself. Harvey would have been proud of him and I had to choke back my tears when I thought of all that Harvey had been denied as a husband and a father.

I presented the diary I had kept, minus the months Marcus had smoked, along with my sketches to the Naval Museum at Garden Island in Sydney in 2006 and every year, on September 17, the anniversary of my rescue by the USS *Queenfish*, I have phoned my good friends, John Bennett and Charlie Levine at their respective homes in San Diego and Chattanooga to talk over old times and to thank them both, along with the United States Navy, for rescuing me. We have met many times over the years and our families and theirs have become very close.

Years after I returned from the war and was accountant of the bank in Albany, I bumped into Dennis Robinson with whom I had messed in my early training at Leeuwin Naval Depot as a communications cadet. Dennis and I had a few beers together and talked of old times. He told me that he, along with all the others in my induction squad, had been shipped to Melbourne after training at Leeuwin and had never left the country.

'Imagine, Arthur,' he said, 'if you hadn't had those carbuncles and been sent to the sick bay, you'd have never been on the *Perth* and gone through hell on the railway and in the sea.'

I hadn't thought about it much, but he was right. A simple quirk of fate had sent me on another path and into another life. If I was able, would I have missed all that happened to me? It's difficult to say. I saw some terrible things: men bashed to death, good mates fighting over a few grains of rotting rice, men with terrible diseases dying in agony. Yet the experience made something of me. Some say it made better men of us. I don't think that. I don't think I'm a better man. But I do think those terrible years taught me how to endure; to believe that I could come through anything. It definitely helped me through our dark family tragedies.

Many couples split up after the death of a child. Mirla and I didn't. We clung together. I knew we would come through. So did Mirla, though she was always stronger than me anyway. In many ways the bad things that happen to us can make us stronger. That was true in the camps and was true in our family. Suffering and tragedies forced us together, strengthening the bonds of love and mateship, squeezing out the irrelevancies like status and money and possessions.

I guess if I've learned anything from my life it's that it is possible for the human spirit to prevail – and that what enables us to prevail and endure is each other. That is all we have. I learned that on the *Perth*, and in the camps where mateship was everything.

I reckon so long as we Australians still have that, we'll be right.

Mirla's Story

When Arthur proposed to me and I said yes so quickly, he told me to hold my horses. There was something he had to tell me. Apparently the navy doctors told him that because of the diet he had been on in the Japanese camps it was possible he would not be able to have children: certainly not for a while, and maybe never. Well, I was in love with him so I married him anyway, though in the four months between our wedding and his discharge from the navy he was away for more than two of them. Yet, by the time we went for our second honeymoon in Kalmunda, I was pregnant. I waited another month to be absolutely certain before I told him. After that I never set much store by navy doctors.

I suppose my story ends about now. I did have a separate story while Arthur was away at the war, but once he was discharged from the navy and came home to me, then, as Mrs Mirla Bancroft, my story became his and his mine. Which is not to say that I didn't have a life separate from his or that I didn't have my independence. But our lives became more and more intertwined as our family grew.

Our first daughter, Dianne, was born in early April 1946; a second daughter, Vicki, in 1948; Toni, another daughter, in 1953 and Colin, our son, in 1958. We raised our family and moved about the country a lot as Arthur was promoted from one bank branch to another. By 1990 we had seen all our children happily married and were settling into being grandparents when tragedy struck: Toni was diagnosed with a malignant brain tumour. I nursed her for months, as well as taking care of her children, before she died. It was the hardest thing I ever had to endure.

Four years later, Vicki became partially blind in one eye and was diagnosed with a brain tumour. The prospect of losing another daughter to such a terrible death was almost more than I could bear, but the tumour was benign. After many months of treatment with natural therapies Vicki regained full vision. Not long afterwards, Cameron, Dianne's son and her second child, died of an accidental overdose at just twenty-two. The loss of their loving son was terrible for Dianne and her family, as it was for all of us. He was a fine, caring young man, and a talented musician.

Another grandson, Simon, had a horrific accident when he was run over by a train, and his left arm and right hand were amputated. Through the miracle of microsurgery the surgeons attached his left hand to his right arm, and now Simon has recovered and is enjoying life. Yet, throughout those dark years of tragedy, the family held tightly to each other and came through.

Arthur and I fell in love at the start of a terrible war and stayed in love, loving and supporting each other, through both the many good times as well as the tragedies of the past several decades. We built a wonderfully happy family, having four children, nine grandchildren and now two great-grandchildren . . . which is not too bad for a man the navy doctors said might not be able to have a family.

What kept us together was affection and love. It was mateship that saw Arthur survive the Japanese camps, and it was love that saw our family come through its tragedies.

For people like us, love endures. It never goes away.

ACKNOWLEDGEMENTS

Many people have contributed both to the concept and to the publishing of this book. Without some of them I would not be here; without others, this book would not be here. I wish to acknowledge them all.

Firstly, I wish to acknowledge Mirla, my wife of sixty-five years. Without the knowledge that one day I would see her again, I may not have been able to survive either shipwreck or my life in the camps. And without her wonderful love and continuing support and companionship, I may not have been able to survive all these years until now. It is to Mirla I owe everything.

I also wish to acknowledge all our children, not only for their love and support but also for their practical help in making this book a reality: to our eldest daughter, Dianne, who not only took my original pencil-scribbled diary pages and typed them up but also provided undying enthusiasm for this book; to our daughter, Vicki, who started the whole chain of events that led to the publication of *Arthur's War* by presenting my diary to Commander Shane Moore at the Royal Australian Navy Heritage Centre, Sydney, and who, after producing a copy of the diary for the family to keep, collated so much material and photos for the publishers. I thank Colin, our son, for his deep and continuing involvement with the next generation of HMAS *Perth* Survivors' Association and the Naval Cadets' Training Ship *Perth* at East Fremantle, as well as also providing photos to the publishers, and finally to our daughter Toni, now sadly deceased, who always showed such a keen interest in her dad's war history and who introduced her children to their grandfather's story by taking them to the War Museum in Canberra and by always attending the Anzac Day services.

I would also like to acknowledge all our grandchildren: Karen, Michael, Kirsten, Cameron (who, sadly, has also passed away), Daniel, Simon, Emily, Stephen and Matthew, and to thank them for their continuing interest in and love of hearing their hero (Pop's) stories. Also, my acknowledgement and thanks to our great-grandchildren, Kacey, Joshua and Arlo, who, as the next generation, are continuing in the tradition of listening to my stories.

I could not, in all conscience, have my story published without acknowledging those of my mates who did not make it back home. All of them in their own individual way helped me soldier on and survive and I wish to say a heartfelt thank you to the memories of Harvey Gilbey and Merv O'Donohue, who died in the POW camps, and to Harry (Lofty) Nagle, who was lost in the South China Sea. There isn't a day goes by when I don't think of them.

I would also like to especially acknowledge my mate Marcus Clark, who not only survived and made it back to Australia, but came home bringing my diary that he had hidden from the Japanese, at great risk to himself, for over twelve months.

I would also like to mention some of the POWs from the USS *Houston* with whom I became good mates in the camps, namely: Otto Schwarz, Jack Feliz, Lloyd Willey and Skip Schilperoot.

No list of acknowledgements concerning this book would be complete without mentioning some of the American crew of USS *Queenfish*, without whom I would not be here. They literally saved my life and I wish to say thank you to Commander Charles (Elliott) Loughlin, John Bennett, Charles Levine, Artie Grandinetti and Pharmacist's Mate 'Doc' Dixon.

I also wish to acknowledge and say thank you to Commander Shane Moore, Director of the Naval Museum, Garden Island, Sydney, who received my diary for placement in the Museum.

My thanks and acknowledgement must also go to Stephen Taylor, Producer of Channel Nine's *60 Minutes*, who thought my story was worth telling, and to the show's reporter, Tara Brown,, who was so charming when she interviewed me.

I cannot conclude without saying a big thank you to all the folks at Penguin Books who provided so much enthusiastic encouragement and support throughout the entire publishing process. They are: Rachel Scully, Publisher; Saskia Adams, Senior Editor; and Sally Bateman, General Manager, Marketing & Publicity.

Finally, my deepest thanks must also go to the author of my book, John Harman, whose fine writing has brought my story alive and who left no stone unturned in our numerous hugely enjoyable interviews. Also my thanks to John's wife, Abigail, a professional photographer, for her excellent photographs.

INDEX

= POETRY =

— The THING THEY CALL A WAR — By J. Léar.

You've heard about the Aussies
Who wanted blood and gore
To fight for dear old England
In this thing they call a War
Sons of Sunny Australia
How proud they seemed to be
Dressed up in their uniforms
And sent across the sea

To Countries tho' so far away
In Honour bound they go
To fight for love and liberty
Against all fighting foe
The rifle held with flashing steel
They fight their way to fame
Lives are lost, blood is shed
But they always played the game

But after months of Warfare
And the glamour starts to wear
They think of dear old Aussie
And the loved ones waiting there
After years of fight and hardship
(Some were laid to rest)
They will land back in Australia
After having done their best
And when the summing up is done
For all their blood and gore
Many a sad story they will tell
Of the "Thing They Call a War"

— FIELD ARTILLERY —

Some sing about the Infantry
With dirt behind their ears
The A.S.C. and Cavalry
And God darn Engineers

But on the right of every line
There marches right fully
The tractors, guns and gun
Of the Field Artillery